Penguin Books
The Phone Book

Ian Reinecke was educated at Melbourne and La Trobe universities. He worked as a journalist in Britain before joining the *Australian Financial Review* in 1977 to write about computers and technology. In 1981 he became publisher of a group of technical magazines produced by Thomson Publications, where he also edits *Communications Australia*. He is the author of *Micro Invaders*, published in Penguins in 1982.

Julianne Schultz was educated at the University of Queensland in Brisbane. She has worked as a journalist for the *Australian Financial Review*, ABC radio and television, and as a freelance writer for leading publications in Australia and abroad. She now teaches journalism at the New South Wales Institute of Technology in Sydney.

To Aidan & Kate,
    So that ET can phone
home...
        Ian & Julianne

The Phone Book
The future of Australia's communications on the line

Ian Reinecke and Julianne Schultz

Penguin Books

Penguin Books Australia Ltd,
487 Maroondah Highway, P.O. Box 257
Ringwood, Victoria, 3134, Australia
Penguin Books Ltd,
Harmondsworth, Middlesex, England
Penguin Books,
625 Madison Avenue, New York, N.Y. 10022, U.S.A.
Penguin Books Canada Ltd,
2801 John Street, Markham, Ontario, Canada
Penguin Books (N.Z.) Ltd,
182-190 Wairau Road, Auckland 10, New Zealand

First published by Penguin Books Australia, 1983

Copyright © Ian Reinecke and Julianne Schultz, 1983

Typeset in Plantin by Dovatype, Melbourne
Made and printed in Australia by
Dominion Press Hedges and Bell

CIP

Reinecke, Ian, 1945-
The phone book

ISBN. 0 14 006710 8
1. Telecom Australia
2. Telecommunication — Australia
I. Schultz, Julianne
II. Title.

384'.0994

Contents

Chapter One
What's at Stake?

Telephones are the nerve ends of modern society. Through them information is detected, monitored, measured, transmitted and collected. Like the body's central nervous system, telecommunications systems are networks of control. The way those systems are organized reflects the society in which they exist and its social, political, economic and defence priorities.

For Australia, the distances within the country and from the rest of the developed world have made good communications even more important than they would be to a small, densely populated country in the middle of western Europe. The national myth of egalitarianism has put an extra premium on ensuring that communications of equal standard are available to almost everyone at a similar cost. To make this possible, corporate and business telecommunications users have generally subsidized domestic subscribers. Similar subsidies have been used by telecommunications administrations around the world to enable as many people as possible to have access to the communications network. Throughout the developed world, telecommunications systems have been provided by the state, reflecting national priorities and ensuring defence integrity. Of the major economies, only the United States has a telecommunications network provided exclusively by a private-sector company, although it is a company so large and heavily regulated, and so closely connected to national defence and law administrations, that it takes on some of the characteristics of the state. In the Third World, however, it is not unusual for private companies - often US corporations - to own the telecommunications network: International Telephone and Telegraph and United Fruit are two important operators in central and South America.

In Australia, the commitment to a universal, low-cost telephone service has existed since before federation. Rapid expansion in telecommunications since the mid 1970s now means that most Australians have a telephone which they can afford. This expansion was made possible by a combination of new technology and improved productivity. These two factors have also made telecommunications important to large corporations. The technology combines telecommunications and computers and makes the publicly developed communications network an invaluable resource. This combination has the potential to improve the quality of life for everyone, or to manufacture vast profits for a few. The exploitation of this potential can either take into account national priorities and benefit all, or be left to a handful of powerful organizations.

The decision now faced by Australians is as fundamental as this. Its resolution will determine the nature of Australian business and society into the next century.

In many ways, the public and most politicians are ill equipped to make this decision. Concerted and partisan government intervention has skewed the debate, as has misleading reporting in the media and the traditional reluctance of the public sector to defend itself when it is under attack.

This book aims to bring home the importance of the debate to all Australians and to provide the information needed for informed and rational decisions to be made.

Australians are now being told that allowing private companies to compete with Telecom Australia will make the country's second largest enterprise more efficient and result in improvements in the telephone service. This suggestion is both misleading and deceptive.

The attempt to introduce competition into telecommunications is nothing like the competition between Chinese restaurants in Dixon Street or Little Bourke Street. It is different from the proposal put forward, when aviation was booming, to sell off TAA and Qantas. It is different from the competition on the roads between cars, trucks and motor bikes which kills thousands of people in Australia every year. An analogy could be drawn between competition in telecommunications and competition between roads and railways, competition which the railways lost when road transport started to carry most of the freight, the profitable transport. The public was left paying the bill for passenger railways of millions of dollars each year; passengers alone will never be profitable.

The battle over telecommunications is one which will determine whether the fastest growing and most important industry of what is called the Information Age remains in national public control or is handed over to private companies, many of them subsidiaries of foreign corporations.

Telecommunications will be the pivotal industry for the rest of this decade and probably for the next as well. The 'knowledge business' and 'information business' are catch phrases dreamt up by Madison Avenue advertising agencies. There is not another industry which remains untouched by them. Telecommunications is like electricity, but its potential keeps on expanding. Sometimes it is referred to as 'the infrastructure of the Information Age'. This means that the grid of cables, microwave towers, telephone exchanges, data links and transmitters which criss-cross Australia are the routes along which information will travel. Information is increasing in importance to large and small corporations. Just as the Industrial Revolution could never have happened without railways to transport manufactured goods and raw materials across nations, so the Information Revolution needs a communications network to transport information within countries and around the globe.

This communications network in Australia, as in most other countries, has been built up at vast public expense over more than a hundred years. Most of Australia's trading partners – Japan, Britain, France, West Germany, Italy, Sweden, New Zealand – have developed telecommunications networks comparable to Australia's, also at public expense. In those countries where telecommunications is not in the public sector, a national network has been developed and the private companies controlling it, such as American Telephone and

Telegraph (AT&T) in the United States, resemble quasi public organizations. AT&T, the biggest company in the world, has developed a communications system without rival. The only reason, however, that AT&T's network reaches as efficiently into the back blocks of Colorado as it does into downtown Manhattan is because of government intervention. During the 1930s depression, Roosevelt's New Deal government formed the Federal Communications Commission (FCC), directed AT&T to provide a national service, and placed it under rigid surveillance to ensure that it did.

The suggestion that the most profitable areas of telecommunications should be annexed by competition from private corporations has only arisen in the last five years in Australia and elsewhere. As trends so often do, this one started in the United States. Telecommunications increased in importance with the spread of computers in US business, and AT&T strayed outside its role as a telephone company to compete in computing markets with the giant of data processing, International Business Machines (IBM). While this was happening, other large corporations saw advantages in wresting control of their telecommunications traffic away from AT&T's Bell System. Without having to support a national network, independent carriers could offer lower tariffs than the established providers of telecommunications services. The appeal to international companies of introducing that competition on a world scale was obvious. With the skills that have made the United States the most formidable country in the world today, this ethos was quickly exported and sold to the rest of the world. As with most exports, this one had greater success in some countries than others.

In Britain, the concept was very tempting to a government which was committed to denationalization, especially of those industries which made money. Cable and Wireless Pty Ltd was floated on the London Stock Exchange in 1981, and encouragement was given to organizations setting up competitive networks with the national telecommunications carrier. British Telecom entered a joint venture with the IBM-backed Satellite Business Systems for transatlantic traffic.

But this was not sufficient, and in the northern summer of 1982, Prime Minister Thatcher signalled her intention to sell off British Telecom, after the next general election.

Britain was the only country in Europe that was denationalizing its telecommunications network. In all the other western European countries, the pressures from 'user groups' encouraged governments to guard their national telecommunications network. France continued the massive upgrading of its communications network begun in the days of former President Giscard d'Estaing. West Germany announced plans to exclude all private involvement in crucial areas of telecommunications – to the extent of introducing a deadline for the removal of all private modems (devices which enable the telephone network to carry computer data). The same pattern was repeated in other European countries which jealously protected their national telecommunications networks against the mounting campaign of 'user groups'.

The companies which were leading the onslaught against the national public telephone and telegraph administrations (PTTs) operated under the guise of 'user groups' in many countries. User groups sprang up throughout western Europe, as well as in Australia, New Zealand and other developed countries. Almost invariably, the user groups posited an alternative of a freer, more competitive national telecommunications network. But they were not inspired by national companies. Although the concept was quickly adopted by large domestic companies, the user groups tended to strongly represent US-based transnational corporations operating through subsidiaries in the target countries.

In West Germany, the founding chairman of the user group was the communications manager of John Deere, the giant manufacturer of farm machinery, and among the top hundred of US Fortune 500 list of biggest companies. This man now heads the International Telecommunications User Group based in Paris. In Australia, this approach eventually spawned a lobby group, Business Telecommunications Services (BTS), which was headed by a director of IBM Australia Limited. The same pattern was repeated all over the world.

The move to introduce competition into the most lucrative areas of telecommunications stood to benefit the transnational corporations most. Towards the end of the 1970s, it became obvious to these corporations that telecommunications was a vital aspect of their businesses. Telecommunications costs rose to second or third place in corporate expenditure charts, beaten only by property and wages. This was caused less by rising prices than by demand increasing astronomically. Telecommunications made it possible for a head office in New York to know at the beginning of every working day precisely what was happening in each of its subsidiaries around the world: production, pricing, costs, expenditures, targets, taxes, wages, government decisions and tariff changes. This made global control possible in a way which could never have been dreamt of by the old trading companies of colonial times. Access to information gave the organization control over itself in a way which would have seemed astounding even a decade earlier.

This control facilitated what economic historians have already called the New Corporate World Economic Order (NCWEO). If the NCWEO controls the world's economy, it is in the hands of increasingly fewer corporations. Australia is important in the NCWEO simply because the level of foreign control is so high. According to Professor Ted Wheelwright of the University of Sydney, the figures for foreign control of Australian industry are astounding: advertising, 51 per cent; merchant banking, 62 per cent; finance companies, 34 per cent; computers, 84 per cent; cotton fabrication, 38 per cent; vegetable products, 75 per cent; flour milling, 38 per cent; bread, biscuits and cakes, 25 per cent; confectionery, 68 per cent; canned fish, 51 per cent; soft drinks, 53 per cent; wine and brandy, 27 per cent; tobacco, 100 per cent; electrical goods, 46 per cent; chemicals and refined products, 78 per cent; chemicals and pharmaceuticals, 78 per cent; chemical fibres, 57 per cent; automobiles, 100 per cent and oil refining 90 per cent. This level of foreign control has been growing for decades, but in the latter half of the 1970s it escalated.

Telecommunications has promoted the growth of new

industries. Without access to 'real time global money' the phenomenal growth in the short-term money market would not have been possible. Every day $500,000 to $1,000,000 million floats on that market. 'Stateless money', the US magazine, *Business Week*, called it:

a vast, integrated global money and capital system almost totally outside all government regulation, that can send billions of Eurodollars, Euro-marks and other 'stateless' currencies hurtling around the world twenty-four hours a day. Huge amounts of these Eurocurrencies have leaked across national boundaries and out of government hands.

If there was further proof needed that corporations could, with the touch of a computer key, circumvent national governments, it was provided in 1982. Citibank, the second largest bank in the United States, was taken to task by a US congressional committee for keeping two sets of accounts to minimize foreign exchange earnings in Europe and shift the profits to the tax-free Bahamas. Its mastery of telecommunications networks had enabled it to bypass government regulations and avoid paying massive quantities of tax while reaping $46 million in windfall profits from currency transactions.

In 1980, Bernard Ostry, Canada's deputy minister of communications, commented:

90 per cent of the flows which we and others in the world are concerned about result from in-house activities of multi-national organizations, and do not relate to services purchased on the free market.

Not surprisingly, as these corporations came to depend more and more on the telecommunications links which made it possible to control their operations, they also wanted to ensure that they had control of the links themselves. This was the only way of guaranteeing that national governments would not interfere in their business. The Europeans had already started to query the flow of data out of the EEC and implemented data privacy protection laws to cover and regulate transborder data flows. Many of the US companies in the global club of the 450 largest corporations regarded this legislation as an attempt to suppress free speech. The first amendment of the US constitution, which putatively guarantees freedom of speech in that country, does not apply, however, in the rest of the world. It is also debatable whether the authors of the amendment would have approved of this interpretation of it in the late twentieth century. It is unlikely that these corporations will give up their battle with the Europeans until they win, obtain substantial concessions, or find ways of circumventing the legislation.

In Australia, no transborder data laws have been enacted. Communications traffic is not restricted flowing in and out of the country. Companies with predominantly national interests also wanted to be able to move information around the country at whim, and at costs that they determined.

It was out of this desire that the Australian domestic satellite was conceived. Although it was sold to the people of Australia on the basis that it would provide better television, more significantly, the domestic satellite had the capacity to break Telecom Australia's monopoly on telecommunications. The promoters of the satellite recognized early that it was potentially an alternative carrier of data, television and telephone communications. In 1982, the Australian government signed a contract with Hughes Aircraft, the aerospace and defence company formed by the reclusive Howard Hughes. For $400 million, Australia was to get the model T of satellites by 1985. The satellite did not promise to provide services significantly cheaper than Telecom's terrestrial network, but it did allow other organizations to become involved and make money out of communications.

With the decision to proceed with a domestic satellite, it first became apparent to Telecom Australia that Malcolm Fraser's conservative government was actively siding with the competitors – 'scavengers' Telecom managers called them – and against the national network. Not only did the satellite project proceed despite its questionable economics, but it coincided with a government funds squeeze. Telecom was refused permission to borrow enough money to improve its network, refused the right to employ the number of people it needed, refused permission to negotiate and settle directly with its unions, and prevented from moving into new areas.

These knockbacks mounted quickly. By 1981, there was no question left in Telecom's mind that it was on a collision course with the government. The final alert came at the end of that year when the federal government announced the formation of the Davidson Committee of Inquiry into Telecommunications Services in Australia. The Davidson committee was required to determine the extent of private-sector participation in the provision of telecommunications services.

Responding to this challenge, Telecom's most senior management went to ground and began working behind the scenes. They also began to acknowledge loudly that maybe a little competition would be a good thing. Many of them seemed to think that a little competition would calm the government and placate Telecom's critics, allowing it to get on with the job of providing national telecommunications. But they misjudged the severity of the assault they were under.

This became patently clear when the Davidson committee handed down its three-volume report in November 1982. The report recommended a fundamental restructuring of Telecom Australia and the telecommunications system in the country, not only permitting competition between Telecom and the companies supplying handsets and private automatic branch exchanges (PABXs), but competition between networks.

The recommendations threatened to undermine the national network. Telecommunications is provided on the basis of an elaborate cross-subsidy between city and country which Telecom costed at approximately $290 million. That means that nearly $300 million is drawn on each year from the profits in intercapital business traffic to offset losses in other areas (all telephones west of the Great Dividing Range and many suburban areas dominated by domestic subscribers). The cross-subsidy is as complicated as the make-up of an organic creature – or the ecology. An assault on one area affects all other areas. At about the same time as Davidson recommended that Telecom's cross-subsidy should be quantified and the unprofitable areas financed by direct government subsidy, AT&T gave up a ten-year project to cost precisely its cross-subsidy. Apart from the financial problems posed by unpacking the cross-subsidy, it also posed enormous political problems.

If those wanting to operate competitive networks for their own and other company's data and telephone traffic between capital cities succeeded, they were likely to remove the profit-able areas and leave the unprofitable ones. There would need to be a subsidy to ensure the operation of a national system.

If this occurred, rates would have to rise to cover the loss of revenue caused by the diversion of business traffic. As rates rose, the concept of a universal public service would disappear. Telephones would become a luxury item at a time when telecommunications promised to reorganize and possibly revitalize western society.

Within a short time of the restructure of AT&T, this trend became evident in the United States. Greater competition 'threatens to undercut this nation's basic telecommunications policy' (of universal service at reasonable rates) according to the US House of Representatives' Government Operations Committee.

The clash between the goals of competition and universal service remains in the future, but is rapidly approaching. The possibility that rural consumers may be unable to afford telephone services in the future as a result of industry restructuring is real.

The attack on Telecom, spearheaded by BTS and its twelve members, BHP, CRA, ACI, AMP, ACP, Myer, IBM, AWA, James Hardie, Ampol, CSR and TNT, hurt the people who worked for Telecom. In the seven years since the commission was formed in 1975, productivity improvements, bettered only in the mining industry, occurred in telecommunications. Productivity in Telecom improved by about 5 per cent, compared with a national average of only 2 per cent. The 6.7 per cent contributed to the gross domestic product by telecommunications also exceeded the national average of 4.2 per cent; again only mining did better with 8.7 per cent, based on 1979 figures. There were no increases in Telecom's charges from its formation in 1975 until the end of 1981, and its growth rate was more than 10 per cent a year.

There was no other industry which was recording such large improvements, year after year, and the people who worked for Telecom were justifiably proud of their work. But it was these very improvements which made Telecom such an attractive target for the 'corporate raiders'.

Although the people working for Telecom were proud of their achievements, they were subjected to a barrage of media criticism. Telecom employees were criticized for being lazy, industrially militant, unproductive and probably dishonest, because SP bookies had telephones. In reality, most Telecom employees were committed to their work and the concept of providing a national telecommunications network.

But the criticisms took their toll, especially in the light of the management's reluctance to defend publicly the nearly 90,000 people who worked for the commission. These people, the public face of Telecom, those who installed phones and answered queries for numbers, became confused and resentful. The anti-Telecom campaign started to have an effect, and some Telecom people became ashamed and apologetic about working for the commission.

Despite this demoralization, Telecom's people started to fight against the threat of denationalization. The unions, the Australian Telecommunications Employees' Association; Professional Officers' Association; Australian Postal and Telecommunications Union, Australian Public Service Association, Australian Clerical Officers' Association, Australian Telephone and Phonograph Officers' Association, Association of Drafting, Supervisory and Technical Employees, Union of Postal Clerks and Telegraphists and the Telecommunications Traffic and Supervisory Officers' Association, organized a 'Make Telecom the Australian Connection' campaign and criticized the management for not having the courage of its convictions and defending Telecom and the people who worked for it. Most of the senior managers who had authority to speak out if they chose were happier to operate out of the public arena. But these managers, accustomed to direct and indirect government intervention, were surprised at the vehemence of the campaign against them and the use of 'dirty tricks' to discredit Telecom. They were not prepared to play 'dirty tricks' themselves, but soon realized that if that was to be the style of the game, they would also have to play it.

The concept of a universal low-cost service was being sorely tried by the end of 1982. The convergence of computers and communications which triggered this assault on Telecom was also reaching into home entertainment and information services. In mid 1982, cable television, which promised this combination in the home, was recommended by the Australian Broadcasting Tribunal for early introduction. This recommendation also needs to be seen in the context of international corporations anxious to compete and participate in the Australian media industry. Similar developments were occurring in Britain. Until the Australian Broadcasting Tribunal's suggestion, the media in Australia, although effectively controlled by four companies, was still exclusively Australian. The mass media was generally seen as being too important to be allowed to slip under foreign control. But with the recommendation to allow cable television to proceed, this too threatened to change. The Australian Broadcasting Tribunal's cable television report, which preceded the Davidson report by a couple of months, also put paid to the concept of a universal cable television service available to all Australians. Instead, it restricted the potential of cable television to more affluent, densely populated areas – those in poorer and sparsely settled areas would inevitably miss out, without some form of government intervention and subsidy. This would mean not only missing out on an extra forty television channels, many of questionable value anyway, but also relinquishing two-way services, such as the 'tele' services, which enable banking, betting and shopping from home, aided only by your television set and a credit card.

The only way of ensuring universal access would be through a single national carrier, able to offset losses in one area against profits in another. With one organization exclusively responsible for the physical network, the programme content could be separated from the means of distribution. This separation would make it much easier to withdraw the licences of programming companies which failed to live up to the promises they made when they obtained licences.

But this egalitarian suggestion was not before the government at the end of 1982. As a result, Australia stood to make the same mistake with cable television that it made with commercial television. The same policy blunders were made in the United States with cable television, where there were plenty of companies only too happy to provide cable television to affluent midtown Manhattan, but none too keen to cable the depressed South Bronx.

The rush to make money out of the telecommunications industry virtually obliberated concepts such as national benefit. The Davidson inquiry equated the national interest with the self-advancement of private-sector organizations wanting to cash in on communications. That is so partisan a view of what constitutes the greatest benefit for most Australians that the term 'national interest' becomes a slogan to express one's view of the world. If that expression ignores the consequences for most people in Australia, it ought to be treated with the greatest scepticism. The Davidson report abandons the notion of a universal, low-cost telephone service for most of the population in preference to serving the interests of those groups who are already the most powerful in national commercial life.

By the beginning of 1983, Australia faced the prospect of seeing the mistakes of the past repeated in national telecommunications. Like the railways, the private-sector plan for Telecom was to reduce it to a service starved of funds, spurned by most sections of business and providing a barely adequate facility for the less privileged. By allowing road transport lobbies to dominate the political decision-making process, and to annex the carriage of freight, the losses incurred by the railway network became a constant drain on public funds. The carriage of passengers alone was insufficient to sustain an economic and efficient service, and government subsidies, reluctantly granted, were used to prop up the railway network. That same fate could be in store for Australian telecommunications if the lobbyists for private-sector interests have their way.

What stands in the way of those ambitions? Like the railways, an inadequate defence is likely to be mounted by those who head the public-sector telecommunications authority. With few exceptions, they are reluctant to engage in active rebuttal of the campaign to soften up public opinion and pave the way to sell off Telecom Australia. It is the people of Telecom who are likely to prove the greatest obstacle to attempts to break up the national telephone network. Their commitment to an organization which has not always treated them well is firmer than many of the private-sector aspirants anticipated. Mass meetings in all capital cities of Australia have attracted thousands in the wake of the Davidson inquiry. Discussion of the issues at those meetings has been neither superficial nor ill-informed, as opponents of Telecom have alleged. Responsibility for organizing opposition to the plans of private interests has fallen to the trade unions within Telecom. It has been their efforts which have forced the issue into the public gaze, in much the same way as it was the Telecom unions in 1978 which first alerted Australians to the social and employment costs of computer technology. For most of the public, the issues surrounding the Davidson report, and the attempt to remove a publicly funded enterprise to the private sector, are shrouded in complexity.

The first requirement for anyone wanting to understand what has happened in communications in the last few years, the forces at work and the issues involved, is information. Ralph Nader, the US environmentalist and public interest campaigner, has described the non-reporting of issues in telecommunications as the greatest failing in the US media. As in many other areas of national life, what is true of the United States holds for Australia. Telecommunications is not a subject which should be cloaked in technical words and mind-dulling expressions. If it is the lifeblood of large international corporations, it is too important a matter to be left to the boffins and the corporate users of telecommunications. Its future direction will determine the ability of people to communicate, to be informed, and in some cases to act. A paralysis of democracy could be no more effectively achieved than by denying people the means to communications. That is what is at stake in the battle for Telecom Australia.

Chapter Two
Inside the Empire

When Mr and Mrs Ernest Snell of Enmore in Sydney's western suburbs became Australia's four millionth telephone subscribers in November 1977, the attention lavished on them came as a complete surprise. Not only did they receive flowers, certificates and one year's free rental, but a high-powered group of executives made the presentation, including Telecom Australia's chairman, Bob Somervaille. Their luck was even recorded in the Annual Report. A little over three years later, John and Lee O'Farrell of Bunyip, 80 kilometres east of Melbourne became subscribers number five million. And although they were rewarded for their luck, the celebration was a low-key affair, with the acting state manager in Victoria supervising the installation of their chosen Wallfone. They didn't rate a mention in the Annual Report.

The different treatment for subscribers number four million and five million illustrates how Telecom lost the spark and enthusiasm it began with in 1975. Although it went on meeting targets and breaking its own records, the barrage of pressure it was under took its toll, and by 1980 Telecom was a much more defensive organization than it had been five years before. In the year the Snells got their telephone, about sixty-five in every hundred Australian households had a telephone, and by the time the O'Farrells were connected, more than eighty households in every hundred had the phone on. Telecom's corporate plan, drawn up in 1977-78, called for nine out of ten households to be connected by 1987. By the end of 1982, the 1987 target looked set to be met at least one year ahead of plan, unless the economy collapsed completely.

This growth was phenomenal. In 1950, there were only 700,000 telephone subscribers in the country. By 1970, there were 2,700,000 and over the next decade they more than doubled. This put Australia, with only 2 per cent of the world's telephones, in the top seven countries on the register of telephones for every hundred people. Not surprisingly, the United States, with 38 per cent of the world's telephones, topped the list, followed by Sweden, Switzerland, Canada and Denmark. New Zealand, with fifty-five telephones per hundred, just beat Australia, with fifty-three per hundred.

In recession-buffeted Australian industry of the early 1980s, not many other industries recorded the 10 per cent plus annual growth rates, and productivity improvements in the range of 5 per cent a year. By 1982, telecommunications was a lonely bright spot on the dim corporate horizon. At a time when retrenchments, short working weeks, and voluntary redundancies were common in almost every section of the workforce, Telecom Australia was notable for not engaging in similar practices; indeed, it was actively recruiting staff. Depending on the measure used, Telecom is either the largest or second largest enterprise in Australia, after BHP.

Despite the general buoyancy in the telecommunications sector in late 1982, the number of people employed by Telecom had actually declined from 88,690 in July 1975, when it was formed, to 85,641 (plus 2,454 on long-term leave) in June 1982. In the previous year, the government had directed Telecom to cut its staff by 2,000. This was part of a general public service cut, but its impact on Telecom was severe. It meant that, for the first time since 1975, the demand for new services was not being met.

Telecom Australia is the most recent organization to deliver telecommunications to the nation. For the seventy-four years following federation, telecommunications services were provided by the Post Master General's Department (PMG), via the Australian Post Office (APO). Before federation, communications links were provided by the states, each of which had an extensive telegraph and nascent telecommunications capacity.

The decision to form Telecom Australia had been under consideration for some years before it occurred. Senior people employed by the PMG had anticipated the move away from a department of state since the late 1960s. For the largest enterprise in the nation to be a department of state was both unwieldy and inefficient.

In February 1973, halfway through its short term, the Whitlam government commissioned Sir James Vernon to investigate the structure of the PMG and APO. The letters patent that Senator Don Willesee sent to Sir James and his fellow commissioners, Jim Kennedy and Bernard Callinan, asked them to:

report . . . in the public interest, what changes if any should be made in the organization, administration and operations of postal and telecommunications services (including overseas services) provided in Australia.

Sir James had retired as general manager of CSR in 1972 and was willing to undertake the task provided he had an assurance from the government that whatever he and his committee recommended would be implemented. Sir James Vernon has had reason to doubt the commitment of governments to inquiries and commissions it established. In 1963, he was asked by Sir Robert Menzies to head a committee of economic inquiry. This committee, with exceptionally wide-ranging terms of reference, covering the entire economy, had some distinguished people on its panel: J. G. Crawford, Professor Peter Karmel, Kenneth Myer, D. G. Molesworth. Over two years later, the committee presented the government with a 10 centimetre thick document, which it completely ignored. Nearly twenty years later, when the tax-avoidance issue dominated Australian political life, the first Vernon report was resurrected. Commentators observed that if it had been implemented, tax avoidance may not have reached the level it did.

In the folklore of Telecom Australia, Sir James Vernon stands as a giant. He is revered as an individual who had the foresight, independence and intelligence to recommend a system of organizing telecommunications in Australia which would serve the country well. During the fourteen months in which his committee sat, Sir James and his fellow commissioners received submissions from scores of organizations and individuals, travelled extensively overseas and commissioned consultants' reports. The key recommendation was in keeping with world-wide trends at that time: to separate the postal and telecommunications functions and remove them from the confines of the bureaucracy. The bundling together of postal and telecommunications functions in a multi-headed department of state had long been a source of discontent, particularly on the telecommunications side. A trade union official who was working as technician at the time said:

We were happy to support the formation of two commissions, largely for selfish motives. Telecommunications offered more for our members than postal. We thought it would give us a better position – be a dream world even.

Support for the split of postal and telecommunications came from many quarters but not from the upper echelons of the PMG's department. The most senior management of the organization was deeply divided. The majority, dominated by people from the postal side, felt that there should be no division. They felt that the APO should remain intact and provide both postal and telecommunications services. In the end, its submission was silent on the most important issue before Vernon and his committee.

At the time of Vernon's deliberations, Jim Smith was the head of finance and accounting for the PMG's department. After Vesting Day, when Telecom was formed, on 1 July 1975, Smith became deputy chief general manager. A reluctant participant in the APO acrimony, Smith said that the difference came down to 'genuine differences of philosophy, personal ambition and power and influence'. His concern was that, without the separation, the managerial talent needed to run the organization would not have been available in Australia.

Despite the division within the organization, Vernon eventually found that:

The APO is responsible for the provision of both postal and tele-communications services throughout Australia – services which differ widely in respect of technology, capital investment requirements, growth rates and employment characteristics. Each of the services is a large and important enterprise in its own right, and the Commission considers that the time has come to place them under separate administrations ... two statutory corporations should be formed to administer respectively the postal and telecommunications services. Both are essential community services, but have the basic characteristics of commercial enterprises. The Commission does not consider that they should continue to be administered as departments of state. Corporate structures will give the two managements the authorities and responsibilities considered by the Commission to be necessary for the organization and administration of the enterprises.

Vernon also recommended that the new corporations should meet financial objectives and have complete responsibility for determining pay, classifications and conditions of employment. These recommendations guaranteed the support of the unions for the new corporations. One union leader said:

We supported the move to a commission. We believed we would move into an area with no restrictions, we would be able to negotiate directly with management, and not be inhibited by the Public Service Board ... it was to be a wonderful fairytale land, not inhibited by government. It was a real world of optimism we were moving into.

Meanwhile, the executives who had opposed the split of the two organizations were overruled by the successful minority.

In a little over twelve months after Sir James Vernon reported, the APO split, and Telecom Australia and Australia Post were formed. Vesting Day, 1 July 1975 is a day of great significance to people working for Telecom. At a senior management level, it is a rare conversation which does not include some reference to 'V. Day'. 'V. Day is terribly important to us, but no one else seems to know what we mean when we mention it,' Roger Banks, director of business development, said.

On Vesting Day, there were 3,538,948 telephone services in operation, 14,766 telex services, 6,019 datel services, 5,772 telephone exchanges, 114,145 broadband relay systems, 41,380 trunk circuits, 399,396 junction circuits, 81,754 kilometres of ducts, 31,774 kilometres of coaxial cable and 26,099,754 pair kilometres of wire in cables. It was an organization worth $5,000 million.

Within seven years, the dramatic growth of the new organization was recorded in the 1981-82 Annual Report:

More than 80 per cent of homes in Australia now have telephones connected. The corresponding figure was 62 per cent in 1975. During these past seven years the telephone network has expanded 50 per cent, local calls have increased by 60 per cent, STD calls have increased by 90 per cent and international calls by 400 per cent. The number of manual exchanges reduced by 50 per cent since 1975, and it is planned to phase out the remainder during this decade.

Turnover now topped $3,084 million.

On Vesting Day, every position in the organization was declared vacant and all the nearly 90,000 people were reassigned to jobs from the top down.

Jack Curtis, who had been one of the three deputy director generals in the PMG's department, was appointed managing director and charged with the task of overseeing and directing the formation of the new commission. For a man who had risen through the ranks of the public service bureaucracy, after training as an engineer, this was the pinnacle of his career. Not many managers, even in these days of mergers and takeovers, get the opportunity to start such a large organization from scratch.

With the formation of Telecom Australia, the engineers who had dominated the organization before Vesting Day were seriously challenged. The most senior troika only included one engineer. Although Jack Curtis had risen through the ranks as a planning engineer, neither Bill Pollock, the general manager, nor Jim Smith, the deputy general manager, was an engineer by profession. Pollock had joined the PMG as a mechanic, changing his career after World War II. After leaving the army, he studied for a commerce degree and returned to the PMG. Jim Smith also had a general background when he joined the Commonwealth Public Service at the end of the 1950s.

Before the changes which followed Vesting Day, the engineers ran everything. But with the change, regional managers no longer needed professional engineering qualifications. Although at head and state office levels many middle and senior managers were recruited from the ranks of the engineers, others were also considered.

Curtis and his team were aided in restructuring Telecom by a proposed management and organizational plan which Sir James Vernon had included in his report. In keeping with established management theory, policy was to be consolidated and determined at head office and decentralized on a branch basis. Since federation, telecommunications in Australia had been delivered on a state basis. The states branches were all-powerful, semi-autonomous operations which decided the way they should be managed, how they were managed and what they did next without excessive head office intervention. Consequently, the level of services was not uniform throughout the nation, and some states, notably New South Wales, lagged as others progressed.

In forming a national commission, this changed. Policy was centralized at headquarters in William Street, Melbourne, and field operations were decentralized to a district level. Before the reorganization, there was little co-ordination between divisions. This caused overlaps and lags in response to new technologies and market demands. Even engineering planning was separated from engineering works. At a state level, the problems were worse. The assistant director engineering and the assistant director telecommunications reported separately to the state manager. Both the divisions were sub-divided geographically, but the technical and commercial functions of the telecommunications business in a state were only brought together at the level of the state manager.

This structure was obviously unwieldy, and Vernon included a revised district organizational structure in his report.

Jim Smith was assigned the task of overseeing the internal reorganization of Telecom:

It was a classic approach to decentralization in a big organization, but in the early days a lot of people were strongly opposed to it. Managers believed in centralization; they didn't want to lose power, and genuinely believed it wasn't the best way to organize things. Particularly, the engineers and the Professional Officers' Association were opposed to it, because they saw it as the first loss of functions which had been controlled by engineers; they believed it wasn't an appropriate way to organize the field operations.

The district organizational plan aimed to centralize all the functions provided by Telecom in one area into one office. It meant that there would no longer be several divisions dealing with subscribers, but all these activities would be combined under a district telecommunications manager, who was not necessarily to be an engineer.

In the 1976 Annual Report, the chairman, Bob Somervaille, wrote:

The district organisations will carry out the day-to-day work now performed by the present engineering and customer services departments. These include installing external plant and telephone and other facilities for subscribers, repairing faults, handling complaints and applications for service, carrying out smaller new works and marketing services and equipment. There will also be decentralisation of other key work areas such as telephone accounts from state head office to local areas.

Overall the new form of organisation will promote a much greater responsiveness to customer needs and the making of decisions at the local level where customer needs and services are best understood. Some 96 per cent of people will be within 80 kilometres of a district office.

In March 1977, the first eight districts were established in Canberra, Wagga Wagga, Camberwell, Ivanhoe, Frankston and Metropolitan Central, North and South in South Australia. The next batch were established in July, and within fifteen months Australia was divided into eighty-three districts.

Behind the enthusiasm for the district organization displayed in the Annual Report and other official publications was bitter opposition to the restructuring from the engineers. It was only after a series of hearings in the Conciliation and Arbitration Commission and a High Court decision on the Conciliation and Arbitration Commission's jurisdiction that the plan was finally implemented. Jim Smith recalled:

The opposition was overcome in 1977 by sheer dint of argument; we soundly defeated the engineers. In the end, I think it was our evident determination to carry it through – it was going to be and that was that – which won out.

What distressed the engineers was the erosion of their authority implied in the district plan. Before Vesting Day, all supervisory management positions went to engineers. The district plan turned this hitherto natural progression on its head, and the engineers quite rightly saw an inevitable waning of their responsibility and authority. The decision to restructure the organization, and particularly the decision to grant people other than engineers access to middle management positions, was a conscious and considered one. The management consultants Vernon engaged, Cresap, McCormick and Paget, suggested that the district telecommunications managers should be drawn from clerical, technical divisions as well as from engineering, so that the position became 'a true management position and not a position where professional engineering qualifications should be regarded as essential'.

This was the first time that the engineers' authority had been eclipsed. Access to management by virtue of engineering qualifications was no longer a right. Despite their numbers – about 2,000 in 1974 – the engineers had always dominated the organization. In part, this was because telecommunications had always been technology driven, and telecommunications planning, until the late 1960s, was constrained by the available technology. But this changed, and by the time Vernon handed down his report, telecommunications planning was no longer determined solely by the technology that was available.

This new approach to planning was publicly acknowledged

in 1975 when the 'Telecom 2000' report was released. 'Telecom 2000' was an examination of the role of telecommunications in the society of the future. At this time, the possibilities created by joining computers and communications technologies were emerging. Inside Telecom, there was a growing awareness that the telecommunications systems chosen for the future would have a large impact on the society the country would have.

Although 'Telecom 2000' was a long-term outlook, not a detailed series of objectives, it turned an exclusive engineering planning model on its head. It drew on a number of disciplines and advocated open planning and community involvement in decisions about its future.

Despite the formal diminution of engineering authority within the organization, engineering's legacy still remains. Kevin Fothergill, the Victorian secretary of the Australian Telecommunications Employees' Association believes:

Even in Jack Curtis's days, engineering was the most powerful section . . . the gear came first, second and third, and it was a nuisance that people had to get in the way to look after it; this was a pretty general attitude. The requirements of the network were always seen by engineering as taking priority over human beings, and this made it very difficult to negotiate with them.

Developing the districts was not the only reorganization which occurred after Vesting Day. The Melbourne headquarters and state offices were also restructured, and this reorganization was still not complete at the end of 1982. The Melbourne headquarters were divided into seven departments: accounting, engineering, industrial relations, personnel, research, information systems and customer services. But Telecom was still criticized for not being sufficiently responsive to the demands of the market place.

Much of this criticism came from the business sector. By the end of the 1970s, the importance of telecommunications for business efficiency was apparent to even the smallest companies. As the computer industry boomed, the need to be able to link computers became crucial. At the same time, the PABX market started to grow rapidly. The private automatic branch exchange was going to the top of many corporate lists of needs. As these pressures mounted, the new commission came under considerable strain, especially as it coincided with government restrictions on independence and resources.

At the end of 1979, Telecom, in conjunction with the government, appointed international consultants, McKinsey and Co. Inc., to investigate the likely future demand for telecommunications facilities and the best way of financing this development. Two years later, the McKinsey team reported, that telecommunications services in Australia compared satisfactorily with major overseas administrations, and that the operations of the organization vitally affect 'the effectiveness of the public and private business sectors of the economy as well as individuals and groups in social and commercial spheres'. McKinsey concluded:

Telecom has improved its performance and today the nation is receiving substantially greater value from its telecommunications investment . . . notwithstanding an improvement in the provision of new types of services since 1975, Telecom needs to invest increased resources in the development and provision of new types of communications services, not only to meet the needs of business and industry but also to further improve the financial and economic efficiency of the total service . . . and Telecom needs to adopt changed management policies and a moderate increase in capital spending in order to improve and extend its services in the light of new telecommunications developments.

As a result of this report, Telecom re-examined its responsiveness to business demands. The year before, plans to introduce a Digital Data Network and a Packet Switching Service were announced. A decision to introduce a commercial services division was made after an internal investigation into the organization of AT&T and other large telecommunications administrations. By November 1980, the nucleus of this division was operating at the William Street headquarters in Melbourne. By 1981, product management groups were incorporated into the commercial services division. These groups – telephone, data, telex and telegram, local network services, trunk network, PABX, small business systems and directory services – all had specific commercial, information and marketing aims. In response to McKinsey's criticism that it was slow to respond to the needs of business, seventy key account managers were appointed to administer the telecommunications needs of Telecom's biggest business clients. Meanwhile, a business development directorate, answerable to the managing director, was established at headquarters. Roger Banks assumed the position of director and with it responsibility for business and corporate planning.

By 1981, corporate planning within Telecom had changed dramatically. Vernon's rosy promise of an organization free from government intervention had been demolished. Time and again the government interfered, seriously inhibiting Telecom's ability to meet the targets it set for itself and the demands of business and domestic subscribers. Even the McKinsey report, which was commissioned by Telecom in conjunction with the government, was kept secret for six months. The government was not prepared to release it. The report found that Telecom was doing a satisfactory job; the only significant inhibition came from the government's refusal to permit Telecom to borrow the money it needed to do its job properly.

When Telecom was formed, expectations within the organization were high. There was a very real feeling that at last the organization would be able to do what it did best without petty government interference. But year after year this enthusiasm waned, until 1982 when a 'climate of unease' predominated in the organization. Although targets continued to be met, the uncertainty started to affect morale.

Within six months of Vesting Day, the government changed. After the election of the Fraser government, at the end of 1975, the climate of Australian public life changed dramatically. Telecom was not excluded.

The new commission had a charter to provide telecommunications services for all Australians. It was required by law to meet the social, industrial and commercial needs of the nation, within the context of financial objectives. Revenue was to cover current expenses each year, and no less than half the capital needed was to be generated internally. This requirement was accepted, although in the preceding decade the APO had never generated more than 47 per cent of its capital internally.

When Chairman Bob Somervaille's first Annual Report was tabled in Parliament in October 1976, it included severe criticism of the government. The new Fraser government had directed Telecom to find 55 per cent of its capital funds internally and to reduce its staff. Somervaille wrote:

While such an arrangement may be necessary in times of economic difficulty the Commission firmly believes that savings and economies should be available to minimise price rises to customers, rather than to increase the percentage of internal funding. Telecom Australia had been cutting back on staff numbers, reducing overtime and closely examining its investment programme from Vesting Day. The Government's mid year decision to reduce sharply public employment produced a significant and sudden reduction in staff for the Commission which had an object to increase its outputs in the form of services to the community by 7 per cent. This further reduction in staff had not been achieved without some effect on the programme of service improvements. Some slowing and capital investment below planned levels was also unavoidable ... There are, however, limits to what can be done and access to sufficient finance, without increasing the degree of internal funding, will be of crucial importance if the Commission is to continue with its programme of service improvements and cost and price containment through exploitation of modern technology. Indeed the Commission would wish to be able to move toward 50 per cent internal funding rather than increasing above the 1975-76 level of 55 per cent.

Rather than decreasing, the level of internal funding rose dramatically. The next year, 57 per cent of capital works were funded internally; by 1978-79, it had jumped to 79 per cent and included its contributions to staff superannuation. For the following two years, it fell to 73 per cent.

Being forced to generate hundreds of millions of dollars

internally placed the organization under considerable strain, but that was not the only government financial constraint. Between 1979 and 1982 Telecom was refused permission to borrow more than $220 million a year, a drop in real terms each year of about 10 per cent. At the end of 1981 came the king-hit.

Cabinet decided, without consulting Telecom, that it would unilaterally increase the interest rate on long-term loans which had been negotiated in the past. Although the loans had been negotiated with a fixed 7 per cent interest rate, in August 1981, the commission was told that the rate was going up to 10 per cent in the new year. This action was contrary to commercial practice, but with the government playing both judge and prosecutor, Telecom had no choice but to accept the increase which added $58 million to 1981-82 repayments and $133 million to the 1982-83 interest bill.

This decision finally forced up the rates for telephone calls and rentals. A major plank in Telecom's corporate plan had been that the real cost of telecommunications services should decline. Despite the financial pressure, Telecom's growth and productivity improvements enabled it to hold prices constant from 1975 until 1981, when they rose for the first time.

The demand that Telecom finance so much of its growth out of internal funds presented a public relations problem. Each year Telecom reported massive profits ranging from $164 million in its first year to $275.1 million in 1981-82. And each year the media commented on the size of the profit and the cost of services. 'If Telecom makes so much money, why doesn't it put its rates down,' was a constant refrain. The reason it didn't lower tariffs was that its profit was being used to finance other developments. As Bob Somervaille observed in his final Annual Report in 1978-79:

... it is difficult to explain a shortage of resources to customers in need of services, particularly in view of the reported profit ... a higher borrowing level would have enabled a better balanced construction programme to be implemented.

Every year the commission attempted to explain this, but

the explanation was not particularly suited to tabloid journalism, already hostile to public-sector bureaucracies. Chairman Bob Brack retaliated in 1982:

Telecom is sometimes criticised on the grounds that its profits are too high. Those who suggest that Telecom should operate at a lower level of return fail to appreciate that the consequent reduced cash flow would mean a reduction in funds available for expenditure on the expansion and maintenance of the network and would make Telecom's task of improving the standard of customer service more difficult than it is now.

Despite the government's intervention, the most senior managers of Telecom were reticent about publicly defending the commission, allowing the criticism of Telecom in the media to continue unabated. Those working for Telecom were criticized for being lazy and unproductive, despite the second largest productivity increases in the Australian economy occurring in telecommunications.

The media criticism reached a peak in May 1982 when the top rating television programme, '60 Minutes', featured an item about Telecom in which it was argued that the commission was not doing its job as well as Bell Canada; that it was more expensive, generally unresponsive, and inefficient. The programme was attacked for not comparing like with like and not putting the situation of would-be telephone subscribers in Sydney's western suburbs into its proper perspective. Quite a deal of the criticism of '60 Minutes' stuck, not least because the programme was then sponsored by BHP and broadcast on Channel TCN 9, which is owned by Kerry Packer's Publishing and Broadcasting Limited. Both BHP and Publishing and Broadcasting were members of the consortium leading the attack on Telecom, Business Telecommunications Services.

This constant attack started to affect the morale of the nearly 90,000 people who worked for Telecom. One technician who had worked for most of his life on the central coast north of Sydney found that his status in the town started to slip dramatically. 'We used to be on a par with the policeman and the town clerk, but things started to get so bad in that area that you just didn't say you worked for Telecom or you'd be abused,' he said.

Jim Smith believes that if Telecom had not been formed telecommunications in Australia 'would be in a great mess'. He believes that a department of state could not have provided the *esprit de corps* and structure to cope with the commercial and political pressure the organization has come under. 'The district organization was designed to charge people up to meet new objectives and targets,' he said.

For people brought up in an organization which provided an essential public service, the idea of being 'charged up' to meet 'new objectives and targets' was one which many found difficult to accept. In areas which were growing quickly, including the New South Wales central coast, the western suburbs of Sydney, and the Gold Coast, the demand for services could not be matched by Telecom, which was denied resources and was not prepared to fight publicly.

Telecom employees started to feel defensive and uncertain. Telecom management had consciously decided that the way to gain the support of the government was not through a public campaign but through a quiet approach, lobbying politicians and trying to influence the political climate from the inside.

Whatever the merits of this approach, it was not one designed to instill confidence in the workforce, which felt it was being buffeted on all sides and not properly defended by management.

Roger Banks was one of the architects of this approach to the defence of Telecom. He believed it was the best way to ensure victory. To make a song and dance in the hope of changing a situation is anathema to Banks, who believes 'if you let the press get involved you lose control, and if you lose control you can't win'. Nevertheless, Banks concedes the damage this has caused a virtually undefended Telecom workforce:

The trouble is our people, our best people, the ones who now feel a bit let down, have gone on all their careers to date, wanting to provide a service. They joined Telecom because they wanted to do this and they still do. Coming out of the previous cocoon has not been easy for many of them. There is a very high degree of commitment. Because our people are committed to delivering a service, they are frustrated when they can't, when they are so often exposed in the press as being lazy and uncommitted, when such biased muckraking as the '60 Minutes' programme is shown on television. Our people used to trust the political process to work, but frankly, the political process has come under a bit of a cloud in recent years. It is an uneasy situation, no matter what you think is right; we have never before been subject to such caprice. Management has handled things on an objective professional level and that is why we have a world-wide reputation for telecommunications, because we are judged on the merits of the issue. It is hard won and sore when put at risk. It is a very sad about-face, that changed environment; we have a very good heritage and the last thing we want is to see that broken down.

Not only did the most senior management at Telecom find it difficult to adequately defend the people whom the public sees as the enterprise - those who install and connect telephones, drive the orange vans, crouch under tents on footpaths, answer operator queries and accept payment at Telecom Business Offices - it was unable to negotiate as freely with its staff as it had expected. The absurdity of this was recorded in the 1977-78 Annual Report. That year Telecom had offered its staff cheaper telephones:

When a company . . . markets goods or services, it is a common practice for the staff to be able to obtain these at a concession rate. This is true of major retailers and manufacturers, airlines, and public transport. It is a practice in many overseas countries in relation to telecommunications.

The proposal was that staff with at least five years' service be given a concession on metered-call charges. The minister of the day, Tony Staley refused, saying that the 'proposal was not warranted in the present economic situation' and that it should be re-examined later.

All these events sapped the morale of Telecom employees.

It was only in times of national emergency and regional disasters that they were given credit and praise.

It is surprising, then, that surveys of domestic telephone subscribers do not reveal the same criticism of Telecom. The attitudes which recur are that the service is seen as being thorough, consistent, unbiased, and expert. Domestic subscribers understand that Telecom 'will always be there', will 'always be able to supply parts' and 'provides excellent consultancy services'.

The Australian Consumers' Association found that most criticisms of Telecom revolved around telephone bills. Seventy per cent of respondents to a survey it carried out were dissatisfied with the information on their bill, and 65 per cent said that they had had cause to query it at some stage or other. Telecom, however, only received queries from less than 1 per cent of its more than five million subscribers, and only between 5 and 10 per cent warranted action. Most errors were the result of clerical mistakes, which are automatically corrected with the next bill.

The other source of complaint is about installation time. This is directly related to the commission's lack of financial and staffing autonomy. In those years when it had inadequate staff and money, the average waiting time for connections grew (depending on the demand in particular areas). But 90 per cent of new connections are made within ten days. Although this length of time is not ideal, it represents a good use of resources. If the waiting time were much shorter, it would mean that people and machines would be sitting, waiting for the next request for a telephone to be connected.

Surveys conducted for Telecom by marketing consultants showed that the confidence in Telecom was so high that people would be prepared to pay considerably more to buy a Telecom phone than they would pay for a 'Joe Bloggs decorator' telephone. This survey presupposes that people can buy their telephones. This is one of the most consistent criticisms of Telecom, and one which has the most support within the organization. Telecom, like most of the other telephone authorities in the world, has traditionally leased its telephones. The rental charge then covers the cost of the handset, its installation, service and maintenance and the subscriber's contribution to maintaining the network. But as the move to introduce competition into telecommunications gathered pace, the notion that a telephone was a decorative item gained support. This has been resisted in most countries. In Britain, approved attachments are permitted as long as the first phone is a British Telecom handset. In the United States, AT&T initially fought the issue but then backed off. It now plans to phase out all leasing so that US subscribers will no longer have the choice between renting or buying.

Much of the concern about non-standard handsets was based on fears of the dangers of technical incompatibility both to individual subscribers and the network. Because of the dangers of incompatible equipment, Telecom Australia, like telephone companies in other countries, has reserved the right to approve attachments. This has raised the ire of the new breed of telephone entrepreneurs, and Telecom, aware of this criticism, approved 6,300 different items for direct supply by the private sector – from Mickey Mouse telephones to PABXs – in the year between Vesting Day and 1982.

Initially, most of the pressure had come from suppliers of office and business equipment, but by 1982 the would-be suppliers of alternative domestic telephones were beginning to make their presence felt. This new era was heralded by extensive media coverage for a man called Sir Ronnie Dias and his company, then called Bell Telephone and Communications Systems. Sir Ronnie, a cigar-smoking man, who hailed from London's East End via New York, Atlantic City, Las Vegas, Israel, Eastern Europe and Sydney's Kings Cross, was an unusually colourful arrival in the normally staid telecommunications industry. Some of his early authority waned when it became known that his knighthood was not bestowed by the Queen of England, but was bought from an order known as the Knights of Malta. Sir Ronnie wanted to sell his fully imported telephones through department stores but encountered numerous obstacles, not all of them in Telecom.

Sir Ronnie was a new breed of telecommunications entrepreneur and one who did not make the established executives very happy. Telecom's 'Buy Australia' policy has enabled seven of the world's big telecommunications manufacturing companies - L. M. Ericsson, NEC, STC, Plessey, Philips, AWA, Siemens - to set up plants in Australia. Telecom buys at least 75 per cent of their output. This relationship had difficulties when the suppliers operated a cartel to divide the market between them. Selection by Telecom of seven suppliers of PABXs to provide the systems caused dissension within the industry association, which eventually collapsed under the strain in 1980.

Although only one of the manufacturing companies, AWA, is not a subsidiary of an overseas based transnational corporation, considerable Australian expertise has gone into adapting and modifying the equipment bought from the companies for Australian use. Most of the technical standards for this modification and adaptation are set in Telecom's Research Laboratories at Clayton in Melbourne. The laboratories' extensive grounds resemble a university campus, and house some of the most talented electronics researchers in Australia.

At the time of the Vernon committee's investigations, Telecom's Research Labs had developed a world-leading digital telephone exchange. There was a suggestion at the time that Telecom should copy the AT&T model, expand the Research Labs, and develop a manufacturing capacity locally. Vernon recommended that 'manufacture of limited quantities of telecommunications items should be further examined'.

This was one of the Vernon proposals which never materialized, owing largely to pressure from the local suppliers. In 1977, Telecom agreed to spend $500 million buying a digital exchange, ARE 11, from L. M. Ericsson, which used similar technology to the one which had been developed by Telecom's Research Labs.

Telecom has a close relationship with the suppliers, who recognize the importance of the commission to their continued operation in Australia. Although there have been commercial conflicts between the suppliers and Telecom from time to time, the relationship has not resembled the 'dirty pool' which has characterized the behaviour of some of the newer entrants to the industry. Talking about the BTS lobby group, Roger Banks said:

What disturbs me about the interest groups and pressure groups lobbying, quite apart from the techniques used, is that they have shrouded their true motivation in a rationale which is less than candid. These lobby groups have advanced plausible but misleading arguments. But they knew before they started what they wanted and that's dirty pool . . . dishonest even. If they are to go on playing dirty pool, we are prepared to play too, which is something we haven't done in the past. When the name of the game changes, Telecom will be able to change to optimize its position. Competition is good if it means improved efficiency, but that ignores the efficiency improvements in Telecom over the last few years. If we start playing dirty pool it could well happen to the detriment of subscribers. Some would have to suffer if the rules change.

The suffering Banks predicted was, by the end of 1982, starting to affect people working for Telecom. As senior executives were saying loudly and often that they felt Telecom 'had the knowledge and talent to do very well in a competitive situation' and that people would prefer to do business with Telecom, the message started to filter through to the staff. The senior management was committed to competition. But many people working for the telecommunications authority were less convinced.

In an attempt to counter this lack of enthusiasum for competition, a motivational campaign was adopted in Victoria in 1982. Featuring a 'football coach', it urged the staff of the Victorian districts to 'get out there and keep going 'til it hurts, get out there and sell'. It was a campaign designed in the words of the video star in the footy jumper to prepare Telecom employees 'for any competition game enough to come our way'. Although the incentives only included boxes of chocolates, bottles of wine and wooden spoons, the sales figures for Victoria went up. Many were not so sure of either the desirability of competition or the commission's ability to win, especially if 'dirty pool' became the norm. They argued that the notion of being able to compete could lull Telecom into a false sense of security.

Although Roger Banks was convinced of Telecom's ability to beat any competitors, he said:

If we aren't stopped we can go on improving our efficiency and performance, making us more efficient, cost effective and relevant. But by one means or another they will try and hobble us. As we go forward into the end of the twentieth-century economy, to suggest any impediment to the full exploitation of this resource would be limited and parochial – an un-Australian motive which should be seen as such.

Telecommunications is one of only a very, very, few bright spots in the economy, yet those guys are wanting to destroy it.

Chapter Three
Its Master's Voice

Telecommunications in Australia has always been politically contentious. Long before any thought was given to dismantling the publicly owned national network, telecommunications was occasionally a hot political issue. Partly because of Australia's size and population distribution and its distance from Europe, telecommunications links have been of crucial importance since the days of the first white settlements. In solving these problems, Australia has developed an outstanding international reputation for the standard of its telecommunications network.

Only nine years after Samuel Morse first used a telegraph line in the United States, the fledgling colony of Victoria built Australia's first telegraph line in 1854 between Williamstown and Melbourne. In 1880, only two years after the first telephone exchange was built in the United States, Australia's first telephone exchanges were opened in Melbourne, Sydney and Brisbane. By 1872, a telegraph line cut Australia in half and connected Adelaide and Darwin. One of the first automatic telephone exchanges in the world opened in Geelong, Victoria, in 1912. By the late 1970s, Australia was again a world leader, one of the first countries to introduce digital exchanges.

The first Australian to head a United Nations agency was Dick Butler, a former PMG engineer. In October 1982, Butler was elected general secretary of the International Telecommunication Union (ITU). The ITU has considerable power for an international agency, and Australia has had a long association with it, all the states being members before federation, when the commonwealth became a member.

The political kudos which politicians should have given the people who made this world-leading telecommunications network possible has always been slow in coming. But politicians have never been slow to realize the importance of telecommunications to members of their own electorates. In a study which Telecom undertook in the late 1970s, to assess outback demand for satellite television, the respondents said that they wanted a telephone first, a telephone that worked second, and a telephone that worked all the time third.

The provision of telephones in the cities, country, towns and new developments is an important electoral issue. Politicians may not have lost their seats over the rate of telephone connections in their electorates, but their lives have been made uncomfortable by it. One senior Telecom executive described the political importance by saying, 'Each phone – especially in sparsely settled areas – is a vote. The connection rate is a very political matter.'

With a degree of integrity rare in some private-sector companies, Telecom has not used its control over the connection rate as a political weapon to obtain what it sought from its political masters; whether it is money, staff or autonomy. Its political masters, however, have not displayed the same reluctance. Indeed, some politicians have used their positions to obtain so many telephone favours that at times Telecom, and the PMG before it, was seen as a private lollyshop for politicians. These accusations flew thick and fast during the years of the Liberal-Country Party coalition government before Telecom became a commission. In those days, as a government department, the PMG was susceptible to political pressure, although the favours it offered politicians were rarely repaid.

Although general accusations have often been levelled at Telecom and the PMG, particularly in relation to granting requests from National Country Party members, the specifics of cases have been hard to document. But at the end of 1981, a case came to light which had all the right ingredients, and there were documents to substantiate the political direction involved. The case concerned a politician, his father-in-law, a small holiday island, and more than one million dollars.

In this case, the politician was the minister for communications at the time, and the deputy leader of the National Country Party, Ian Sinclair; the small holiday island, Lord Howe, 700 kilometres north east of Sydney; and Stan Fenton, Lord Howe's first postmaster and radio operator was the father-in-law.

It took six months from the time the island's management committee first approached Telecom for approval to be granted for a new telephone link with the mainland and a local automatic telephone exchange.

Not all the 270 residents on the island were convinced that the million-dollar telephone would be a good thing. Lord Howe island is best known as a holiday resort for businessmen and politicians 'who want to get away from the phone' and some of them, including New South Wales Premier Neville Wran, were less than impressed. Wran was one of many people who signed a petition opposing the installation of the telephone. Many of the islanders liked their quiet, peaceful way of life, where people visited each other rather than relying on the telephone. Others were concerned that the four 29 metre radio towers needed for the new link would be unsightly and take up too much room because of the guy wires needed to support them. Some just felt that the noise and cost of cabling through the rocky island would be excessive.

But Stan Fenton was among the island's telephone enthusiasts. At the time he said:

I have two sons and two daughters, all of whom live on the mainland. My wife Gladys has grandchildren in England. That is why we think the phone is a great idea for Lord Howe. Imagine what it is like to prepare for bowling day and drive down to the club, only to find the game has been called off, when one phone call could have saved us all the time and trouble.

But if the Lord Howe telephone demand was causing conflict on the island, it was nothing compared to the flurry within Telecom.

In November 1980, the island's management committee approached the New South Wales manager of Telecom, Ken Douglas, and requested an improved telephone service. Shortly afterwards, Douglas asked his chief engineer in New South Wales, Bob McCarthy, to assess the earliest possible completion date. At this time, Telecom was under severe pressure from the government. The 'climate of unease' generated by ministerial veto of the preceding years had made Telecom managers uncertain. In the same month as Douglas asked McCarthy to look at the Lord Howe request, the government announced the formation of Sir Phillip Lynch's Razor Gang. The Razor Gang was designed to cut the numbers of people employed in the public service and hand over profitable public-sector activities to the private sector. Prime Minister Fraser made this clear when he announced its formation. 'There is a need to avoid intruding into areas of activity capable of being performed efficiently by the private sector,' Fraser said. As Australia's largest enterprise, Telecom, and the PMG before it, was always a prime target when governments wanted to cut public service numbers. So, when the Razor Gang was formed, Telecom management and staff rightly feared the worst.

Over the preceding years, the amount of capital funding generated internally rose, so that by the end of 1980, the rate of new connections failed to keep up with demand by the biggest margin since Vesting Day. This delay was particularly bad in Sydney's rapidly growing western suburbs, Penrith and Campbelltown, the central coast of New South Wales, around Gosford, and the Gold Coast in Queensland. Government decisions delayed Telecom and detracted from the service it provided. Nevertheless, during the 1980-81 financial year, Telecom spent $2,376,900,000 and connected 552,369 new telephone, telex and datel services.

It was against this background that Bob McCarthy replied to Ken Douglas's query about the earliest possible starting date for the new radio telephone link to Lord Howe Island. McCarthy wrote in December 1980:

The earliest practicable date would be eighteen months from now, and although not included in the 1981-84 DCWP [draft capital works programme] as just written it is recommended that action be directed towards equipment delivery in 1981 for installation early in 1982-83.

The installation of the SCAX [small country automatic exchange] is seen as part of the rural plan and is supported by the chief manager, customer services department. It would be included in the 1982-83 program in lieu of another SCAX item.

McCarthy's nomination of 1982-83 as the earliest possible date was dependent on the Electricity Commission installing new generating equipment, the Department of Communications allocating HF radio frequencies, and agreement between Transport Australia and the Overseas Telecommunications Commission on technical and commercial aspects of installing the radio links.

Following McCarthy's recommendations, a letter was drafted for Ian Sinclair to pass on to the leader of the National Country Party and deputy prime minister, Doug Anthony. The practice of drafting letters for the minister to sign is a function performed by both the public service and semi-government authorities. In part the letter Telecom drafted for Sinclair to sign said:

Preliminary planning has been undertaken on this project, but some delay will be inevitable in procuring the necessary equipment and installing and commissioning the plant on the island. It is currently planned to complete this work during 1982-83 and every effort will be made to meet this schedule.

Sinclair refused to sign the letter. In the margin adjacent to this paragraph Sinclair scrawled: 'This date is unacceptable – try again.' He also drew two lines through the 1982-83 date and wrote underneath: '1981-82'.

Sinclair's intervention sent Telecom management into a panic, as only the most basic preliminary planning had been made at this stage. An urgent telex from the Transmission and Line Planning Department at Telecom's headquarters in March 1981 ran through the planning undertaken so far and suggested an urgent meeting of the seven other departments involved in the project:

In order to frame a reasonable reply [to Sinclair's direction] it will be necessary to accurately tie down target dates for all aspects of the overall installation, together with a listing of variable factors that may cause delays – a critical path diagram would be appropriate.

By the beginning of 1982, Lord Howe Island got its telephone link with the mainland, although according to women working at the International Manual Exchange in Sydney's GPO, the quality of the link was 'hopeless'.

The link was also not without its trade-off cost. Nineteen other centres due to receive SCAXs that year missed out. In Telecom's Annual Report for 1980-81, the acting chairman of the commission, Tom May, wrote:

Good progress has been made in meeting the rural conversion program and during the year the number of manual services was reduced by 11,650 to 61,709. The rural program is a high cost area and further progress in meeting the overall objective of providing a universal standard automatic telephone service throughout Australia depends to a large extent on the finances that can be made available for this task. Extensive cross subsidy from the profitable services is an essential ingredient.

Lord Howe's meagre population ensured that it would never be a profitable service, and the urgency with which it was implemented meant that nineteen other centres in New South Wales missed out, including some in Sinclair's own electorate of New England. The irony of the Lord Howe installation was that despite some of the islanders' impeccable connections with the National Country Party, they are part of the electorate of Elizabeth, one of the safest Labor Party seats in Australia.

Not all the government intervention in Telecom since Vesting Day has been directed towards party political gain. But a great deal of it has been.

When Telecom announced plans to close sixteen Manual Assistance Centres (MAC) in New South Wales and Victoria at the beginning of 1982, telephonists mounted an unprecedented campaign to save the centres and their jobs. One of the most successful campaigns was waged in the western Victorian town of Hamilton. There the telephonists lobbied their local member, the prime minister, Malcolm Fraser. This lobbying had an effect. When Telecom and the Department of Communications decided which MACs should be saved, Hamilton was on the list. Fraser was notified of the salvation of the Hamilton MAC just two days before he was due to meet another deputation on the matter from his electorate.

Another instance of the political sensitivity surrounding Telecom affected a technician in Melbourne. A woman subscriber in the wealthy South Yarra suburb had complained about a fault. When the technicians came to repair the fault, they found that they did not have the right equipment or the time to do the job that day, so they returned to the exchange planning to complete the job on the following day. Later the woman phoned the technicians to find out why her telephone had not been repaired that day. The technician informed her that this was because of a staff shortage as a result of government policy. The technician felt that he had received a sympathetic hearing and had made the problems, caused by government intervention, clear to another member of the public. The subscriber, however, had rather better connections than the technician anticipated. When her husband was informed of the day's events, he phoned the prime minister to complain – not about the cuts to Telecom, but about a technician commenting on government policy. Shortly afterwards, the technician was 'counselled' – a management euphemism for reprimanded – and his employment file marked accordingly.

As a statutory commission, Telecom's relationship with the government is prescribed by the legislation under which it operates. The *Telecommunications Act* 1975 requires the commission to perform its functions in such a manner as will best meet the social, industrial and commercial needs of the Australian people for telecommunications services. It is required to take into account the desirability of improving and extending its telecommunications services in the light of developments in the field, the need to operate its services as efficiently and economically as practicable, and to take account of the special needs for telecommunications services of Australian people who live and work outside the cities. Section 7 of the act provides for the minister to give directions in writing about Telecom's functions and the exercise of its powers as appears to the minister to be necessary in the public interest.

The government has not, however, given Telecom the independence those working for it felt had been enshrined in legislation applying after Vesting Day in 1975. This independence from the government was one of the selling points of splitting the PMG into Australia Post and Telecom Australia. The independence, however, was short lived. By 1982, some senior Telecom executives were saying that they had more independence as a department of state than as a statutory commission, that in the old days of the PMG ministerial veto was rarely used, compared with its frequent use since 1975. Although this recollection owes something to rose-coloured glasses, in the old days the people making the requests were also providing the advice. Now Telecom still advises the minister, but there is an additional advisory buffer in the Department of Communications, which has been a source of considerable friction in recent years.

On the evidence of interference after the Vernon report, Telecom management and employees were sceptical that the freedom from government intervention promised by the Davidson report would eventuate. For a Telecom which had been directed by the government to cut its staff by an arbitrary 2,000 in 1981, the comment of the communications minister, Neil Brown, to the National Press Club in November 1982 must have rung a little hollow. 'You will not have that growth in employment if you have the hand of government strangling the whole operation perpetually,' Brown said.

The government certainly exercised a strangling hand in the years of the late 1970s and early 1980s, interfering in everything from the purchase of property, industrial relations, wages, staff numbers, policy decisions about changes to the network, to restructuring loans without consultation and declining contracts. The cabinet, under the leadership of Malcolm Fraser, has tended to act as a superior board, passing judgements and reserving the right of veto on decisions made by senior management and the board of the commission itself. Although it is clear that Telecom must be subject to democratic control, under the Fraser government that process has been partisan and party political.

One senior Telecom executive described the relationship with the Fraser government thus:

It hasn't been easy. We keep changing ministers which isn't easy at all. Since Vesting Day we have had four ministers in this government. They have a problem when they come to this portfolio because it is such a difficult area – not only telecommunications, but broadcasting and postal as well – it has got to be a problem. It takes them a while to come to grips with it. Meanwhile the day-to-day business must go on. We are an $8 billion enterprise, earning close to $3 billion a year with a cash velocity in and out of the doors of $6 billion. There are a lot of real time problems which need to be solved immediately; it is a continuous flow. When you consider it, we spend $800 million on materials every year and every contract over $500,000 has to be signed by the minister. Now ministers are cautious people concerned about snakes in the grass, so they ask questions, but first they have to figure out what questions to ask about gear they may not have the vaguest clue about. So they ask questions and things are delayed. But for us it is just one speck in a continuum.

This day-to-day interference reached a new peak when Neil Brown took over the communications ministry in May 1982. Intervention was Brown's ministerial style, and it had created opposition from the bureaucrats in his previous department, employment and youth affairs. Brown's style came as a further shock to a Telecom uncertain about what the Davidson committee would recommend; the 'climate of unease' grew. One of the early indicators of Brown's intentions came when he delayed signing an order for Mitsubishi vans. Telecom managers concluded that Brown's reluctance was sensitivity to a charge of conflict of interest. One of his predecessors, Tony Staley, sat on the board of Mitsubishi.

It was during Tony Staley's time as minister for communications that relations between Telecom and the government started to sour. Staley was responsible for the selection, promotion and development of the concept of an Australian communications satellite. This satellite was recognized quite early as a means to break Telecom's monopoly. Staley also made a number of other decisions which have had a lasting impact on Telecom. It was his decision to prevent Telecom entering the market for under fifty line PABXs, answering phones and national facsimile. These decisions were made in direct response to lobbying by private industry groups, some of which have now been disbanded.

Jim Smith has been the deputy chief general manager of Telecom since Vesting Day. He believes that the Staley decisions created a 'climate of unease' which has been exacerbated by subsequent decisions by other ministers:

The Staley decisions on facsimile and answering phones were not very significant in a market satisfaction sense, but they were symbolic. Symbolic of restrictions on Telecom. There has been increased unease since, but that was the trigger.

Smith believes the reasons for government intervention in Telecom fell into two major categories:

The first is a genuine political ideology in favour of private enterprise versus public enterprise. Secondly and just as importantly, it [the government] reacts to lobbying by vested private interests: the Office Machines Association with the answering phones – they have now disbanded; Keith Rosenhain from Myer with the videotex decision [where Telecom's videotex plans were stopped by the government]. Also with the decision not to let us sell multi-feature phones it was because of lobbying by companies marketing similar instruments. In particular cases the lobbying effort argue a case strongly and get what they want. I fear that inside Telecom undue weight is given to the knock-backs, rather than putting them into the perspective of approvals. The small business market is far far bigger than any of those areas we have been refused and the premium telephone and other telephones, data, Austpac and a number of new services. It is just a question of how it is perceived.

In terms of lobbying success, one of the biggest was the victory Kerry Packer and Keith Rosenhain (former managing director of Myer) had over Telecom on videotex. Videotex is a key to the telecommunications potential of the Information Age. It is a system which connects telephones to television sets with the aid of a converter, which then enables a two-way flow of information. This information may range from stock exchange listings, to airline timetables, news stories, or food and wine catalogues. Videotex first got underway in the United Kingdom where, developed by the British Post Office, it was called Prestel. Although Prestel was originally aimed at a mass market, its main users are business customers. In Canada and France, other videotex systems have also been developed, and a tussle for world domination has developed between the competing, incompatible technologies.

Videotex is particularly attractive to two established industries: publishing and retailing. Publishers see a need to protect themselves from the inevitable competition of screen-based information providers, and retailers see a future way of selling without expensive department stores and costly overheads.

So it was not surprising that the two companies in Australia most interested in videotex were Kerry Packer's Publishing and Broadcasting (a subsidiary of Consolidated Press) and The Myer Emporium, which had recognized the need to diversify because of contractions in the retailing industry by the end of the 1970s. Telecom had been conducting trials with Prestel for several years, but Myer was more interested in the Canadian Telidon system which, it claimed, provided better graphics. Publishing and Broadcasting was noted for its general enthusiasm about the new communications technologies.

Late in 1980, Telecom put a proposal to the government whereby it would provide the basic network facilities and computer data base, and private enterprise would provide the information and the terminals. The weight of overseas evidence was that the national telecommunications carrier needed to be involved if there was to be national access to videotex. Despite this advice, letters from Telecom's chairman, and the advice of the department of communications, the government decided not to give Telecom the go ahead for videotex.

Ian Sinclair made this announcement at an anniversary celebration at J. N. Almgren's Sydney plant one spring afternoon in 1981. Industry representatives at the event were stunned. The decision to exclude the public sector was clear-cut; videotex, Sinclair said, was best left to the private sector. In the meantime, Packer's Publishing and Broadcasting group had secured the Australian end of international rights to Prestel.

But it was a Pyrrhic victory for Kerry Packer. Armed with the support of the cabinet, his executives did their sums a little more carefully. They found that without Telecom's involvement videotex was not viable as a nationwide service. One Telecom executive recalled that within a couple of days of the decision he was summoned to the Hotel Australia in Melbourne by Kerry Packer. Packer said that he now realized that videotex would not be viable without Telecom's involvement and maybe an agreement could be reached between them. The executive replied that he would only be too happy to negotiate if Packer first obtained a letter from the minister giving Sinclair's approval to the discussions. He suggested that Packer seek the letter as he had more success with the government than did Telecom.

The cabinet has not been slow to exercise its power in other matters, in particular its right to appoint commissioners. This has contributed greatly to the climate of unease of which Jim Smith spoke.

This practice first became apparent when the founding chairman of the commission, Bob Somervaille, a leading Sydney lawyer and company director, read in the *Australian Financial Review* that his appointment had not been extended. Tony Staley only notified him later in the day that it was the government's intention not to reappoint him as chairman. Somervaille was angry and hurt by the decision, especially as he thought it was taken because he was doing his job: promoting the best interests of Telecom. Tom May, a company director in the construction and transport industries, succeeded

Somervaille as acting chairman, but his term was shortened to a two-year period.

Cabinet again demonstrated the control it wielded over Telecom when in 1981 the founding managing director, Jack Curtis, resigned a year early when he was told he had lost the confidence of the prime minister after a cabinet room showdown. This came at the end of a protracted industrial relations dispute in which the government delayed ratification of a pay settlement which had been negotiated between Telecom and the ATEA contrary to the rules of wage indexation then applying. As a result, the network came to a virtual standstill, and wage indexation, which had survived for several years, was abandoned. After this fracas, the prime minister wanted blood, preferably that of Jack Curtis and Jim Smith.

Both Curtis and Smith are reluctant to talk about what happened in the cabinet room that day. 'You'll have to wait for my memoirs for that – I kept a minute by minute diary of what happened,' Smith said.

It was a time of hurt and disillusionment for Curtis, Smith and other senior executives. Curtis was by all accounts a skilled and brilliant manager and leader, a public servant in the old school of cautious gentlemen. In some senses, he was also a father figure for the group of younger men he had around him. In the turmoil leading up to the splitting of the PMG, Curtis had been a calm, determined leader. At that time, the knives were drawn – most of the senior managers did not want to see the PMG split into Australia Post and Telecom Australia, but Curtis and those in favour of the split prevailed. This personal fondness and respect made Curtis's departure a year early an extremely difficult pill to swallow, and many senior managers blamed the ATEA, rather than the government for causing the crisis, which had brought the matter to a head.

Jim Smith is a tough executive, who jokes that his nickname is 'Axeman', but the toughness he saw in the cabinet room that day took him by surprise. Smith recalls:

We expected a rough time and we got it. Other people in the public and private sectors have had a rough time from the headmaster

[Fraser]. It is very hard to recapture the atmosphere of those times, the emotion was so high, it was a very emotional and harrowing time. Jack Curtis resigned; he was not sacked. I believe you never offer your resignation . . . they might take it. A different power did apply because I was a career officer rather than an appointee. Let's just say I didn't feel a need to resign. It was a very harrowing experience. It was certainly the nearest thing to a star chamber I can imagine.

Following Curtis's departure from the twentieth floor of Telecom's headquarters in William Street, Melbourne, the question of a replacement was anxiously discussed. After the carpeting he received in the cabinet room, it was obvious that the government would not consider Smith as Curtis's successor. The gaze then fell on Bill Pollock (chief general manager), Gordon Martin (general manager, engineering), Roger Banks (director, business development) and Tony Newstead (assistant general manager, Hong Kong Telephone Company).

Tony Newstead, like Jack Curtis, came out of the PMG's Queensland organization. He was well regarded as an administrator, engineer and planner. He was responsible for the highly acclaimed plan, 'Telecom 2000'. When Telecom was commissioned, Newstead was tipped as a possible managing director; it was a choice between him and Curtis. When Curtis was appointed, Newstead took up a position with Hong Kong's telephone company. Hong Kong Tel is a privately owned telephone company, which provides for the telecommunications needs of Hong Kong's five million people. Although Newstead had settled in Hong Kong, by the end of 1981 he was thinking of returning to Australia. He was a logical choice for Curtis's job. He was flown back to Australia for a series of interviews in both Canberra and Melbourne. He felt sure he had the job; it had been virtually promised him. Twice his name went before cabinet and twice it was rejected. Eventually Bill Pollock, with the backing of Sir Phillip Lynch, one of the strongest organizational men in the Liberal Party machine in Victoria, got the numbers and the job. Gordon Martin was promoted to Pollock's old job of chief general manager.

The promotion was to one of the most difficult jobs in Australia. The Chanticleer columnist in the *Australian Financial*

Review, the chronicler of Australian business and politics, wrote that at the time of his resignation Jack Curtis 'was under more pressure than most managing directors ever experience'. Chanticleer wrote a fictitious job description on the day of Curtis's resignation:

WANTED: Managing director for Australia's largest business. Unfortunately there may be changes in the organisation, but we are not quite sure what they will be or whether bits will be sold off. There will soon be an inquiry by somebody or other and successful applicants will learn of the terms of reference of the inquiry and who will conduct it, if they read the newspapers.

Assuming the organisation remains intact, the appointee will report to a chairman when one is found. He will also report to a Minister, a group of commissioners, numerous members of the Departments of Communications, the Prime Minister, Treasury, Sir Phillip Lynch, interested backbenchers, Bill Mansfield, Kerry Packer and Doug Anthony.

If he has the time, the managing director will administer 88,000 people, a cash flow of $12 million a day and the most complex technological changes Australia has ever seen. Salary for this important prestige position has just been increased by 20 per cent to $72,000. This unfortunately is about half the total package that applicants would receive for comparable jobs in private industry, does not include housing loans, education for the children or a limousine, and everyone will always know your salary.

However, we can offer the best superannuation scheme in Australia and $3,500 in allowances, as long as you don't spend it all at once. Changes in operating policy of the organisation, as they affect the managing director, will be announced by the Minister in public speeches from time to time. Appointees should watch the newspapers for meetings of bodies such as the NSW Birdwatchers Society, Ballarat Grain and Feed Association and the Liberal Party Mothers' Guild – addressed by the Minister from time to time. Applicants should write to Spencer Stuart, stating name, number of days residence in Australia and reason for wanting the job.

In Australia, the status accruing to senior managers of public-sector organizations is not quite equal to that of their peers in the private sector. The reason for this is complex and has little to do with the personal attributes of these people, many of whom have a more difficult job than their counterparts in similarly sized organizations. Accountability to a government which changes its mind, reassesses its priorities, seeks favours and maintains the right of veto is more difficult than accountability to shareholders once a year. Not surprisingly, those who make it to the top of these public-sector organizations are among the toughest operators in the country. One man who has worked closely with chief executives of several of the biggest companies in Australia said that he had never met anyone as tough, shrewd and cunning as Bill Pollock.

At the most senior levels of public-sector management there is often a certain ambivalence towards working outside the private sector, as though somehow it is not the real thing. Although this depends to a large extent on the personal psychology and politics of the individual, the bureaucracy impinges more on the life of a public-sector manager than it does on those in the private sector. In a setting reminiscent of The Club in the 'Yes Minister' television series, one senior Telecom manager spelled out the problems of nominally not being a department of state, but still effectively being under the thumb of Canberra's bureaucrats. Sipping his tea from a fine bone china cup, he said:

They seem to regard policy as their area, as though we are people in boiler suits who screw phones on walls. I think that that is the common bureaucratic misconception. They don't seem to realize that to run an enterprise like ours you must have something going for you. We make decisions and then a class seven clerk starts asking questions about it as though the decision was not made on the best possible basis. That is no way to run a bassoon factory let alone the biggest enterprise in the country.

Another senior executive said that there was a fair degree of ill-disguised antipathy between Telecom and senior to middle ranking bureaucrats, especially in the departments of finance, treasury and the prime minister: 'They pretend to understand and become instant experts. Not surprisingly our contempt for them is often ill disguised when we meet them.'

This somewhat uneasy relationship between the bureaucracy and Telecom has made the task of preparing for a future dependent on political whim particularly difficult. When Telecom's most senior managers opted for a behind-the-scenes method to try and exert political muscle, they first had to overcome this mutual antipathy.

It would be unfair to say that this is all one sided. Telecom managers, in general, tend to think that if left to themselves they could manage telecommunications better than anyone else in the country. Although there may be elements of truth in this, it suggests a world dominated by a technocratic élite who would prefer not to be answerable to anyone. As the biggest organization of government – a large earner, employer and spender – Telecom is obviously scrutinized carefully by the government. Any organization of the size – public or private – would be. For the bureaucrats charged with ensuring that government policy is upheld, whether that is in industrial relations, wages, staff ceilings, purchasing policy, or loan raising, it is crucial that the second largest enterprise in the country be seen to abide by the guidelines, however much the managers and staff feel that this is against the interests of the organization.

Public servants anxious for career advancement learn early that the key to success is not to put up proposals which are unacceptable to the government. So when the government's intention to scale down Telecom became clear, it gave bureaucrats in government departments opportunities to settle old scores which had rankled over the years as Telecom treated them with contempt. Although many of them fought against the recommendation Jim Davidson made that the public service should not review his committee's findings, seeing in it a very real threat to their role, others were quite happy that Davidson had done the work for them. 'He's drafted the legislation and done a good job that the government likes, why don't we just implement it all?' a first assistant secretary in the Department of Communications told his staff.

There is, of course, a positive side of Telecom's accountability to government and that is that its charter requires it to provide a universal telecommunications service for all Australians, taking into account the 'social, industrial and commercial needs of the Australian people'. If the government were equally committed to this principle, it could mean that Australians would have an unrivalled telecommunications service. It would also mean that the common good would have to be put before profits, empire building or petty conflicts. But for the government to impose a set of circumstances – cutting staff, arbitrarily raising interest on outstanding loans, refusing to approve contracts, refusing permission to raise the capital it needs to do its job, refusing to approve settlements of industrial relations problems – and then to turn around and say that these things happen because Telecom does not run as a business is hypocritical. The government has posited a solution which would prevent interference without acknowledging who was doing the interfering in the first place. Its solution in the Davidson report means that the social needs of all Australians will be downgraded in the future. That is a dangerous preamble to Australia's hopes of participating in next century's Information Age.

Of the most senior executives in Telecom, Jim Smith has made the strongest statement of commitment to telecommunications remaining primarily in the public sector. Before the Davidson committee reported to the government he said in an interview:

I have a belief in the public enterprise, because it would have service as the keyword in its charter and in the process it would need to meet financial objectives, not putting profit making first. It's a belief that public utilities are able to do that better than private enterprise because the objectives are different.

We have been surprised by the tactics some of our opponents have used. It is like we are boxing using Marquis of Queensberry rules and they are using Thai boxing. The tactics in planting stories and misrepresentative programmes, bringing experts in from overseas, and so on, these tactics have surprised and disgusted us. If these are the standards they use to get their own way, what standards of business behaviour will they bring with them to telecommunications?

These standards are not universal in the private sector; but look at Costigan and the meat substitution row; nothing like that has happened in telecommunications.

It is the objectives that are important. Telecom is an organization designed to provide a service to the people of Australia. When Telecom starts thinking of itself as the number one objective, things get lost. The service to all Australians must remain paramount.

Chapter Four
Rest of the World

'Look what's happening in the rest of the world!' has always been a powerful argument in public discussion of important issues in Australia. The reasons are clear. Australia is isolated geographically from the societies of North America and Europe which it admires and imitates. There is no white culture older than 200 years and many of its social manners and political attitudes are drawn from other countries. In an economic sense, it is heavily dependent on the owners of US, UK, European and Japanese capital, and control of that investment is exercised by the presence in Australia of all the major multinational commercial empires.

The result not just in economic and political activities but in the arts and in social issues is a diffidence towards developing new ideas. Nowhere is this more true than in technology. Australia does not have an indigenous computer industry big enough to fill a decent-sized building in California's Silicon Valley. Yet it is not for want of a sufficiently large market to buy the goods. As a consumer of computer imports, Australia ranks number eleven in the world, above some much larger countries which depend less on the foreign manufactured products of transnational electronics companies. It is true that all the big names of world electronics are represented in Australia, their corporate names and logos are prominent in the skylines of North Sydney and South Melbourne. For the most part, they have no commitment to local manufacture, nor is there an active government policy to encourage them. Some of those international companies do manufacture or assemble electronics systems in this country, but it is only because Telecom Australia insists on it. Without Telecom's telecommunications contracts to justify local manufacture, there is no incentive for those companies to operate anything more than shop-window operations. The Australian content in most electronic systems sold locally is confined to advertising, sales, freight and packaging.

In many other countries, that dependence on overseas sources of supply in an era of swift technological change might be examined and debated in public as a national malaise. In Australia, it is not. Computer companies pride themselves on the degree to which they have educated the Australian market to accept high-technology products. They even bestow the accolade of simultaneous product releases in the United States and Australia. Sydney and Melbourne are routinely included on their launch schedules, fitting in between Los Angeles, Chicago, Florida, Toronto, Singapore, Hong Kong and Tokyo. In the marketing divisions of most of the US computer companies, Australia is classified as an off-shore island of the United States, a little larger and more distant than Hawaii.

The lonely voices of dissent in cultural, social and political matters, which insist there is an Australian identity, are opposed by some of the dominant forces in national life. Conservative governments since World War II have, almost without exception, slavishly identified themselves with the United States and Britain. The most divisive political issue in that period, the Vietnam war, was one of a long series of commitments made on behalf of the Australian people to serve the narrow political interests of the government of the day. The business community has an almost automatic reaction to people, products, services and ideas imported from overseas. Although less publicized than their colleagues in the arts, there are many entrepreneurs who have had to establish their credentials outside Australia before being accepted at home. Because some of the largest companies in Australian business life are controlled from abroad, it is there that the centres of excellence are assumed to rest. Corporate executives who spend their working lives guessing the desires of boards based in London, New York and Tokyo look with great suspicion on any suggestion that Australia not toe the line of international corporations. The very worst insult that can be aimed at an opponent at the top levels of Australian business is that he or she is parochial, inward-looking, unwilling to accept innovation. In most cases, what that means is diffidence towards the transnational view of the world.

Telecommunications has been a source of frustration to those who seek to spread the blanket of international corporate hegemony over Australia's economic life. It has caused carping from the local representatives of those interests, who adopted Telecom as a bogy figure well before its formation as a separate commission in 1975. Telecom embodies the very antithesis of the values which the international corporate states seek to implant. It is, like most telecommunications organizations in the western world, in the public sector, an automatic cause for offence to the corporations. It does not primarily operate on the profit motive, for it must fulfil the obligations in its charter to provide communications services in an equitable fashion to most people. And it is a monopoly, not achieved by the operation of market forces which creates a Broken Hill Proprietary Company Ltd in Australia or an American Telephone and Telegraph in the United States, but by legislative fiat. In a very important ideological sense, the nationally owned telecommunications authorities are a primary target for international companies.

During the second half of the 1970s, there was an international build up of pressure from transnational companies aimed at wresting influence from the suppliers of telecommunications services. It has been seen in its most overt form in the United States, where the word 'deregulation' has been elevated to a statement of virtue by large corporations. In its other forms, the same sentiment has entered the language as 'liberalization', 'relaxation' and 'increased competition'.

The reasons why the process to which those terms refer is occurring in the United States are complex and often only partly understood by those outside the telecommunications industry. They have generally been represented in simple concepts. Telecommunications is due for a shake up we are told by the Australian experts in US deregulation. The virtues which should predominate are private-sector enterprise, competition and proliferation of suppliers. The effect will be the quicker introduction of services and products (to keep up with the rest of the world), lower tariffs and greater freedom of choice for the consumer. It is imperative to follow the US experience, we are told, down a path which leads to the nirvana of the Information Age. The United States is held up to Australia as the new model for Australian communications. It is time to scrap more than a century of the development of telecommunications in the public sector in Australia and don the new robe of deregulation, liberalization, competition.

The most enthusiastic advocates of that course of action were not evident at a major conference on the future of Australian electronics, held in Melbourne late in 1977. They would have heard an American, Malcolm Macaulay, then managing director of a small electronics company in Canberra, deliver a public rebuff to Allan Moyes, who at that time was chief executive of IBM Australia Ltd. After listening to Moyes's fervent endorsement of the international IBM corporate line, with liberal references to the virtues of free competition and lack of regulation by government, Macaulay took the platform. 'I always welcome the opportunity,' he said, 'to learn from Australian experts on American free enterprise.' He then proceeded to attack Moyes's position with relish, detailing the degree of government intervention in the US electronics industry, from defence department contracts to the Buy America policy, which discriminates against foreign competition. Macaulay exposed the selective account that Australians who support US free enterprise present.

It is a point more pertinent in the early 1980s, after an intense corporate campaign to portray recent events in US telecommunications in simplistic and misleading terms. There has been a powerful appeal to Australians to accept that there is a trend sweeping the world, with the United States in the vanguard, which will revolutionize telecommunications. The same advocates can be observed at work in Canada, the United Kingdom, Europe, Japan and elsewhere. And as usual the carping cry of those who would have Australia follow the leader is that to do otherwise is to be parochial and backward.

The first fallacy in this suggestion is that what is happening overseas in telecommunications is not what the proponents of private-sector competition in Australia say is happening. And the second fallacy is that even if what was happening overseas could be transplanted to Australia, that alone is insufficient reason for doing so. On both points, the Australian outriders for the international corporate cavalry have failed to make their case.

In addition to being the largest in the world, the US telecommunications industry is one of the most complex sectors of that nation's economic life. Based on assets, profits and number of employees, it sustains the world's largest company, AT&T. Unlike Telecom or the PTT organizations in Europe and Japan, AT&T is owned by private investors. A staggering three million of them own a total of 750 million shares. Annual meetings are media events, requiring venues capable of holding thousands. The 1982 annual meeting in Baltimore attracted 5,100. With assets from the telecommunications network and its manufacturing subsidiaries, AT&T's installed base of assets is about $120 thousand million. It is the world's single largest corporate employer, with more than a million on staff. Since its beginnings in 1877 as the Bell Telephone Company, AT&T consolidated and absorbed its competitors until it held a stranglehold on US telecommunications. It has grown beyond the dreams of one of its original shareholders, Alexander Graham Bell, inventor of the telephone. It remains integrated in the US corporate structure by about forty direct cross-directorships with other large companies and more than 900 indirect common board positions.

AT&T is, like Telecom Australia, a monopoly, a position it has protected by its pricing policies, its attitude of relentless opposition to its competitors and by political power. The nature of Bell's monopoly has absorbed two government agencies which have attempted since the 1930s to contain the company's power to dominate telecommunications. Until the late 1970s, the efforts of both agencies, the Federal Communications Commission and the Federal Department of Justice, met with less success than the time invested by their staff warranted. But, in January 1982, a dramatic announcement was made in New York which has resulted in what has been described as the greatest corporate reorganization in US business history. Ma Bell, as AT&T was known, was to be broken up; competition was to be encouraged. It appeared on the surface a victory for those conflicting corporate interests in the United States which saw Bell as too big, too powerful and too able to determine the policies of US business. Before examining the new Bell, and the relevance of the decision to break it up in an Australian context, consider AT&T's enormous strength.

Unlike the PTTs in other parts of the world, AT&T is, like some other large companies in the electronics industry, 'vertically integrated'. Bell owns its manufacturing facilities as well as the network, in which many of its products are installed. There are four levels in this hierarchy of ownership. At the bottom is the largest and most successful research and development organization in the world, Bell Labs. With an annual budget of more than $2 thousand million, the Bell Labs develop new techniques, processes and products which feed the rest of the organization with technological expertise. Among the most spectacular contributions made by the Labs to the development of electronics are the invention of the transistor and the creation of the integrated circuit, forerunner to the microprocessor. Such was the importance of the patents filed by Bell Labs scientists to the future of the electronics industry that an anti-trust case brought against AT&T in 1949 obliged it to make all patents available.

If Bell Labs is the ideas department of AT&T, its factory is owned by Western Electric, the manufacturing subsidiary which is the largest telecommunications supplier in the world. In terms of company size, with more than 160,000 employees and annual sales of more than $12 thousand million, Western Electric is one of the largest corporate entities in the United States. It has only one shareholder, AT&T. What the Labs design, Western Electric manufactures. In addition, AT&T is the largest supplier of business communications systems to other corporations. The Bell network itself is the most sophisticated, efficient, and reliable yet devised, and by far the world's biggest. With the number of telephones per hundred of population in the high seventies, Americans are among the world's most enthusiastic users of telephones. The massive volume of voice and data traffic generated by private and business users allows economies of scale to drive down tariffs and enables free installation of telephones and free local calls in some areas. The network was run by twenty-four subsidiaries, called the Bell operating companies, or the BOCs. It is they which exercised the monopoly over US telecommunications, despite the presence of some smaller independent carriers.

The final level of the AT&T hierarchy is its Long Lines division, so named because while the operating companies handle traffic within their areas, a separate structure has been established for trunk traffic. As a return on investment, trunk traffic is the most profitable area of any telecommunications carrier's activity. Much of it is related to business use, and although the vast majority is voice traffic, there is an increasing amount of data between computers. Profits from long-distance traffic allow Bell to keep its rates down across the country, even in areas where it is unprofitable to provide telephone services or where return on investment is marginal.

Bell's is sometimes referred to as a quasi-monopoly, because it does face some competition for the carriage of telecommunications at the local level and for long-distance business. There are a total of more than 1,400 companies which co-exist with Bell in the domestic communications market. All but a handful, including companies such as GTE and Continental, are independent of the Bell network. The independents increased their share of the domestic market at the expense of Bell only a couple of per cent between 1975 and 1980. They are estimated in the early 1980s to have a little more than 15 per cent of the market share; Bell has the rest. There are other competitors providing services beyond the standard telephone, including mobile radio system operators who vie with Bell for business. In the area of long-distance traffic, there are competitors using microwave links and others using satellites to compete with AT&T. Their presence has hardly inhibited the corporation's growth.

The touchstone of US telecommunications legislation is the 1934 *Communications Act*, passed during the Roosevelt administration and one of the last actions of the proponents of New Deal policies. The US government found it necessary because of Bell's reluctance to provide unprofitable telephone services, particularly in rural areas. Acting in accordance with profit maximization, AT&T sought to concentrate on those areas of its business where returns were greatest. Only legislation forced it to act otherwise. The same act established the primary regulatory body for US communications, the Federal Communications Commission. The commission was to ensure the survival of competitive common carriers in a market which AT&T dominated. Without government intervention, a fact conveniently invisible to advocates of the market economy as the most efficient means of economic organization, AT&T's competitors would certainly have perished.

The best known of a series of decisions made by the commission to ensure that Bell's competitors remained alive is the Carterfone case in 1968. Bell contested the accusation by Carterfone, a Texas mobile radio telephone company, that access to the network had been unreasonably denied it. In less publicized instances, AT&T agreed to interconnect other networks to its own system, extending this right to railways in 1960-61 in an attempt to stave off their demands for wider access. And almost a decade before Carterfone, the commission began to license competing microwave operators who challenged Bell for long-distance traffic. The response of AT&T to this loosening of its grip on US communications was not quiet acquiescence. One move aimed against competitive microwave carriers was a service Bell called Telpak, which offered discounted bulk data rates to large corporate customers. Not only were its rates cheaper than the competition, but it warded off the possibility that some of those large customers would seek to establish networks of their own and siphon off revenues from the Bell network. It was not until

1976 that the commission was finally able to outlaw Telpak on the grounds that it was illegal and discriminatory. In areas such as telegraphy, six other carriers were licensed by the commission, and a similar number of competitors were permitted to offer satellite transmission for long-distance traffic.

The pace of the commission's decision making aimed at encouraging competition for AT&T increased during the 1970s, culminating in an agreement that the giant was to be split into a number of divisions. The combined forces of the Department of Justice and the commission were influential in a settlement which has been hailed as the most significant in US corporate history. It is the commission, however, which has made the running, using some of the remarkably wide powers invested in it by the 1934 *Communications Act*.

The basic requirement insisted upon by the commission is that common carriers provide services on request, and at reasonable charges and non-discriminatory rates. All tariff schedules, lists describing services and charges, must be filed with the commission for approval. It is the commission's job to decide whether the charges are just and reasonable. Accounting rules used by the carriers are also determined by the commission, and the larger operators must file monthly and annual financial and operating reports, which are available for public inspection. Depreciation rates used by the larger carriers are also prescribed by the commission. Approval is needed before a carrier constructs, acquires or operates services, and the commission's assent is also required before it can discontinue or curtail services to the public. If carriers merge, consolidate or acquire each other's facilities, the commission must also give its stamp of approval. Although the Bell system is its major concern, there are more than sixty companies in competition with it which have annual operating revenues of more than $1 million.

When Australian proponents of competition in telecommunications hold up the United States as a model of a free market place, they seldom acknowledge the role played by the commission. No telecommunications market is more closely regulated than the US one, and the powers of the commission make those of the Australian government over Telecom look feeble. The purpose of that regulation, as recognized in the 1934 *Communications Act*, has been to keep Bell in check, ensuring there is at least some competition. The market, left to its own devices, would act in a way contrary to the spirit in which the commission was established. There is no doubt that if the Bell system were freed from FCC controls, it would move quickly against its competitors to put them out of business. The means at their disposal are many, ranging from rate cutting, creating delays in connecting competitors, structuring the cross-subsidy to block the opposition, and restricting entry to new areas, such as electronic publishing. AT&T would use its size to reach out and crush its opponents. Without the intervention of the commission, with its annual budget of $80 million and its 2,000 employees, the operation of a free market would end competition virtually overnight. It is not competition which has kept telephone rates down in the United States, but the very considerable influence of the commission. When proponents espouse the virtues of deregulation in other countries, that point is seldom made. If the efficiency of the US telecommunications industry is a tribute to anything, it is to stringent government regulation, not free competition.

Even the extensive regulation to which the commission has subjected Bell, and the efforts of the US Department of Justice to press anti-trust cases, was not sufficient to prevent an effective monopoly. The role of both the FCC and the Department of Justice is highly political, and the competition which exists is the result of a long series of decisions aimed at thwarting Bell's predominance. Competition has not evolved as a natural condition of a free market. The attempts of the Department of Justice to tackle the anti-trust nature of Bell's domination resulted in a consent decree in 1956 and a prosecution in 1974. In a variation of the original decree in January 1982, agreement was announced between AT&T and the Department of Justice to settle all pending cases. It was preceded by a decision of the FCC, called Computer 11, which set the scene for the 1982 agreement to break up Bell. The Computer 11 decision, made in May 1980, insisted that if Bell were to enter certain new markets created by the convergence of computers and communications it would have to be through a separate subsidiary company.

The FCC distinguished between basic and enhanced telecomunications services, the latter being those which went beyond the provision of telephone lines and equipment. The distinction was necessary because, although the telephone industry was regulated, the computing industry, where many of the enhanced services existed, was not. To recognize the difference, and having no wish to regulate data processing, the FCC insisted that AT&T form another company, which became known as Baby Bell. Faced with that decision, AT&T was under some pressure to reach a settlement with the Department of Justice and to stave off a flood of anti-competition cases if the prosecution launched in 1974 eventually proved successful.

The consent decree shocked world telecommunications by the dramatic nature of changes the Bell system would have to undergo. Not only was a separate subsidiary formed, but AT&T ceded independent existence to all its local operating companies. The twenty-four local telephone companies owned by Bell encompassed the United States, accounting for 80 per cent of its capital investment and 800,000 employees. They were to operate as twenty-two companies in the immediate wake of the decision, with the aim of amalgamating them into seven separate companies within a few years. A separate subsidiary was formed to administer the rest of AT&T, later to be called American Bell, and a new subsidiary was formed under the name of AT&T International to carry the flag in other countries. This was an important departure for AT&T, which had made a deal in 1925 with its rival, International Telephone and Telegraph (ITT), which confined Bell to the US domestic market. Although the 1982 agreement meant Bell no longer provided local calls, it did not cede its Long Lines division to the operating companies. Long Lines remained, guaranteeing a continuous source of income from the single most profitable area of the communications business. Bell Labs also remained within the fold, providing the technological expertise and innovation which had provided the backstop to the commercial acumen of the organization since Alexander Graham. The other layer of vertical integration was also retained; Western Electric could continue to manufacture communications products, such as switching exchanges, for the local operators, and could also launch a whole series of new equipment aimed at the business market. News of a PABX, which could handle both voice and data, soon leaked out from American Bell. Micro- and minicomputers for the business market were also tipped.

The settlement was welcomed by both the Department of Justice and AT&T, with the FCC chiming in its approval. For the Department of Justice, it was as good as it could hope to achieve, given the long and only partly successful attempts to curb the Bell system. As far as AT&T was concerned, it meant an end to costly and time-consuming litigation, which had been a significant drain on its corporate resources over many years. In a business sense, it also meant that the proportionately less profitable activities of the Bell operating companies were disposed of. In return, Bell could concentrate on profitable long-distance carriage of traffic and on selling the goods produced by the joint efforts of Bell Labs and Western Electric. And for the FCC, under the chairmanship of Reagan appointee Mark Fowler, the settlement furthered its aims of reducing government regulation in telecommunications. Fowler has been a keen advocate of the 'let the players play' approach, urging withdrawal of government intervention in the market place.

As for Bell's competitors, many were unconvinced, with the prevailing doubts, perhaps best summed up by George Knapp, vice-president of ITT, who said:

The ITT companies which compete with the Bell system may benefit from the divestiture of Bell operating companies from AT&T because it is more likely they will eventually have normal business relations with local operating companies. However, it would be naive to believe that all telecommunications problems would be solved by the proposed settlement. In fact, without changes by the court or corrective legislation, the proposed settlement represents a decisive victory by AT&T over consumers, competitors and even the Bell operating companies.

If free and open competition had genuinely been the reason for the existence of Bell's competitors, why would they deplore the removal of government regulation? The answer, ignored by the free marketers who press deregulation in other countries, is that without continued careful regulation, the notion of competition in US telecommunications would be empty. The reason for maintaining competition in US telecommunications is political, a fact recognized by successive administrations.

That same exercise of political policy making can be seen in even clearer focus in Britain, under a government of similar ideological hue to that of Ronald Reagan.

Confronted with a publicly owned telecommunications monopoly, the Reagan administration would probably have acted in just the way the Thatcher government in Britain has acted. With some evidence of overt pressure from the international companies which stand to benefit from pushing telecommunications into the private sector, the Thatcher government has rushed to weaken British Telecom's hold over communications. As an entity separate from the Post Office, British Telecom was less than two years old when the UK secretary of industry, Patrick Jenkin, announced that it would be sold off. The announcement followed a report commissioned by the government which recommended a loosening of British Telecom's control of the terminal equipment market and an end to its exclusive right to carry telecommunications traffic. In Britain, the process has been described by the government and its supporters as 'privatization', a rolling back of the nationalized sectors of the economy. It is significant that another target was Cable and Wireless, the British telecommunications systems supplier in which the previous Labour government had taken a majority stake. The reason that the Thatcher government could so confidently predict there would be investor interest in telecommunications is that it, virtually alone among the nationalized industries in Britain, has the potential for considerable profits.

The transfer of telecommunications to the private sector in Britain has been lumped together with the regulatory changes in the United States as evidence of a trend for greater competition. That trend is presented as a global movement fuelled by technological developments in communications which lead to greater efficiency and lower tariffs. The US and the British experience in telecommunications is quite different. Whereas Britain has had a state-owned monopoly, the dominant carrier in the United States is a private corporation. The British have had a single entity responsible for telecommunications, not a variety of smaller independent operators which have existed in the United States as local telephone companies. Britain has had no competitve common carriers, using either microwave, leased telephone lines or satellite on the major trunk routes. As a consequence, there has not been the need in Britain for a regulatory authority such as the FCC. Tariffs have been set by British Telecom, and before it the Post Office, with reference only to a users' committee, which includes community and business representatives from outside the telecommunications industry. And an effective cross-subsidy has balanced profitable against loss-making routes, with the aim of a universal telephone service for Britons at a reasonable price.

In Britain there is no parallel to the forces in the United States which have exerted pressure on the government to diminish the influence of AT&T. So who then had the Thatcher government been listening to in framing policies which, if implemented, will introduce the most radical changes in the structure of British telecommunications?

The answer to that question in part is that the Thatcher government has been listening to itself. Its monetarist rhetoric requires the government to adopt a prejudicial attitude towards state-run enterprises. Given that its anti-public sector stand has won it the support of British business and of a majority of voters at the polls, the government has little incentive to engage in public discussion, least of all about the effect of its measures on most of the people who use telephones, the domestic subscribers.

That attitude was clear in the study it commissioned into British telecommunications by a professor of economics at the London School of Business, Michael Beesley. It recommended changes which could easily have come from a government policy statement. Beesley's was recognized as an insubstantial report, completed in very short time. Among the many criticisms directed at it was one from the consultants Coopers and Lybrand who accused Beesley of basing the report on assumptions about profitability and competition which were simply not justified. The Beesley report relied heavily on presenting the US experience as one which was valid for Britain, arguing that competition in the supply of terminals and telecommunications services was desirable. In political terms, it was an eminently acceptable document for the Thatcher government.

The equation of private-sector competition with lower tariffs and a greater variety of services was promoted by industry groups in Britain, such as the Telecommunications Managers' Association and the Telecommunications Users' Association. Although there had been minimal pressure from large British enterprises which were not heavily dependent on international communications, there were some private-sector supporters of the notion of alternatives to British Telecom. Their presence was less overt than their counterparts in Australia, but influential nevertheless. London has long regarded itself as the financial and commercial centre of Europe, as a crossroads through which information flows. It is the telecommunications capital of Europe. The pre-eminence of London has been the subject of some jealousy from other European countries, notably Switzerland, which announced late in 1982 that the upgrading of its telecommunications system was aimed at challenging London's dominance. In addition to traffic within Europe, London is the gateway for about 60 per cent of all transatlantic communication links used by private corporations based in Europe and North America. Any restrictions placed by British Telecom on the transfer of telecomunications traffic between the outposts of those corporations would be keenly felt. US experience with European transborder data flow legislation has been represented as an unwarranted interference in their internal corporate affairs. The very existence of nationally owned telecommunications authorities is regarded as a potential threat to international corporate telecommunications traffic.

The most significant common carrier competitor to emerge against British Telecom, known as project Mercury, has had enthusiastic support from the government, through the Department of Industry. Its promoters include Barclays Bank, Cable and Wireless and two public-sector organizations, British Rail and London Transport. Their aim is to use railway ducts in which to lay optical fibre cables between the three main business centres in Britain, London, Manchester and Birmingham. Although the practical difficulties of using fibre optics proved too great for the initial phase of Mercury, and it resorted to microwave links instead, its tariffs were pitched 10 per cent below those offered by British Telecom. The telecommunications authority has responded by offering high-speed data services, the best known of which is called X-Stream. British Telecom's other responses include a joint venture with the IBM-backed Satellite Business Systems (SBS) to provide a transatlantic route for corporate traffic.

The real effect of those competitive challenges can be seen in British Telecom's tariffs, where the profits from heavy traffic business routes have subsidized a universal low-cost telephone service. The pressure of competition will force British Telecom to push up domestic tariffs and rentals and to hold down increases for business users. The cross-subsidy, which has underpinned the economics of telecommunications in Britain, is being dismantled. In mid 1982, British Telecom announced relatively small rate increases, but they demonstrate the trend. The average increase on telephone bills as a result of the rise was estimated at 3.3 per cent. That was made up of an increase on residential tariffs of 5.5 per cent and a rise of just 1.5 per cent for business subscribers. In the event of a victory by the conservatives at the British election due in 1983, British Telecom will be floated on the London stock exchange and just over half the total shareholding will be offered for sale. The vast majority of investors who have expressed interest in the shares of the new enterprise are institutions and pension funds, not small investors or members of the public. With a market capitalization of about £6 thousand million, and the prospect of a very low return on capital, even the boldest of investment fund managers may not be tempted by the float.

In the terminal area, British Telecom has retained the right to install the first telephone into premises, but after that there is open competition by private sector suppliers. Despite opposition by the three entrenched suppliers of handsets, GEC, Plessey and Standard Telephones and Cables, imported equipment will compete without being penalized by import duties. The result will be a flood of foreign products onto the British market, in line with competition that US manufacturers experience from telephone suppliers in Japan, Hong Kong, Taiwan and Korea. Declaration of open season for terminal equipment in Britain also creates opportunities for US companies, but in business attachments, rather than handsets for the home. The provision of PABXs and terminals which hook into the telephone network for business purposes promises to be a lucrative market for suppliers currently shut out of Britain by the British Telecom approvals system.

The demand which corporations began to voice in the United States from the 1960s onwards, leading to the establishment of competitors to the Bell system and their protection by FCC fiat, took two decades to reach Europe. And in spite of limited pressure from home grown corporations, the Thatcher government has received the message from international corporations that British Telecom stands as a potential threat to the movement of information across national borders. Because telecommunications is one of the few profitable sectors of a British economy based on heavy engineering and manufacturing, the attack on British Telecom is politically convenient for the Thatcher government. The business needs of transnational companies have coincided with the Thatcher government's ideological platform.

Despite the best efforts of international business and the sympathetic response their demands evoke from many governments, there has been only minimal movement in other countries to emulate the restructuring of regulation of US telecommunications. Some countries have strengthened their commitment to a nationally owned telecommunications network and encouraged integration of the public- and private-sector activities of the equipment and terminal suppliers. The call for regulatory change which US transnational companies are attempting to export has met strongest resistance where there is a nationally based telecommunications industry to protect. Britain can be counted the greatest success in the campaign to re-create the regulatory freedom which large companies in the United States have achieved in telecommunications. The tide in Australia, where there is not a strong nationally based telecommunications industry, has been running heavily in favour of US transnational users of communications services. One reason is that six out of the seven largest domestic equipment suppliers are owned by companies based outside Australia.

In Europe, the task of introducing US-style regulation is made easier by the strong position of US-based electronics companies. About thirty of the largest electronics companies in Europe are US owned. Of the total market in 1982 of $100 thousand million, US companies either imported or manufactured within Europe $31.5 thousand million worth of electronics goods. The next largest national group was West Germany, with $19.2 thousand million, followed by Britain, France and the Netherlands, whose shares were between $11 and $12.3 thousand million. In addition, US-based companies are estimated to control 80 per cent of the European computer equipment market.

Given that economic power, US companies have been influential in pushing for regulatory changes in Europe. In West Germany, minimal changes have been made to favour US proponents of competition with the national common carrier, Deutsche Bundesposte. The most strident advocate for change is the users' group, Deutsche Telecom eV, which has a membership dominated by subsidiaries of foreign companies. In addition, about half the membership consists of national companies with international subsidiaries. Its chairman represented the agricultural equipment manufacturer, John Deere, ranked number sixty-six in size among US transnationals. A group with a similar membership operates in Switzerland. Germany made an extensive study of the future of telecommunications in a government commission established in 1973, which formed a number of working parties to examine aspects of communications. After detailed examination, they concluded that there was need for no significant change. The only sign of relaxation of the monopoly role of the Deutsche Bundesposte has been the removal of standards approvals to an independent government authority. But the Bundesposte has also tightened its control over modems, demanding those not supplied by it be removed from the network by 1985.

The country with the highest number of telephone services and handsets per hundred of population, Sweden, has similarly discovered little rationale for change. Its state-owned telecommunications authority, Televerket, is integrated with a strong domestic industry which exports to other European countries, South America, the United States and the Middle East. Similar integration of the state authority and its suppliers is increasing in Italy, where the three largest telecommunications suppliers have been invited to work as a consortium to modernize the Italian telephone network. The aim is to build up a domestic base for export and the three companies, Telettra (owned by Fiat), GTE (a subsidiary of the US company) and Italtel (state owned) between them account for 70 per cent of telecommunications manufacturing in Italy. The Netherlands also shows few signs of acquiescing to US corporate pressure. Its relationship with the largest electronics company in Europe, the Philips Industries group, strengthens the integration of network owner and equipment supplier.

Perhaps the clearest example of the rejection of US pressure has come in France, in a process which was begun not by the present socialist administration of Francois Mitterand but by his conservative predecessor, Giscard d'Estaing. In 1975, the French government decided to revitalize the telecommunications and electronics industries by a massive injection of state funds. About $10 thousand million was set aside for a five-year plan which introduced electronic switching into the network and encouraged greater use of the telephone. As a result, the number of telephone lines in those five years trebled, to eighteen million. A further commitment to state-backed growth in high technology industries was made by the Mitterand government, which ear-marked $20 thousand million of state funds for the electronics industry in the five years from 1985. Rather than regulate to create competitive common carriers, the French government has permitted its telephone authority to plan a telecommunications satellite, called Telecom-1, which will be co-ordinated with the existing terrestrial network.

Outside Europe, despite the hopes of the US competitors of Japanese electronics and telecommunications companies, there are few ripples of change in Japan. The only sign of the foreign pressure succeeding has been the report of an administrative reform committee recommending minimal moves towards deregulation. Because of the close co-ordination between private and public high-technology sectors in Japan, it is unlikely that competition, particularly involving foreign companies, will be allowed in either the network or terminal equipment areas. Where carriers are in private hands, such as in the Japanese international telecommunications body, KDD, the government, at local and national level, participates as a stockholder, and foreign stakes are banned. The authority which handles all domestic telecommunications traffic, Nippon Telephone and Telegraph, is owned by the state.

One area where the export of relaxed regulation policies from the United States could be expected to take healthy root is in Canada, which is heavily influenced in all areas of its economic life by its southern neighbour. The fragmentation of Canadian telecommunications ownership bears some resemblance to the United States, but a direct parallel is misleading. Whereas the Bell system controls more than 80 per cent of all traffic in the United States, its former subisidary, Bell Canada, accounts for only 60 per cent. The rest is made up of a mixture of privately owned and state-owned operators, including GTE in British Columbia and the provincial governments in Saskatchewan and Manitoba. There has, as in West Germany, been a transfer of technical standard approvals to the department of communications, but the major regulatory body is the Canadian Radio and Television Commission. In the period of greatest pressure to weaken its US equivalent, the FCC, the Canadian regulatory body has strengthened its position, exercising greater control than ever before. The vertical integration of Bell Canada with Northern Telecom, Canada's largest telecommunications company, and with the research facilities of Bell Northern Research, resemble AT&T's former structure. There has been a long programme of co-operation between private industry and the Department of Communications, without whose support there would be no domestic satellite industry, one of Canada's strengths in telecommunications. Unlike the FCC, the Canadian commission has not slavishly followed the dictates of the advocates of market-place economics and has used its power to trade off the corporate aims of companies against the public interest. An example is its requirement that television companies provide remote-area programmes through direct satellite broadcast in return for being allowed to operate profitable pay television services in the cities.

As in matters of war and commerce, Australia has been the most pliable of US allies in the business of communications. With neither a strong sense of national identity nor a healthy domestic electronics and telecommunications industry, it has acquiesced in the Davidson report to a role of supporting actor. It has gone even further than Britain, which does at least have some nationally based industry in telecommunications to protect, in accommodating the desires of US transnational companies. For those international companies, the United States is only part of the market. The nature of their business means that regulation of their activities may have to be loosened at home first, but then it has been fervently pressed on the rest of the world as the appropriate model to follow. Along with those major companies, transnational service industry sees the need to break the restraints of regulation, especially when exercised by national public authorities. Among those service companies are advertising agencies – of which eleven of the world's dozen biggest are US based – public relations companies, insurance companies, and computer software and international accountancy companies. It is the needs of those companies and their host corporations which are being met by US demands for changes in regulation. And it is their need which has led to the demand for re-regulation in other parts of the world. Whenever international corporations in Australia call for support from politicians and the business community, there is a ready response. The spectacle of Australian business executives blindly doing the bidding of New York, London and Tokyo is not new. In the matter of telecommunications, it can be argued that they have never served their traditional roles so well. But the words they use and the thoughts they express are, like many of their other attitudes, imported from across the Pacific.

Chapter Five
Techno Telephone

If it were left to the ordinary domestic telephone subscriber to demand a different sort of telephone network, technological change in telecommunications would be slow. The reason is that telephone subscribers are unlikely to clamour for something which brings them few advantages. And since the 1870s, the telephone in Australia, and other developed countries, has served its users adequately. It has provided, at relatively low cost, a reliable means of communication which is easy to use and which reaches most people. Ordinary subscribers in metropolitan areas have noticed over the last few decades that the quality of the telephone line has improved and that it is now possible to dial long distance direct rather than through an operator. They have happily used the standard telephone handsets which differ little in the 1980s from models introduced fifty years ago. It was not until very recent times that fancy handsets, such as the Mickey Mouse and Snoopy models, have been on sale. Only a small minority of subscribers use them in Australia, although the marketing effort behind feature telephones in the United States has been much more intense. From time to time, telephone subscribers have complained that they do not receive an itemized account which allows them to keep track of the amount they have spent on long-distance calls. But there has been no widespread, concerted call for the technological improvement of the telephone service by private subscribers.

There are at least two ways of interpreting that situation. Either the public is unaware of benefits that new technology in the telephone network will bring, or so slight are the improvements that it is difficult to regard them as sufficiently important to raise as demands.

Change is clearly not coming from domestic telephone subscribers. Any dissatisfaction they have with the service they are receiving is insufficient to force the transformation of the telephone system occurring in most industrialized economies. Private telephone subscribers perceive the necessity of few improvements beyond making the same system work better, and there appears to be little enough demand for that.

Why then did Telecom Australia in 1977 commit itself to spending hundreds of millions of dollars to install computerized telephone exchanges? Why is much of its more than $1 thousand million annual capital expenditure devoted to introducing digital networks which will mean little detectable difference for the domestic telephone subscriber?

The answer is that telephone administrations have two sorts of customers, one spending proportionately more on telecommunications than the other. Although the vast majority of those who have telephones use them for private purposes, the smaller group of those who require them for business is much more active. Revenues for the administrations come not so much from installing handsets as from the amount of use they receive. And based on the number of calls made, business telephones generate vastly more traffic than the average private telephone. So although they may not be the largest group of telephone owners, the business community and government certainly produce more profits for telecommunications carriers. There has been an astonishing growth in both the number of telephones installed and the amount of traffic carried on the network within the last twenty years. Much of that increase is the result of a greater reliance by industry, commerce and government on the telephone; more than 80 per cent of their communications in Australia is estimated to be by telephone. Apart from that increase in voice traffic, there has been an explosive increase in the use of computers. The introduction of computers sets those in commerce and government apart from private subscribers.

The result is a paradox. The sort of telephone network we

have was determined by people's need to talk to each other, whether in their private lives or in the course of their jobs. But the most influential group of telephone users, the small businesses, large corporations and government departments which use the network the most, have a need beyond voice telephony. They also want a network which can accommodate communications between computers. For some fairly basic technical reasons, which will be examined, telecommunications networks designed for voice produce inefficiencies when computers are at either end of the line.

The imperative felt by businesses and government to have a network which can efficiently move data from computers around is that data processing now represents a major cost for any large organization. The improvements in productivity which computer users, justified or not, attribute to electronic data processing demand that they seek similar results from the telephone network. The economic and political power of those organizations are the moving force behind technological change in telephony, sometimes in the face of reluctance by common carriers to satisfy their wants.

In order to explain how those changes are taking place, it is worth tracing the course of the development of telephones from the time they began to be assumed to have at least some place in human discourse. There were, of course, doubters who said the new technology of telephones would never establish itself in the face of entrenched competition from very efficient, poorly paid messenger boys. Alexander Graham Bell proved them wrong.

In the course of doing so, he also displaced telegraphy, which in the way it transmits messages is more similar to modern digital communications than the telephone network Bell's invention created. Although Bell is the best known of the early telephone pioneers, partly because his name was used by the company which later became the largest communications corporation in the world, he was one of a group of inventors all working towards the same end. Of the others, Thomas Edison, who developed the telephone mouthpiece which is still widely in use, was the most famous. Bell's claim to have made the important breakthroughs in the development of the telephone was staked in the courts as much as the laboratory. He fought and won numerous patent cases, some brought by him and others against him. But the technical principles his work resulted in became the basis of the telephone system now in use.

The word most often used by technical people when they describe the telephone network is 'analogue', as distinct from the digital networks designed for data communications between computers. The word 'analogue' describes how human speech is converted into electrical impulses which are then sent through the telephone network. The sound patterns of speech are converted into impulses which are mirror images of those patterns. They are an analogy of human speech which enables the sound patterns to be sent along a telephone line and converted back to speech at the receiving end. No matter what the sound, whether human voice or music, the telephone network converts it to electrical impulses and then back again. Two-way communication is achieved by using one wire into the telephone and another out, so that incoming and outgoing signals do not cause interference. The telephone line is, for that reason, referred to by technicians as a 'twisted pair', because the wires are twirled round each other and encased in plastic. The telephone cables which carry signals throughout the network contain hundreds of twisted pairs, coloured differently for identification. A cross-section of cable, cut to expose the wires within, reveals a technicolour confusion of strands, each of which has to be joined up when cables are jointed.

Bell's use of an electrical analogue of the human voice on the telephone network was only half the solution to the problem of enabling people to communicate. The first telephone networks were unwieldy affairs, because although signals could be sent point to point, they had to be switched by manual operators. If you wanted to call someone on the other side of town, you rang the operator and asked to be connected. The operator took a lead connected to the twisted pair which fed into your telephone and plugged it into a socket on the switchboard which connected the caller and the receiver. Early manual exchanges employed large groups of operators, mainly women, to perform that task for local calls.

Had that way of doing things remained, it has been estimated that all the adult women in the United States would now need to be employed to do the work. A US undertaker averted that possibility. His name was Strowger and as his use of the telephone in business became greater he sought a way by which calls could be switched more quickly. He developed the earliest automated telephone exchange, which automatically connected callers with the numbers they dialled. Strowger's exchange used mechanical means to make the connections, but it ran on electricity. It is thus described as the first of the electromechanical systems. The calls were connected by electrical impulses which triggered mechanical relays one after the other, in a step-by-step fashion. Telephone exchanges which use Strowger's invention, or variations of it, are commonly called step-by-step exchanges. Step-by-step equipment is still used in a large proportion of telephone exchanges in developed countries; Britain and New Zealand, in particular, have high percentages of them in their networks.

As the quality of telephone instruments improved, from candlestick models, where the speaking and listening devices were separate, to the sort of handsets we have today, so did engineering in the network. More reliable repeaters were developed, which boosted the electrical signals on their way through the network. Better quality sound was achieved and people no longer had to shout their messages into the mouthpiece, a lesson it took some telephone users longer to learn than others. Improvements in switching also occurred, replacing Strowger's exchange with systems which, although still electromechanical, enabled calls to be switched more quickly. The new generation exchanges were called 'crossbar', a reference to the way in which they connected relays a group at a time rather than in sequential steps in the way Strowger had envisaged.

Towards the end of World War II, when the first computers were being developed, analogue networks and step-by-step exchanges were installed in most developed countries. The telephone, as a device for communicating in the course of business, was firmly entrenched. In private homes, it was increasingly common, particularly in the houses of wealthier families. The advances in electronics, which led by the 1980s to pressure for change in the way that telephone networks operated, did not come on the telecommunications companies unannounced. The communications groups were themselves responsible for some of the most important developments as they sought greater efficiency, particularly in switching. The invention of the first transistors occurred in the Bell Labs subsidiary of AT&T, in the tradition started by Bell. The integrated circuit, which later made possible the microprocessor, was also the work of Bell Labs. In both cases, its scientists were seeking a way to switch electrical signals more quickly, enabling connections between callers to occur more swiftly.

The importance of computers to the future of telecommunications did not, however, begin to blossom until data processing became a feature of commercial life in the 1950s. Most of those computers were large, cumbersome machines by today's standards, but they did create a need which telephone carriers had not met before. Computers needed to talk to each other through telephone networks designed for the human voice. Instead of speech patterns, the telephone network had to carry the streams of data flowing between computer systems. At about the same time, other forms of telecommunications traffic, particularly between business and government, began to flourish. Among them was telex which, like computers, did not communicate by sound patterns. Another was facsimile, where machines scanned pages of print and pictures, encoded them into electrical impulses to be sent through the network and created the same image at the receiving end. Instead of being routed like telephone calls through the network, switched by exchanges on the way, most of that traffic was carried on private lines. These were telephone links leased from the communications carriers, which connected business houses directly and were not switched through exchanges. As non-voice traffic built up, computers used the network like telephone users, on what was described as a 'dial-up basis'. This trend accelerated in the 1960s with the introduction of mini-computers.

Mini-computers were smaller and less powerful than the mainframe machines which preceded them in offices. They depended on communications even more because they were used in distributed systems where the aim was to spread processing and data storage capacity throughout a network. The branch offices of large companies, for instance, might all have a mini-computer rather than, or in addition to, a large computer at head office. Using computers in that way placed greater reliance on communications. The amount of data in relation to voice carried on the telephone system increased rapidly.

In order for traffic between computers to be transmitted on the telephone network, a device had to be used to convert the signalling method of computers to that of telephones; the function which in voice communications was performed by the telephone handset. The devices introduced to allow computers to communicate had to convert the digital signal of data processing machines into the analogue signal of the telephone network. The devices were called 'modems', shorthand for the modulation/demodulation process which occurred in converting the signals. Modems were literally black boxes which were linked by cable at one end to the computer and at the other to the telephone network. The modems were owned and installed by the telephone carrier and leased by users of computer systems. Modems were needed at each end, and their use enabled telecommunications carriers to attract more traffic but retain their control over what was transmitted on the network. That was a matter of some frustration to organizations heavily dependent on data communications and an increasing source of friction between the provider of the service and the users.

Telecommunications became more important to corporate and government organizations which had adopted computer systems. The cost of communications between computers became a factor in their budgets which was beyond their power to influence. Tariffs were set by the carrier, and if the customer thought it too high, there was no alternative to turn to. Unlike their use of data processing systems, which was subject to no regulation at all, their use of telecommunications was closely regulated by the provider of the service. The stage was set for a confrontation between the corporate world and the telecommunications carrier. In Australia, that tension between the two camps intensified in the mid 1970s, after the formation of Telecom Australia.

While voice communication in business was still predominant, data communications increased in importance, growing in Australia after 1975 by more than 30 per cent each year. And while the cost of processing data declined, a point made relentlessly by the computer suppliers, the cost of communications showed no comparable tendency to come down. It was not a trend which made data processing managers, or accountants, happy, and it was exacerbated by the lack of expertise in communications within companies. There were also restrictions on corporate use of communications which did not exist in data processing. Once mini-computers were wheeled in the front door, they needed only to be plugged in and switched on. Their operation was a good deal more complicated, but their installation was not. By contrast, arranging communications links was a more complex process.

Application had to be made to the telecommunications carrier, technical standards had to be met by the machine before it was connected to the network, and there was often a waiting time for installation of modems. Some of the delay was the fault of business organizations, which expected the same procedures involved in installing computers to apply in telecommunications. The result was frustration with the carrier, leading to demands that corporate users of computer equipment be freer to decide what could be plugged into the network.

The telecommunications carriers, in the meantime, were engaged in their own introduction of computers, both in conventional business applications and, more dramatically, in the networks. The conjunction of telephone and computer, described variously as computercations, telematics and telematique, was approaching.

The main interest of the communications carriers was in the introduction of computer equipment into telephone exchanges, a development which occurred in two phases. The first combined computer technology with electromechnical telephone exchanges. If computers were used to control the switching in exchanges, the carriers could derive a number of benefits. Computer-controlled switching required fewer staff for installation and maintenance and less space in exchange buildings, because electronic circuit boards were smaller than electrically operated relays. Greater reliability and easier diagnosis of faults were also claimed as advantages. Telecom Australia began to install computer-controlled switching in the late 1970s, until its efforts were interrupted by a national dispute with its technicians. It concerned exchanges in which new equipment had been installed. The exchanges were known as ARE 11, a term which received a wider airing when the Australian Telecommunications Employees' Association argued that they destroyed the skills and jobs of its members. The disagreement in 1978 over how the exchanges were to be manned and how maintenance was to be conducted took four years to resolve.

The dispute also involved the use of more full-blooded computerized equipment in exchanges which were known by the term 'AXE', a name also coined by L. M. Ericsson. AXE exchanges were computers which took over the old methods of switching, both Strowger's step-by-step method and the later crossbar system. Their introduction caused wider alarm among technicians than the computer controlled ARE 11 exchanges, because the proposed maintenance arrangements in AXE systems significantly eradicated technical skills and jobs. Diagnosis of faults was to have been carried out at a central point by a computer connected to groups of exchanges. The staff in the exchanges would then be instructed to perform tasks such as changing circuit boards. The dissatisfaction with ARE 11 and AXE and the dispute it provoked was of sufficient significance for the federal government to establish the Myers committee of inquiry into technological change which was asked to examine the effect of introducing a much wider range of technology.

In the network itself, changes were being made which brought the technologies of the telephone and the computer closer together. The first was a technique which enabled computers to communicate without the modems which converted digital signals so they could be carried on analogue telephone lines. Using copper cables, a different method of signalling was introduced. It was called 'pulse code modulation', or 'PCM' for short, and it enabled digital signals to be sent directly between computers. PCM is only a small proportion of the Australian telecommunications system, although the longer term aim of Telecom and other carriers is to convert their networks for digital use. Introducing digital transmission, as opposed to switching equipment, is a massive task, because it involves replacing eventually the entire maze of cables used to carry telecommunications traffic.

Some cable replacement has begun, using a thicker cable with a solid core which is able to carry much more traffic, whether the signals transmit conversations, computer data or television pictures. The newer cable is known as coaxial, and its main advantage over conventional cable is that it has wider bandwidth. When telephone calls are transmitted, they occupy a relatively small part of the bandwidth of coaxial cables, so many conversations can be packed on to them. The result is cost saving for the carrier, because instead of many cables being laid, a single cable is installed. Coaxial cable can carry television pictures, which use up vastly more transmission capacity than voice. Coaxial cable enabled the first direct broadcast of television pictures between Sydney and Melbourne, and it is also used for voice and data traffic.

Other means of transmitting signals have been introduced in the last couple of decades. The use of radar and military radio communications systems during World War II introduced microwave which offered some clear advantages over cable. Microwave systems transmitted signals in the same way as radio stations; they were picked up by antennas every 60 kilometres or so, amplified and sent on to the next antenna. The type of antenna used is a dish which collects an incoming signal, the strength of which is indicated by the dish's diameter. A microwave system introduced by Telecom in the 1960s stretched across the Nullarbor Plain, connecting West Australia with the eastern states. It was at the time one of the most ambitious uses of microwave ever attempted.

Although most people's conception of a telecommunications network is based on images of cables in ducts underground, microwave carries a large proportion of trunk traffic in most modern systems. In Australia, more than 70 per cent of interstate traffic is carried on microwave links. The towers used in transmission can be seen strung along mountain ridges between the Australian state capital cities. Microwave does not automatically eliminate the need for modems, because the signals carried between the dishes are almost all in analogue form. For the same reasons as signalling by cable is converting to digital, traffic on microwave links will increasingly be digital.

The other new medium for carrying signals is the satellite, and since the first communications satellite was launched into the geostationary orbit in the 1960s, it has been joined by dozens of others. Because satellites in that orbit remain in fixed relation to the earth, they can be regarded as similar to giant transmitter towers, without the steel superstructure to support them. Satellites perform precisely the function of microwave towers. They pick up signals from earth, amplify them and send them back. Compared to the cost of installing terrestrial telecommunications networks, whether from cable, microwave or a combination of both, satellites are cheap. Some telephone carriers, such as the Bell System in the United States, adopted them as a transmission medium which broadened its mix of cable and microwave. Other carriers have seen satellites used to break their monopoly carriage of telecommunications. In this regard, Australia represents the clearest example in the world. Both satellites and microwave systems use radio signals for transmission, but higher frequencies are being used increasingly in space. Most microwave systems operate in the 4/6 gigahertz range; the newer satellites use the 11/14 gigahertz band. As the majority of microwave links are operated by existing carriers, their competitors using satellites have opted for the higher frequency, thus avoiding interference, on both the technical, regulatory and political fronts.

What has all this meant for the private telephone subscriber and what will the changes underway mean in the future? The answer, surprising to some, is very little. The major beneficiary of the transformation of the telephone network will be large corporate users, in the way signals are transmitted and switched and in the greater range of equipment they can attach to the public telecommunications system. If they do not own a computer, or constantly use the telephone, domestic subscribers will see few benefits. The quality of the lines over which voice is carried will improve, although nowhere near the rate at which that improvement will occur for business subscribers. People who use the telephone in their social and private lives have little need for the myriad different attachments corporations want to connect to the telephone system. They will be able to acquire fancier telephones which will make dialling easier, but long after those facilities are standard in offices and industry. Some telephones will display the number being dialled on a small screen set in the handset, or record how many seconds the conversation has been going and how much it is costing. Again, these features will be introduced in business first. The display may show the number which is attempting to call in, enabling the telephone owner to decline to answer unwanted calls.

Some domestic telephones will have abbreviated dialling and most will be equipped with push buttons to save the odd second in dialling. That increased speed of keying in numbers is pointless unless the connection between handset and exchange is made more quickly, and even that will be barely detected by most subscribers. The fact that a call connects half a second quicker is of little importance if it takes the ordinary telephone user two seconds to put his or her ear to the telephone. Other facilities that will be put to work in the office first, will enable the telephone to automatically re-call engaged numbers or if dialling is interrupted. Loudspeaking telephones, which first appeared in the offices of business executives, will also be used in homes.

The range of potential uses that private subscribers have for the telephone will always be dwarfed, however, by the needs of corporate users of telecommunications. That is the reason business interests have been the most powerful force in determining the technological direction of telecommunications. Not only are they the largest customer in dollar terms, but they also use the network intensively, making them the most profitable group of subscribers. Apart from their value to the carrier as revenue earners, they need to hook into the network a vast array of computer terminals, from mainframe and mini-computers, to word processors, and high-speed telex and facsimile transmission machines.

Of those attachments, the most strategically important for business users is PABX, the modern equivalent of the switch Strowger developed to facilitate his business communications. Instead of switching calls through the public network, PABXs switch traffic within an office. The operator who answers calls at the company switchboard directs them to the appropriate extension. Older office exchanges, called private manual branch exchanges, or PMBXs, are still in use in many Australian businesses but are now being rapidly replaced by not one but two generations of technology. The plug and cord boards, so named because the operator connects callers by inserting leads into sockets, were first superseded by automatic exchanges. Like their equivalent in the public network, these automated exchanges were electromechanical. Calls were connected by pressing buttons instead of using plugs and cords. The later version of automatic exchange uses electronic equipment which enhances the central role of the PABX in the development of what has been hailed as the office of the future.

When one confronts the profusion of electronic office technology, it is helpful to regard the PABX as the hub of a wheel which connects together a number of spokes. When life was simpler, and most offices had only the telephone for communications, the switchboard operator could direct traffic quickly and efficiently. With the increase in traffic, and the addition of different means of communications, the task became much more complex. A greater volume of voice traffic needs to be handled and other connections must be made: between computers large and small, facsimile machines, high-speed telex machines, word processors and between terminals in one place connecting to computers holding information in another. Although the first electronic PABXs confined themselves to switching voice traffic, newer models claim two advances. Firstly, they are fully digital, meaning that the last vestiges of electromechanical technology have been eliminated from them. Secondly, because they operate in the same way as computers, using the same signalling system, they can handle voice and data traffic with equal ease. They can be used to switch communications, human and non-human, through a central private exchange in the office. Sometimes referred to as integrated PABXs, because they treat voice and data traffic in the same way, these new machines will have a fundamental effect on office work and on the relationship between the business user of telecommunications and the carrier.

A basic attraction of computer systems is that once they have sufficient memory and processing capacity to perform one function they can easily be expanded to take in other tasks. That is certainly true of digital PABXs, which do much more than act as a telecommunications traffic cop in the office. Some of those features may make the telephone easier or quicker to use, and sooner or later they will flow through to domestic telephones.

Because digital PABXs have the capacity to store information electronically, just as a computer does, they can hold in their memory a list of commonly called numbers for each extension. Instead of dialling the full six- or seven-digit number, and the code if the call is a long-distance one, the telephone user dials two or three digits. The PABX's memory does the rest. That is an advantage if you work in an office and dial a few numbers very frequently. The same is true of a feature known as 'repertory dialling', which can save time if you often call numbers which give the busy tone. On some telephone handsets, the time, cost and estimation of the call is displayed on a small screen. If the computer memory is stored on micro chips in the telephone rather than at a central point, those facilities are available without a PABX. But digital private exchanges have other advantages for corporate users beyond the sometimes gimmicky features that computer technology makes possible. PABXs are being sold to managers as weapons which can be used in their battle for control over the workplace, for they are formidable machines for spying on the workforce.

Under the old regime of plug and cord boards, there was a certain autonomy given to office staff in their use of the telephone. Short of the operator listening in, conversations remained private, and there was only patchy supervision of the call's duration and destination. As a device for monitoring staff telephone use, the operators were imperfect agents for management's desire to control the workforce. Monitoring and recording are much more reliable in electronic systems, and this has become one of the main marketing features of digital PABXs. The destination of the calls made from every extension can be recorded centrally by the private exchange and printed out on paper. The duration of each call and its cost can be similarly recorded. The value of calls made from each extension can be automatically calculated, as can the time that they were made. Every time an employee lifts the telephone receiver to dial out, the PABX is alerted to collect this information so that the company can keep a complete record of telephone use.

The arguments advanced by PABX suppliers for monitoring calls appeal to business efficiency. Where cost allocations are made to different departments, the information gathered by the machine allows telephone calls to be totted up. If management suspects that employees are using its telephone to make private calls, it can check the numbers dialled from each extension, or ask employees whom they were phoning. If a department which one would expect to be an intensive user of telephones is revealed as making few calls, the uncharacteristic pattern of use can be detected. Such features enable businesses to be run more efficiently according to the PABX suppliers.

The effect of increased surveillance on staff productivity and autonomy is not considered, however, nor is the basic issue of privacy faced by employers and suppliers. The Telecom trade unions in Australia have been virtually alone in raising the question of the effect of systems which record telephone use. One demand put forward by the ATEA, and accepted by Telecom and the PABX suppliers, is that the last two digits of any number called should be deleted from the systems' records to protect privacy. In large hotels, where recording devices are used to bill the cost of telephone calls to guests' accounts, the unions argued that a warning sticker should be placed on the handset. Because of the lack of awareness by most office staff of the capabilities of electronic PABXs, few have sought safeguards when new systems are installed. And even fewer employers have gone out of their way to warn their staff that their work has been placed under closer surveillance.

If that is possible using digital private exchanges, what is to prevent similar surveillance occurring in the public-switched network? In a technical sense, the answer is nothing at all, and although it is true that there are legislative guidelines governing telephone taps, it is certainly easier with digital exchanges.

In the older electromechanical exchanges, a wire had to be physically connected to groups of relays for telephones to be tapped. This was usually done by selected technicians in Telecom exchanges who had received security clearances and were regarded as trustworthy employees. Because those relays are replaced by electronic circuit boards in digital exchanges, tapping in to telephone conversations can be done much more covertly. Wires do not need to be physically attached to relays; the computer equipment used to diagnose faults in the exchange can gain access to telephone conversations by calling them up from a terminal which need not be located in the exchange. Because digital PABXs operate on the same principles as those exchanges, they can also be tapped without the need for anything so obvious as a wired connection. Tapping conversations in the network is also not as easy to detect, for microwave links can be intercepted without the intrusion required for cable. The attachment of listening devices to telephone cables can be more easily detected because voltage is drawn off from the network. Microwave signals are intercepted in mid air by electronic listening posts and give away no such clues.

PABXs are the products of telecommunications suppliers. The equivalent product of the data processing companies is a technique they call 'local networks'. Local networks carry traffic over relatively short distances; a kilometre or two is usually sufficient to wire the largest office buildings. They can carry data between computers, word processors and facsimile machines, or transmit voice traffic in digital form. Different types of networks are used; some are loops, others are in ring formations around which telecommunications traffic travels. Terminals hooked into local networks deposit data which transmits along a single cable until it reaches the terminal which is its destination. The networks direct traffic in much the same way as PABXs, treating voice and data alike.

Both digital PABXs and local networks allow voice traffic to be treated differently. The vast majority of business communications are conducted in voice form, although it is more efficient for corporations to transmit data instead. The solution is to digitize voice: to break it up into bits and treat it like traffic between computers. That enables the voice equivalent of electronic mail services to be introduced. 'Electronic mail' is the term used to describe messages sent between terminals through a communications network. The terminals may be mini-computers, micro-computers or word processing machines, and messages keyed in on one can be sent to the screen of another. Many terminals sold in offices now have a facility known as an 'electronic mailbox'. When the user switches on the machine, he or she can check whether there are any messages from other terminals. By keying in a code, any messages left in the user's absence appear on the screen. The same can be done with voice messages which have been digitized. Messages are held in computer memory until their recipients call. The claimed improvements of such systems are the elimination of calling back, the necessity of making only one call to contact someone else and accuracy in relaying messages.

Another device introduced into offices which blurs the line between telephone and computer terminals is the display phone which has a screen and keyboard as well as a mouthpiece and number keys. Already operating in the United States and Canada, the devices use two lines, one for voice and another for data. While a conversation is being held, data and text can be displayed on the screen, including charts, graphs, statistics and paragraphs of copy. A small keyboard allows users to key in further information which can then be displayed on the screen. Similar devices are expected to lead the telecommunications manufacturers into battle against the computer suppliers. The aim is to install a terminal on the desk of every executive in large organizations, a most profitable project if achieved.

Many of the functions which can be performed by electronic equipment in the office formerly belonged in the telephone network. Switching calls and billing individual callers can be done, for example, by digital PABXs with equal efficiency as exchanges in the network. That realization has prompted many large corporations to construct national and international networks of their own. The telephone circuits are mostly leased from carriers, but the trend for very big companies is to bypass the carriers and either construct their own systems or use smaller competing carriers. Private microwave links were the first means used to construct such networks, but satellites provide an even greater potential. Satellite Business Systems in the United States, for instance, is one-third owned by one of its largest customers, International Business Machines. The effect of those private networks is to divert traffic from the main carriers, forcing a redistribution of capital spending in the network and interfering with the cross-subsidization between profitable and unprofitable services.

Another medium for those private networks or competing

common carriers is fibre optics, which can carry the volume of traffic transmitted on coaxial cables but which are very much lighter and thinner. Instead of sending electrical impulses along copper cable, the developers of fibre optics used a light source directed down the centre of cables made from refined silicon, or sand. By switching the light sources on and off very quickly, messages could be sent in digital form. Unlike copper cables, no interference was caused by the proximity of other cables and neither moisture nor excessive heat affected transmission. For telecommunications carriers, the added attractiveness of optical fibre cables is that they can be installed in smaller ducts or pulled through channels occupied by conventional cable. Advances in the technology of fibre optics have also extended the distance which signals can be sent before being boosted by repeaters. That means that fewer access points are required and less maintenance in repairing faulty repeaters, a major cost for the carriers.

An important user of fibre optics is expected to be cable television systems which in addition to transmitting TV programmes carry telecommunications services. Cable television systems which take over traffic that would otherwise go to the telecommunications carriers divert revenue which undermines the economics of telephone networks in the same way as competing carriers do. Trial cable television systems in North America measure the amount of gas, electricity, water and other services provided by utilities and transmit the information back to the supplier. Two-way information retrieval services, such as videotex, can also be installed on cable networks. Teleshopping, banking from home, and automatic alarm services for fire and intruders can be supplied on cable systems. All the revenue involved is diverted from the traditional telephone carriers.

How does this affect the private citizen, as opposed to the corporate user of telecommunications? The answer is that domestic telephone subscribers will be classified into the rich and the poor. Those who can afford them will use the new devices and services which the priorities of corporations have made possible. Many wealthier subscribers will be able to enjoy the benefits of corporate networks as part of their employment package. For most people, the range of options will be extended only by the availability of gimmicky telephones at a higher price than standard handsets. Because of the pressure from corporate users of telecommunications to pay less for telephone and data transmission services, the carriers will be forced to charge domestic users more. For most people, the transformation of telecommunications will be seen for what it is, the annexation by business of a service which used to be regarded as a universal right. The telephone may once again be the preserve of the minority in society who can afford it.

Chapter Six
Trojan Bird

Before mid 1977, the question whether Australia should have a domestic satellite was a matter left to Telecom boffins. After that, it became a political matter. The act of intervention which took the satellite question out of one arena and placed it in another was a report commissioned by Kerry Packer, chief executive of Television Corporation Ltd, the operator of Channel TCN 9 in Sydney. Packer was primarily interested in using a satellite for the distribution of television programmes outside existing coverage areas in the major Australian cities. But the possibilities of the satellite being used as a lever to prise Telecom's monopoly grip from telecommunications had not escaped him.

The story of how Australia came to sign contracts for a satellite which will be launched in mid 1985 from NASA's shuttle space vehicle is political, not technical. Although the debate about whether there should be a satellite was intense for five years, it was confined to those who had transcended the barriers of understanding about how satellites worked. Outside a handful of people in private industry and Telecom engineers, the technology of satellite communications was not widely understood in Australia in the mid 1970s. For those able to penetrate the smokescreen of technical language, the decision-making process by which Australia came to acquire a satellite became a case study in how the private sector applied pressure on the Fraser government. That process had an important effect on Telecom, for a number of reasons.

First suggestions by the Packer organization that there should be an Australian satellite were dismissed by Telecom.

Their studies had shown it did not make economic sense, and there were technical difficulties. Those considerations alone were not to determine the outcome of the satellite debate, as Telecom was to learn. The satellite showed up Telecom management's inability to interpret the Australian political process, no matter how great its expertise in technical matters. By the time Telecom took stock of the threat to its operations which the satellite posed, it was too late. As a result, when the Davidson committee sat down to inquire into Australian telecommunications, one of the main questions before it had already been answered. At the top of Davidson's agenda was the question whether Telecom should face competition from other common carriers. The Australian satellite organization, Aussat Pty Ltd, announced during the inquiry that it had signed contracts with Hughes Aircraft Company for a communications satellite system. The question of competition had already been settled.

Although Packer's primary rationale for an Australian satellite was to extend his television distribution, willing allies with other motives joined in his quest. In January 1977, IBM received approval from the Federal Communications Commission in the United States for a satellite project in which it was a partner. The possibility of duplicating that success in Australia very quickly brought IBM into the fray. The other influential force promoting the satellite was the world's most successful supplier of spacecraft, Hughes Aircraft Company. It had briefed all the parties which could influence the outcome of the project after it had sold a satellite system to Indonesia in the early 1970s.

When the government responded to Packer's promptings and announced that a task force would re-open the question of an Australian satellite, the major players were in place. Their submissions were influential in determining the outcome of the task force's inquiry. The task force contained a single representative from Telecom and was chaired by the general manager of the Overseas Telecommunications Commission (OTC), Harold White. The White report was considered by an inter-departmental committee, which was established to report to the then minister, Tony Staley. The enthusiasm of the minister for Canadian satellite systems led to a Canberra workshop at which technologists from that country were given a public platform. It took five years from the time the White task force was announced until contracts for a system were signed. In that time, the stage was set for the Davidson inquiry into Telecom.

The first person to hold the spotlight was Kerry Packer. He set the scene by commissioning a report from US satellite consultant, Donald Bond, who had, in Packer's words, an 'illustrious record in the communications field'. Certainly, Bond was well qualified technically to prepare a document about the possibility of an Australian satellite. Packer's main intention in commissioning the report was, he said, a concern for the communications needs of rural dwellers. Television's existing distribution arrangements did not fully serve rural dwellers, Packer said in a letter to the minister of communications, the late Eric Robinson, in August, 1977. 'I am of the opinion,' wrote Packer, 'that our existing communications network is not satisfactory nor capable of providing such a service to the Australian people'. In addition to suggesting that a satellite be used for network television from the major city channels, he explained his reasons for commissioning a report. They went beyond television distribution:

Having become aware of the use and application of domestic satellites elsewhere with their proven potential to resolve many of Australia's existing telecommunications shortcomings I commissioned a study . . .

Kerry Packer revealed how easy it had been to gain the prime minister's ear. He told *Video Age* in January 1983:

And I went and saw the Prime Minister and I explained to him my understanding of what was happening in those areas and to his undying credit he grasped on to it immediately and said, 'Of course it's what we want. It's exactly the sort of thing we need to stop the drift of people into urban areas. We can keep them informed. We can allow them to participate in whatever's happening around the nation', and he said, 'Can you do more for me on this?', and I said, 'It will take six or twelve months. We will pay for it, then we will put to you a paper of how we see this developing.'

Although the report was mainly about television, the use of a satellite as a lever against Telecom's hold on Australian communications was also of primary concern. The significance of the decision to license Satellite Business Systems in the United States had not escaped the notice of the Packer organization. SBS became the most important model to be used by the forces opposing the Telecom monopoly. Outlining the report's implications, Packer wrote to the minister:

It might well mean a major revision of the television broadcasting frequency plan to accommodate additional re-broadcast transmitters, a reassessment of future terrestrial telecommunication systems, a change in the rights of Telecom as a common carrier expressed in the Telegraph Act and prospects of a more equitable tariff structure for these services.

There was no clearer statement of intention in the debate about the satellite.

Bond's report was primarily a technical document, with little consideration given to the social, political and economic issues of the satellite. It contained no new information of any significance. A series of reports prepared by Telecom about possible satellite systems had been issued beginning in the early 1970s. Less than two months after Bond's report, Telecom released its latest study, which confirmed earlier reports that satellite communication was uneconomic for Australia. Bond described satellite developments in North America as if they were a mystery to Australia. If his report provided new insights for the Australian television industry, there was nothing in it to change the sums done by the national telecommunications authority.

He proffered Australia a satellite model based on current US communications space systems: twenty-four transponder spacecraft operating in the 4/6 gigahertz range. The technology of satellite communications dated back to 1957, with the launch of the Russians' Sputnik, but it had leapt forward when the ideas of science fiction author Arthur C. Clarke were put into practice by Hughes Aircraft in the 1960s. In 1945, Clarke had posited in the technical magazine, *Wireless World*, the possibility of using what he called 'space stations' to send signals around the globe. Three spacecraft located in an orbit above the equator would be enough for radio signals to be transmitted to every area of the world. The orbit became known as the 'geostationary slot' because a satellite located in it remained in fixed relation to the earth. The satellite was like a repeater station located high atop an imaginary tower; it was kept in place by gravity and would last for years before its batteries ran out. It received signals from earth, amplified them and sent them back to ground stations. The receiving and transmitting equipment in satellites was called 'transponders' and the frequency range in which the signal travelled up and down was between 4 and 6 gigahertz.

Bond proposed a standard communications satellite, but the technical nature of space technology meant that few non-technical people understood that he was putting forward nothing that was novel and innovative in satellites. He was merely transplanting US technological solutions across the Pacific Ocean. Not for the first time, that approach proved unsuccessful. Bond recommended planning begin immediately, based on his blueprint.

Bond advanced a straightforward application of existing North American systems. He had recommended the lower 4/6 gigahertz frequency instead of the higher 11/14 gigahertz range for a combination of technical reasons, but in the process ignored the realities of frequency allocation and use in Australia. Telecom controlled an extensive microwave network in just the frequency Bond suggested for the satellite. That became one of the main reasons why the frequency selected by Bond was not the same as the one finally adopted by the Australian satellite system. Higher frequencies for satellites were being explored, although there were technical limitations to them, a point Bond made in his report.

There is a trade-off in satellite technology between the power at which the transponder transmits and the size of the receiving stations on the ground. The 4/6 gigahertz satellite version suggested by Bond transmitted at lower power than the high-frequency 11/14 gigahertz systems. Satellites with lower operating power had the advantage of lasting longer, for up to a decade, compared to high-powered spacecraft which continued to operate for only three years. Balanced against the cost advantages of low-powered, low-frequency satellites was greater investment in antennas on the ground. Whereas satellites in the 4/6 gigahertz frequency range needed dish antennas, 2 or 3 metres in diameter, higher powered spacecraft could transmit to dishes less than 2 metres in diameter and in some applications down to antennas only 1 metre wide. Smaller dishes were considerably cheaper to buy and install.

Bond opted for a lower powered, low-frequency, longer life system transmitting to relatively large antennas. One of his reasons was that under certain conditions, notably during heavy rainfall, the signal from higher powered satellites was severely impaired or even blotted out. SBS had discovered similar results in transmission tests from the sub-tropical Florida region of the United States. Conditions in the due north and the north-east areas of Australia could be expected to produce distortion to the signal from the satellite. This was less important for television pictures, where the quality would decrease but some images would still be seen, than for data communications. Computers communicating in data streams needed absolute accuracy in transmission. A heavy tropical rainstorm interrupting a flow of data from a mining site to a central computer in Sydney and Melbourne would render unintelligible the information being transmitted.

A month after Bond's report had been presented to Robinson, the minister for post and telecommunications, its existence was announced in the House of Representatives, and by December 1977 a task force had been formed to inquire into Australian satellite communications. In October, Telecom produced a report of its own, based on contact with eighteen federal government organizations, eleven state and local government bodies, fifty-one hardware suppliers and systems consultants, twenty-four potential users and other interested parties, including the Federation of Australian Commercial Television Stations, to which Channel TCN 9 belonged; and thirty-four overseas organizations. Its bibliography noted that since the beginning of 1972 there had been thirty-one reports on satellites circulated within Telecom, the majority of which had been produced by staff within the organization. The October report examined the historical background of discussions about satellite systems in Australia, the use of the Intelsat system by OTC, potential applications in Australia, its integration with existing facilities, and the effects of a domestic satellite system.

The Telecom report's findings were unequivocal:

On the basis of these findings, it has been concluded that: it is not possible at this time to establish a quantitative economic case to justify the provision of a national satellite system, although the market for greatly improved TV program distribution at rates which reflect costs is an important factor.

It was also concluded in the report that the market for television distribution by satellite was 'uncertain'. This did not endorse the Bond thesis that Australia needed a communications satellite for television and contained no support at all for the assertion that it was required to diversify telecommunications. The government nevertheless established an inquiry of its own.

The White task force, as it became known, was headed by Harold White, who as general manager of OTC was largely responsible in 1975 for ensuring that overseas telecommunications remained outside Telecom's control. Other members were drawn from government departments but only one, Rollo Brett, the director of planning, was drawn from Telecom. Other members were from the federal departments of post and telecommunications, finance, health, transport and two representatives of the defence department. OTC had two places on the committee, with White being joined by Graham Goswinckel, its assistant general manager. The secretariat was also headed by an OTC man, director of planning, Dick Johnson, who was assisted by representatives from the departments of post and telecommunications and from transport.

When the inquiry began, there was political discussion about its method of holding hearings. In particular, Senator Susan Ryan, spokeswoman for the federal opposition on the media, asked the new minister who was entitled to receive transcripts of what were mooted as public hearings. White had declined to give Ryan access to the transcripts, a matter which the new minister, Tony Staley said he would take up with the inquiry's chairman. The submissions were public knowledge and some parties, such as IBM Australia Ltd, chose to release theirs to the press. Clearly, one of the key submissions was from the Packer organization, which put in two separate proposals for how the satellite could extend television coverage to country areas by licensing additional broadcast stations in rural towns. Hughes Aircraft submitted the most detailed technical document, putting a number of options before the committee.

The transcripts revealed more than the submissions, especially about the committee's state of mind. Even before the task force had written its report, observers of its hearings concluded that it was unlikely to disagree with Bond about the need for a satellite. It was a question of what the satellite system would look like rather than was one necessary. As early as May 1978, White was quoted in the *Canberra Times* as saying a domestic communications satellite was only a matter of time. The comment was made on the eve of the committee's Canberra hearings, nearly six months before White's report was presented to the government. During the appearance of Kerry Packer at the hearings, the following exchange occurred at the end of the media group's evidence:

WHITE: 'Thanks, Mr Packer, and I think at this point I'd like to ask my colleagues if they have any further questions to put. Was there anything further that you would like to put in Mr Packer, at this stage?'

PACKER: 'Just I hope we get a satellite sir, and that we can get a little bit of time on it.'

WHITE: 'We'll get a satellite, the only issues are when, what design, who controls it, how much it's going to cost, who pays for it all, etc, etc.'

PACKER: 'Those sort of minor things that . . .'

WHITE: 'Exactly. Thank you very much gentlemen, we'll rise in ten minutes.'

It was 'those sort of minor things' which concerned IBM in its submission to the task force, prefaced by a letter from its then managing director, Allan Moyes. He made it clear that the North American model served as the basis for IBM's Australian satellite strategy, saying:

During the preparation of the submission, our people here in Australia have worked with colleagues in the USA so that our local perspective of Australian needs, particularly in the business communications field, has been combined with our experience overseas in experimentation with and application of satellite communications systems. The work we have done in the preparation of this document has left us with a high level of enthusiasm for an Australian communications satellite, an attitude which I am sure will be readily evident from our submission.

IBM's submission was a hymn of praise to its parent company's decision to back the SBS venture. It also detailed SBS's use of the Canadian CTS or Hermes satellite for experiments in transmitting data around the United States, using the 11/14 gigahertz frequency. In the process, it took a swipe at Telecom. The IBM submission said:

However, monopoly communications carriers with a vested interest in existing facilities and an obligation to provide nationwide telephone communications appear far less motivated than entrepreneurial entities to bring these applications into commercial operation.

It drew unfavourable comparisons between rates about to be offered by SBS for long-distance communications and those set by Telecom. No mention was made of the distortions introduced into the Australian tariff structure by geography and market size. Satellites were cheaper according to IBM. It urged the Australian government to duplicate its experiment on the Hermes satellite, a suggestion which when later implemented by the Department of Communications, ended in failure. It argued that a separate commission or consortium should be established to run the Australian satellite, and it should operate outside Telecom's control. It also presented an argument, later adopted by Business Telecommunications Services (BTS), of which IBM was a member, that Telecom should lose the right to decide which parties were connected to the network. IBM's qualification that such interconnection was not intended for 'direct competition' with Telecom rang hollow in view of SBS's role in the United States.

The transcript of the White task force hearings revealed in greater detail the company's intentions. The chief witness for IBM was Bob Evans, vice-president of the corporation and one of the executive partners which supervised SBS's operations. Introducing him, Allan Moyes, made clear to the committee the importance of Evans's appearance. Moyes said, 'It is true, I think, to say that Bob Evans has never been very far away from the central thrust of the technological development within IBM. Evans brought along some slides to show the committee, which illustrate why IBM is so bullish in its approach to the future of satellite communications'. Evans took the trouble to explain the IBM corporate view about regulated telecommunications markets, such as that in Australia, saying:

I would say that as you know in the United States, as well as other places around the world, that communications are regulated at the moment; your industry [that is, data processing] is not regulated and so there's a barrier of some sorts in respect of your computers, and computer makers being too interested in communications for the possibility of regulation, which in all honesty, that many computer makers fear might restrict the dynamics that we've seen in this industry through the past twenty-five years, right or wrong.

It was one of the first suggestions that the US deregulation issue was being exported to Australia.

IBM's ambitions were not limited to computers, as Evans made clear:

...we thought that perhaps that the best way to design a system would be to try to design the whole system from end to end, putting what in our view were the right functions in the computer, the right functions in the earth stations, the right functions in the satellite.

Evans cited the case of a large US corporation, which he referred to as 'N' and described the savings which could putatively be made using satellites. In its 1977 estimates, the company decided it would spend $224 million for its communications and computing services. Of that total, $34 million could have some application to satellites and according to SBS, $11 million of that could be saved because of lower tariffs. SBS had chosen 11/14 gigahertz frequency because it reduced earth station costs to users, but Evans had a slightly different concept in mind for Australia, as did the task force chairman, who said:

One of the problems we face is developing what the government called a scenario or a variety of scenarios, which we interpret to mean possible satellite configurations and, as you would know, they'd have to be hybrid I guess in form in order to meet the various requirements that are seen here.

The use of the word 'hybrid' in the task force discussions with IBM was a signpost to the eventual recommendations of its report. A hybrid satellite was one which had both 4/6 gigahertz and 11/14 gigahertz frequencies, in other words, a mix of both high- and low-powered solutions in space and large and small antennas on the ground.

Hughes Aircraft submitted a detailed report on the technical options containing a preface from Albert Wheelon, the man who had designed and built the first geostationary communications satellite: 'It is not our intention to suggest any system or satellite solution.' Hughes had all the options covered, however; not only was it the contractor for SBS's systems but a few years earlier it had sold a communications satellite to

Indonesia, called Palapa, which operated in the 4/6 gigahertz frequency. In its coverage of the options, Hughes, true to its word, did not urge a particular satellite system on the White task force. But it did devote eight pages to describing a satellite in the 11/14 gigahertz frequency compared to three paragraphs to one in the 4/6 gigahertz frequency. It also proposed the same satellite body selected by SBS, rejecting a heavier and more expensive version.

To the surprise of no one who had followed its progress, the White task force recommended that Australia acquire a national satellite system. There were some surprises, however, at the strength of the dissent from the majority committee conclusions, especially from the Department of Finance. The task force recommended a hybrid spacecraft which sought the best of all worlds. It mooted three separate frequencies, including 4/6 gigahertz for regional television broadcasting, 11/14 gigahertz for direct broadcast television and telecommunications, and 7/8 gigahertz for use by the defence department. It revealed uncertainty about the cost of such an innovative use of satellite technology. The engineering problems facing the system designers were formidable. The same satellite required powerful 100 watt transponders for direct broadcast television and telecommunications and lower powered transponders for regional distribution of television. There needed to be a variety of antennas on the ground. The task force was unable to agree on costs for either the space or earth segments of the system and also expressed doubt about the level of demand from potential users of the system.

White recommended a separate authority outside Telecom's control to run the satellite and carry telecommunications traffic in competition with the monopoly carrier. The suggestion that a consortium be empowered to run the satellite system was not adopted. Only later did private-sector interests gain the right to direct ownership of part of the system and representation on the board responsible for the satellite's operation.

The strongest counter to White's report was contained in an appendix which gave the dissenting statement of the

Department of Finance representative, J. P. Coleman, chief finance officer, communications section. Coleman said:

In my view the improvements to Australia's communications capacity which could evolve from the basic model system are marginal improvements to a communications infrastructure which provides already a sophisticated, high quality service by world standards. I am not satisfied that it has been established that these marginal benefits could be provided necessarily at less cost by means of a satellite system.

Coleman suggested that the task force had got its sums wrong and was unduly optimistic about possible demand. He was proved right on the last point within months of the task force's report, when the Department of Defence let it be known that it had no desire to take up the capacity on the satellite which had been allocated to it. Coleman was also to be proved right about the cost of the system overall and of the price at which telephony could be provided by satellite to the outback.

It would be inaccurate to describe the attitude of the then minister, Tony Staley, to the report's content as anything less than enthusiastic. Staley was a fervent advocate of high technology; it became the hallmark of his reign in the portfolio. But according to Staley, the big business interests who had pushed hardest for a satellite really had as their motive the welfare of people living in outback Australia. Tabling the report in Parliament, Staley said that a domestic satellite had many advantages:

Above all, it could be a solution to our problems in providing communications to remote areas and isolated communities. The government is concerned that some Australians still lack basic communications services, do not have television, are restricted in their access to radio, and suffer some cultural and social deprivation because they are beyond the reach of current communications.

It was the lack of services which Staley took up as an insistent theme in his public statements on the satellite.

Two developments had already begun to ease the plight of those in the outback. The first was a rural telephony programme undertaken by Telecom, with the support of the government, especially its National Country Party members. While the satellite was still being debated, the government approved the acceleration of the rural programme, which was scheduled to cost about $500 million when completed. The extension of Telecom's terrestrial network reduced the number of people who could not be reached by Telecom's existing network. Yet the number of those people unserved by telephones was a major reason for the satellite. Staley's concern for the deprivation of outback people in television and radio services also appeared to ignore a project involving Telecom, the Australian Broadcasting Commission (ABC) and the international satellite authority, Intelsat. A series of large earth stations were to be located throughout areas of rural Australia which were not served by radio and television. They would receive ABC radio and television programmes from an Intelsat satellite which were picked up by the large earth stations and re-broadcast by transmitters. Thus many of the supposed beneficiaries of the satellite were likely to be radio listeners and television watchers well before it was launched.

The White task force report signalled an increase in Staley's intervention in the process of acquiring an Australian satellite. Fired with enthusiasm for a satellite, Staley took two further steps. He appointed an interdepartmental group to provide him with another satellite report, and he undertook an overseas tour to examine the options. The interdepartmental group became known as 'the working party' and it produced a blueprint, at Staley's behest, of the satellite which will be launched in mid 1985. The working group ignored much of the work of the White task force and came to conclusions which differed from it.

White was in no real position to respond; he had retired as OTC general manager. His fellow OTC representative, Graham Goswinckel, became the leading contender for the job of heading OTC's satellite involvement, which led to his appointment as the first general manager of Aussat Pty Ltd. Rollo Brett from Telecom became Victorian state manager, and most of the other representatives returned to their former jobs. One exception was Brigadier David McMillen from the Department of Defence. He resigned from the public service to become the Australian representative of the US supplier, Ford Aerospace, which later emerged as one of the three leading contenders to supply the satellite system. McMillen told the press he saw no conflict of interest in the switch.

Staley meantime headed for North America. The Canadian Department of Communications showed Staley a trick that its engineers had developed on the Hermes satellite which IBM had found so useful in trials for its SBS service. Hermes had the most powerful transponder aloft, beaming out 200 watts of power, which allowed television signals and data to be received by dishes only a metre in diameter. By gradually lowering the power from the satellite, the effect could be judged on television picture quality. Down as low as 20 watts, there was some fall in quality, but the picture could still be seen. That, the Canadians assured Staley, was good enough for the residents of their country's far north; was it not adequate for Australians similarly located? The Hermes broadcasts were in the 11/14 gigahertz frequency, which was susceptible to being blotted out by heavy rain. The differences in Australian and Canadian climate were not fully explored.

Staley held a press conference when he reached London and declared that the problems of satellite technology, which had so concerned the White task force, were now solved. Outback dwellers could have a very small dish for less than $1,000, and because lower power could be used in the satellite, its working life would not be restricted to the three or so years, 100 watt transponders were predicted to last.

Staley took his fieldwork back to Canberra to put before the working party, which was chaired by the acting head of his department, Hugh Payne. A report of Staley's visit to British Aerospace's Stevenage facility was sent to the company's Australian representative and it read: 'During our briefing of Mr Staley we spoke of Canadian developments. Unfortunately our disbelief of Canadian claims was misinterpreted as lack of knowledge.' Lest that judgement prove an epitaph to their efforts to bid for the Australian satellite contract, the British company tried to cast doubt on the Canadians' Ottawa demonstration, saying:

However, Canadian claims of ability to provide good TV from 20 watt transponder in satellite to one point two metre dish are based on limited trials and we would wish to see results of one year's trial before accepting feasibility. After seeing Mr Staley we had discussions with several US manufacturers at Intelcom 79 in Dallas and none were convinced it can be done at a price acceptable to domestic customers.

That judgement did not deter Staley who, within a few months, was touring outback centres of Australia citing firm figures for the cost of a small dish antenna to receive direct broadcast television. The lowest bid recorded by the local rural newspapers, for whom a ministerial visit was front-page news, was $400. Staley was not so loquacious about the uses to which a 11/14 gigahertz satellite could be put by business users in the cities. The satellite model he returned with from North America and Europe was almost precisely the spacecraft used by SBS in the United States. SBS was one of the stops on Staley's overseas tour, as was a visit to its suppliers, Hughes Aircraft Company. The satellite which so impressed Staley in its potential for the outback was the 20 watt, 11/14 gigahertz version, which was designed by Hughes for SBS. It became the model system not only for Staley, but also for his departmental working party.

By August 1979, the working party had recommended the SBS satellite model, rejecting the more complex version suggested by White and the lower powered television distribution system promoted by Bond. Not that the working party presented a united front in its advice to the minister. The representative of the Department of Finance again proved to be independently minded, and in a dissenting statement recommended that the whole project be shelved for two to three years. Even the representative of the Department of the Prime Minister and Cabinet thought a decision about the satellite should be put off for a year. A representative from the Department of Finance also disagreed that the satellite operator should be an authority separate from Telecom or a consortium including private interests. According to the department's representative, it should be operated by a subsidiary of Telecom.

It was clear that the minister's visit, and the working party's examination of the US system, had borne fruit. The report noted:

Of particular interest were comments from a number of users of private line networks, especially in the fields of data transmission and computer systems. In addition to the technical aspects of transmitting large amounts of high speed data by their terrestrial or satellite links, these submissions have pressed strongly for relaxation of the regulatory controls applied to the termination of private line networks.

The working party also attempted to correct some of the minister's public inconsistency between approving Telecom's rural telephony programme and promoting the satellite. It recommended that Telecom spending be 'reviewed' because of the advantages it claimed satellites would bring. Of Canadian developments the working party said:

A new development has occurred recently arising from an extensive series of experiments conducted by the Canadian department of communications using the Hermes and Anik B satellites.

After the working party's advisers in the Department of Post and Telecommunications had viewed the Canadian experiment, the working party concluded that television 'could well be' provided to the outback by that method. Harold White said that Staley and the working party had seen nothing that his task force had not been aware of.

Staley, undeterred, said in parliament:

We can no longer ignore the rights of our fellow Australians to equitable access to communications facilities and to those services which cannot be adequately provided with such facilities. No longer can a very substantial group of Australians, who have contributed so much to this nation – and particularly to the development of its resources – be treated as second-class citizens.

He confessed to parliament:

One of the most moving experiences in my public life was to see the astonishment and delight of people from remote areas when they realized what a domestic satellite could mean to themselves and their families.

While the minister was spreading the good word in the outback, his working party had other things on its mind.

Its report said:

A terrestrial digital data network will provide data services to the growing range of small and medium users by means of the terrestrial telecommunications infrastructure. Increasingly however large organisations at least will require for their internal purposes to transfer large quantities of high speed data between a few main nodes distributed around Australia. These services do not need to traverse the general public telecommunications network and for efficiency and reliability reasons should not be required to do so.

A workshop had been organized by the Department of Communications to show off the satellite system about which Staley had become enthusiastic. One Canadian satellite system was thought by Staley and his hosts in Ottawa to be the most suitable. It was called Anik C and was almost identical in design to the SBS system. Both were built by Hughes Aircraft and both projects had satellites launched on the first NASA shuttle carrying a commercial payload, in November 1982. Of the twenty-three speakers at the workshop in Canberra, seventeen were Canadians. The managing director of Telecom, Jack Curtis, pointed out that the satellite was still uneconomic for Australian needs. He said if the government wanted a satellite it had every right to buy one, but that did not change the economic argument against it. It was a speech which did not go down well among the converted. Canada offered to supply an Anik C-style system to Australia, but the proposal foundered on the reluctance of the Department of Communications to circumvent the public tender processes for government contracts. The political consequences could have proved fatal to the project, as it bypassed other suppliers, including Hughes.

The Canadians suggested that the Australian system be prime contracted by their own company, Spar Aerospace.

The government's announcement that there would be a satellite along the model provided by SBS and the Canadian Anik C was a formality. In April 1980, an industry briefing was held by the 'satellite system management unit' of the Department of Communications. Its head was Graham Goswinckel, former OTC representative on the White task force. At the briefing, ostensibly to provide local manufacturers with an opportunity to assess their chances of providing components of the space and earth segments, it was clear that an alternative common carrier had emerged. On the eve of the briefing, the secretary of the communications department, Bob Lansdown, had outlined the ownership structure of the satellite operating authority to a meeting of national advertisers in Canberra. There would be a mix of public and private capital, with the former taking 51 per cent of the project. Aussat, as the new company was to be called, would break away from OTC once the bids to supply the system had been evaluated. The satellite described at the industry briefing was a variation on the Hughes-built spacecraft supplied to SBS and the Canadians. It contained a mix of 30 watt and 15 watt transponders, although all transmitted and received in the 11/14 gigahertz frequency.

Once the satellite design was released, the hopes of non-Hughes contenders dimmed. The specifications closely resembled a Hughes satellite. Nine months later, complaints to that effect by two other leading contenders, Ford Aerospace and British Aerospace, were lost in the publicity surrounding the announcement of the winner and the formation of Aussat. Ford had aroused controversy almost a decade earlier, when it accused Hughes of gaining the Indonesian Palapa contract with the assistance of bribery of officials. Hughes denied the charge, labelling it sour grapes. No such accusation was made in Australia.

A press conference to announce the conclusion of contract negotiations was held in May 1981, with members of Aussat's new board present. Protests from the telecommunications unions that the board was almost completely constituted of representatives of interests likely to benefit from the satellite's use were brushed aside by the government. Questions at the press conference about Aussat's future role as a competitor to Telecom received the reply that the Davidson inquiry would determine the matter. Not even those who believed the satellite project was a political stunt by the government thought Davidson would decide against the need for a satellite. Davidson assumed the satellite was a fact of life and made its recommendations accordingly. Joining the Aussat line-up at the press conference was Albert Wheelon, the man from Hughes, who had signed the company's original submission to the White task force. Neither the men from Aussat nor from Hughes were able to answer questions about the likely cost of earth stations for those in the outback. Rural dwellers were still being claimed as the main beneficiaries of the satellite.

No mention was made of a study of remote areas of the Northern Territory which had been commissioned by Telecom. It showed that demand in the outback was not for radio or television but overwhelmingly for a telephone service which worked. The survey took into account Telecom's development of a digital radio concentrator system (DRCS) which enabled rural subscribers to be given a telephone service using terrestrial means. The report said: 'Based on cost and other data currently available, DRCS should be the technology to be used for remote area telecommunications services.' The report stressed that its information was based on prices in the tender documents for both the satellite and the digital concentrator. They did not change the conclusion it had come to before those prices were available:

Based on present cost estimates made prior to obtaining tender prices, telecommunications services can be provided at all locations at a lower cost by DRCS than any other means, including satellite systems.

There appeared to be little evidence of the rural disadvantaged groups being represented at any level in the discussion about whether Australia should have a satellite. They appear not to be significant beneficiaries of a satellite which will carry ABC and commercial television and which will be used to break the Telecom monopoly on profitable business traffic routes between the capital cities. Telecom's response, to accelerate work on both its Austpac packet switched network and its digital data network, is also not geared to meet the needs of this group.

The sting in the tail of the Davidson report for Aussat is that it would be put in the same position as Telecom, and forced to lease out its circuits to those constructing their own networks. Even a suggestion by Neil Brown, who succeeded Ian Sinclair as minister for communications, did not dull Aussat's disappointment. Brown had conceded that the government was considering a proposal that the satellite authority be converted to a company in which the private sector would have a majority holding. Davidson did not help investor confidence in the project: Aussat was to be used as a 'carrier's carrier', a facility provided, as Telecom was, at largely public expense; it was to be hired out as a private highway by corporations. Davidson gave no credence to the arguments for rolling Aussat into Telecom, a suggestion put forward by the Telecom unions in their submissions. Yet that may well prove the only rational and economic solution for Australia's domestic satellite.

Chapter Seven
Wiring the Nation

Before the beginning of the 1980s, no one really talked very much about cable television outside North America. It had been around for decades, of course, providing television for people who couldn't receive it over the air, but it certainly hadn't made an impression as the new boom industry. In the more affluent years of the 1960s and 1970s, cable television was an occasional gleam in the counter culture's eye. Members of the counter culture recognized early that cable television had the potential to give everyone who wanted it 'access' to television; television would be more accountable and media would no longer be prefixed with the word 'mass'.

By the beginning of the 1980s, cable television was one of the few areas of global corporate entrepreneurial enthusiasm. In the United States, companies formed to capitalize on cable grew in leaps, absorbing smaller organizations in their stride. Stockbrokers were more cautious. Cable television had yet to prove itself. But the enthusiasts were undaunted. Cable was *the* industry of the future. It must be; it combined two of the richest industries in the world: television and telecommunications. By the end of the 1970s, North American companies exported their enthusiasm to willing recipients in Britain and Australia. By 1982, both countries were about to commit themselves in principle to the cable dream, although by this stage the dream was starting to turn into a nightmare in the United States.

In the spring of 1982, both the Australian and British governments received reports recommending that cable television go ahead. At the same time, one of the biggest, most visible, quality cable programming companies in the United States folded. CBS Cable had been formed in 1981, as a subsidiary of the giant CBS broadcasting network in the United States. CBS Cable took the theory of cable television seriously: that it is possible to narrow cast, by screening cultural programmes for smaller, select audiences and make money out of it by advertising. Although CBS Cable's advertising surveys showed it that some of the richest and most important people in the US watched it, the numbers remained small, and the advertisers remained unconvinced. After spending $60 million, CBS's main board closed CBS Cable.

For executives in big companies who were intrigued by the excitement and profitability of television and who recognized the importance of telecommunications to business in the Information Age, cable television was a Godsend. On the one hand, it provided an opportunity for getting in to television and, on the other, it was an entrée to the relatively closed world of telecommunications. In Australia, the companies most interested in cable television, including Myer and Elders IXL, made no bones about the dual reasoning for their interest. But they also accepted the common wisdom that cable would have to be 'entertainment led', that the television component would come before the telecommunications capacity for the two-way services of telebanking, teleshopping, telebetting, and the other teleservices.

Cable's dual capacity in the early 1980s was far removed from its first use in a small town in Pennsylvania on the east coast of the United States. A small appliance store owner, John Walson, in 1948 was having problems selling his main product: television receivers. The reason for the reluctance of Mahanoy City residents to buy television sets had nothing to do with reservations about its impact. It was simply that the hilly countryside made it difficult for people to pick up television that was beamed from Philadelphia, 130 kilometres away. It meant that the investment was worthless. So John Walson, in an oft-cited example of US entrepreneurial flair, organized the local residents to build a community antenna to pick up the Philadelphia programmes, which was then connected to the local homes by coaxial cable. Walson sold televisions, the residents of Mahanoy City could watch television, and cable television, then known as Community Antenna Television, was born.

As well as operating in areas which could not receive or broadcast television, this early form of cable television was used to relay programmes across borders. Canadians watched US television thanks to Community Antenna Television, and Europeans watched the television of their neighbours. These early cable systems had only a handful of stations, generally between four and twelve, quite different from some of the systems today which offer over a hundred channels.

This early form of cable television did not really take off in Australia, partly because the delay in introducing television meant that reception was generally good. Before 1960, the *Broadcasting and Television Act* banned the use of what was known as Community Television Aerial Systems. After an amendment to the act was made, permits were granted in areas covered by existing stations but where reception was unsatisfactory. These permits, however, prevented the operators from importing distant signals. The need to do so was limited anyway. Television throughout Australia was much the same, and no neighbouring country produced programmes that Australians were clamouring to watch. Between 1962 and 1982, the largest operators in Australia delivered television via cable to only 797 households. The most sophisticated systems operated in Adelaide's foothills, but they became redundant when UHF translator services became available.

When Tony Staley as the minister for communications in 1980 came up with the idea of cable television for Australia, it came as a surprise to most. Certainly, Telecom had long-term plans to install a cable television network, but Tony Staley's enthusiasm about cable, gleaned from watching television with scores of channels in North America, was something quite new. Staley said that Australia would be able to lead the world with cable television and optical fibres, creating new jobs, markets and international prestige. His enthusiasm inspired nearly 200 organizations to prepare submissions for the broadcasting tribunal's investigation into cable television. Although many of the submissions said 'let's wait and see', 'we need more information' and 'we don't know', a handful were bursting with excitement and bravado. The resources boom was just around the corner and there was money to be made from what has been described as the 'baubles, bangles and beads' of the Information Age.

But by the time the recommendations to go ahead with cable television were handed down, the scene had changed dramatically. The resources boom had burst before it arrived, the recession was in full swing, cable television was not living up to its promise in the United States, video cassette recorders were installed in 250,000 Australian homes, and there was intense pressure for Telecom to be dismantled.

In addition, the Davidson inquiry had some rather different opinions about cable television from the broadcasting tribunal. From the time that both committees of investigation were underway, it was obvious that they would overlap. For several years, the knowledge that telecommunications and broadcasting would converge and become parts of a whole was accepted by insiders. In 1982, the convergence happened in Australia. Cable television brought telecommunications and television together. Both the government and the chairmen of the committees, David Jones and Jim Davidson, were aware of the overlap. In an attempt to ensure that the two reports did not contradict each other, regular meetings were held in the North Sydney office tower they shared. Despite these good intentions, on the two most fundamental areas of overlap – whether Telecom should operate a common carrier cable network, and the nature of the regulatory body to oversee the convergence of telecommunications and broadcasting – the reports were diametrically opposed. Davidson recommended that Telecom should operate a common carrier cable network, with Telecom retaining exclusive access to its ducts, and Jones recommended that there should not be a monopoly network and that any companies that wished should be able to set up their own systems with access to Telecom's underground ducts. The Jones report suggested that a new telecommunications and broadcasting regulatory authority be set up, based on the Australian Broadcasting Tribunal, to oversee both areas; Davidson's report said it should be left to the minister and the Standards Association of Australia, of which Jim Davidson was a vice-president.

David Jones came to the chairmanship of the Australian Broadcasting Tribunal in 1980, taking the place of his colourful predecessor, Bruce Gyrgell. David Jones was a Melbourne lawyer before his appointment, a man who has retained a gangly schoolboy appearance into his forties. Jones was a diligent chairman without the personal flair of his predecessor. But whenever his report was criticized, he reacted strongly, quickly and personally. It was with shock and hurt that he read Davidson's criticism of his report. He felt that Davidson's criticism came from a misreading of the tribunal's five volumes and said so publicly. 'I thought that there had been consultation and discussion between us, but it was obviously only one sided,' he said.

The contradiction between the two reports was to further delay and confuse the cable consideration underway in the Department of Communications in Canberra. The department had already been surprised by the small number of submissions it had received in response to the cable report and the lack of enthusiasm in many of them. To counter this lack of public awareness and enthusiasm, David Jones was urged to 'sell' his report to the Australian community.

One of the first major opportunities David Jones had to sell his report was at a conference organized by the Australian Cable and Subscription Communications Association in Canberra in November 1982. The association was formed earlier that year to represent the companies wanting to operate subscription and cable television services: Myer Emporium, Hills Industries, Amatil, Nilsen Premiere, Elders IXL, Philips Industries, Townsend Communications, and Stereo FM. At considerable expense, the association brought out a number of international speakers: Walter Cronkite, for thirty-one years one of the most popular and respected news correspondents in the United States, Lord Hunt of Tanworth, a former British cabinet secretary, a director of IBM (UK) and chairman of the committee which investigated cable television in the UK, and Lionel Mudd, a cable television engineer with an impressive array of international credentials. Although the association had hoped that the conference would convince Australians that cable television here would be different from cable television in the United States, the conference rather effectively left cable television in Australia low on the list of national priorities. Almost all of the publicity which came out of the conference was summed up by the front page of the *Canberra Times* on 9 November 1982. It featured a photo of Walter Cronkite in a particularly Uncle Walter pose, pipe in the corner of his mouth and a headline reading: 'No instant benefits from cable.' Members of the association were appalled that, after paying Cronkite a fee, reported to be $70,000, he could publicly discredit enthusiasm for cable television. Cronkite probably felt that as a respected journalist and broadcaster he had an obligation to tell the truth as he found it, however unpleasant that may be to those who paid for his visit to Australia. Cronkite opened his keynote address this way:

I come to you from the land of the satiated eye, of cable seemingly gone berserk. A land of 4,782 cable systems serving 13,079 communities of twenty-nine million homes wired, of fifty million homes passed, of approximately four billion dollars already invested (or should it be 'gambled') on transmission hardware alone, of at least thirty programming networks and at least thirty-five more said to be on the drawing board.

There are cable networks offering standard films – eight or so at last count, three offering twenty-four hours a day of sports events, three offering twenty-four hours a day news, and others offering twenty-four hours a day weather, health and exercise, country music and rock and roll (twenty-four hours a day, yet), cultural concerts and drama, and two networks offering what they call 'adult fare' (when their opponents aren't watching it they call it 'pornography'), and there are the so-called super stations – independents who beam their programmes of old movies and local sports to the satellite for any operator to pick up.

Perhaps never in the history of commerce, and certainly not in the history of communications, has a new technology begun its life in such entrepreneurial chaos. The woods seem to be ringed with those waiting to blast the head off the goose they see there laying golden eggs.

We now have in operation some thirty networks vying for space on systems that have up to a hundred channels. The newer systems have the larger number of channels, obviously, but more than half the systems now operating have twelve channels or less. Experts think it could have five billion dollars over ten years to modernize and upgrade those limited systems.

Cable television only began after a few false starts in the United States. By the beginning of the 1970s, there were a large number of small family run 'mom and pop' cable systems, described by one journalist thus: 'In the early 1970s, however, the wired nation still resembled a medieval fiefdom, with each cable-operator prince in his own domain.' By the end of the 1970s, that had changed dramatically. Now more than 50 per cent of the US cable market is in the hands of the ten largest companies: General Electric, Getty Oil, General Telephone and Electric, RCA, American Express, Gulf and Western, CBS, Penn Central, and Time Inc. The list of the next forty biggest companies involved in cable television continues to read like the Fortune 500.

One of the most important changes in the face of cable television in the United States came from an idea of a man called Gerald Levin. Levin was a lawyer who had had a range of jobs, including working for a consulting firm that specialized in solving engineering problems for Third World countries, before applying for a job with Time Inc. At Time Inc., the giant magazine publishing company, Levin had a bright idea which set the pace for cable television around the world. First of all, he realized that people who had only seen television with commercials would pay to watch television without commercials, and then he gambled $7.5 million of Time Inc.'s money on leasing a transponder (a broadcasting transmitter which receives one channel and retransmits it) on an RCA satellite.

The satellite transponder made it possible for Home Box Office, advertisement-free subscription television, to be picked up by cable operators all over the United States. Home Box Office, with its programming mix of first release movies, sports and specials, boomed. In 1972, it had 365 subscribers. By 1980, it had more than six million. Home Box Office was the market leader of pay cable television, but other companies were fast to follow, copying both the programming concepts and the satellite distribution model. Meanwhile, Time Inc.'s other video company, American Television and Communications, grew to be the biggest cable operator. Time Inc. was no longer mainly a magazine publishing company; the video divisions became the biggest and most profitable in the organization.

Once Home Box Office had broken the ground, there was a boom in programming available to cable system operators throughout the US off the satellites, and the cable television industry grew at a rapid pace. At the same time, the Federal Communications Commission began loosening its control over cable television, both as a result of court challenges and its own determinations. In 1972, the commission had adopted a set of rules which closely regulated cable television. The rules were designed to protect the television broadcasters, and dictated that all cable systems with more than 3,500 subscribers must have four access channels, two-way capacity and at least twenty channels. As the commission slowly ceded its powers, they were taken up by local authorities, and the marketplace went into action. Companies offered increasingly sophisticated systems to ensure winning franchises - deals were done, libraries and civic centres were donated to ensure victory, promises were broken and activities verging on the corrupt became synonymous with the rapid expansion of cable television.

In 1980, the National Telecommunications and Information Administration commented critically on the franchising system. It said:

Important problems have arisen in the current franchising scene in major cities and metropolitan areas and these problems have reached a level of visibility that is causing them to be treated extensively in local newspapers and national general interest publications as well as in the cable trade press. Some of these problems are associated with ever escalating cascades of demands for services on the part of the cities and ever escalating promises of services on the part of cable companies. Others arise from the intensity of the competition for these franchises. This has gi en rise to a series of questionable practices whose extent and pervasiveness is perhaps without modern precedent in the dealings of a national industry with local governments.

At the same time access and minority programming was failing to live up to its early promise. Walter Cronkite read the litany of failure in this to the conference:

Of the almost 500 systems, with a total of 1,500 access channels, barely 5 per cent, or 260 systems, are co-operating in the production of educational programming. On all those 260 systems, educational programming averages just one hour and forty-three minutes a day. With more than 13,000 communities served by cable nationwide, only 50 colleges and universities are actively producing cable programmes, 239 high schools, 139 primary schools and 64 libraries. Of the nearly 5,000 systems, only 86 are producing programmes especially for senior citizens, 90 for women, 96 for children, 56 for the physically immobilized, 25 for the deaf, 84 on health care and medical programmes, 58 doing ethnic and minority programming and 183 systems providing or co-operating in the production of religious programming.

The lesson of access and community programming was that without guaranteed financial support (ideally a percentage of the revenue generated from basic subscriptions) non-commercial programming failed to develop. In some cities, better deals were negotiated than in others, and some cities were better able than others to enforce the agreements. The success or failure of community access and educational programming was directly related to the money and facilities available.

The sort of programmes that cable excelled in were basically the same programmes that network televison had always offered – news, serials, soap operas, sports, movies and game shows. Ted Turner is a maverick in the broadcasting industry in the United States. He is a man almost as well known for his interest in sailing as his interest in television. From Atlanta, Georgia, he runs a superstation, WTBS, which is picked up by more than seven million subscribers to 2,000 cable systems. He also runs two 24-hour news stations, CNN 1 and CNN 2. Although CNN 1 quite often beats the network news teams to stories, it has not adopted a new approach to television news; rather it has adapted the same formula of short items packaged into half-hour bulletins. Although Turner's CNN 1 is hailed as one of cable's great innovations, he does not yet make any money out of it, financing the news operation out of WTBS's profits. When he was asked to describe the types of programmes he expected to show on cable's many channels in the future he replied: 'Do you want to know what tomorrow's cable programmes will be like? Then turn on your TV set now. They're one and the same.'

Cable operators made great play of being able to show movies while they are still in the cinemas, but the number of quality first-release movies is limited, as is the number of quality, sporting competitions, foreign programmes, specials, and cultural events. Advertisers still buy time on the basis of numbers only very cautiously considering advertising to small specialized audiences. Cable cannot deliver network television's mass audiences yet. Although quality programming innovations were the main draw card for cable subscribers, who paid another fee as well as the basic monthly rental to receive them, the programmers were soon running out of quality material, and by late 1982, renewal rates were falling. To retain audiences and keep programme costs down, operators started re-making stage shows such as 'Camelot' and 'The King and I', and commissioning movie producers in other countries, including Australia, to make programmes for cable. They also started serials which combined soap operas with the euphemistically 'adult fare', and 24-hour games channels were developed. Rather than pushing up the quality of network television's programmes, cable television, combined with a deregulatory commission, dragged the network's standards down even lower. Although the drop in cable renewal rates was compensated for by the increasing number of people able to subscribe, US viewers were tiring of the same old television.

As the cable industry in the United States has been a failure and disappointment for all but a very few large companies, many people, including some of the most enthusiastic would-be cable operators in Australia, were dissatisfied when the Australian Broadcasting Tribunal recommended a model for cable television which seemed doomed to repeat the worst mistakes already made in the US. David Jones has consistently maintained that his report does not offer Australians a pale imitation of US cable television, but he has failed to convince everyone.

At the same time as the Australian Broadcasting Tribunal was considering cable television in Australia, a committee in Britain was doing the same thing, although in six months rather than in the eighteen months it took the Australians. (The Australian terms of reference were much broader, encompassing questions of the type of technology, and the social, economic and other issues, whereas Lord Hunt's British committee was only required to examine the impact of cable television on existing broadcasting services and make a recommendation.) What was happening in the two countries was different but there were certain common elements. Deregulation of telecommunications was a principle both governments were committed to. Both governments regarded the marketplace as the best arbiter of public and commercial good, and North American programming and equipment companies were anxious to see new English language markets opened for their products.

Both reports recommended doing away with the hard won local content guidelines which have regulated broadcast television for many years. The committees argued that it would be impossible to fill all the available channels with predominantly local programming. During both inquiries, companies, including Home Box Office, had been assiduous in putting their case for access to channels. For these companies, such access would tie up lucrative new markets for marginal extra cost. The broadcasting and production industries in both Britain and Australia were quick to point out that these recommendations could seriously undermine local industries and national control of the media. In Australia, the media, although in the hands of only four groups, is one of very few industries which is still controlled by Australian companies.

Some of the enthusiastic people involved in developing cable television including Lionel Mudd, former president of the (UK) Society of Cable Television Engineers, saw their job in part as waging a war against what Mudd called STOAT – Same Tired Old American Technology. Mudd and others argued that if US programming was allowed in, as well as US transmission technology, the chances of Britain or Australia developing a national world-leading industry would be foregone forever. This argument revolved around the transmission system which should be used. In the United States, cable systems use what is described as 'tree and branch' technology. The image of a tree with many branches and households as leaves is a good analogy. With this system, all the programmes are sent through the trunk and branches to the subscriber's home, at which point the viewer selects the programmes he or she wants to watch. In the way blood flows through your legs, and your toes, so the same programmes come direct into your home with a tree and branch network. This is the system which was recommended by the tribunal for Australia.

There are considerable problems, however, with the tree and branch system. It means that the converter in the home must be costly and sophisticated. It also creates problems of guaranteeing privacy, and the ability to use the system for two-way 'teleservices' is limited. The Australian tribunal commented on these problems in its report:

A conventional coaxial cable tree network is not an efficient delivery system for interactive services. This is because the network provides a 'party line' type connection and a single subscriber monopolises a circuit throughout the whole system during the time that information is flowing to or from that subscriber . . . Depending upon what bandwidth is allocated for interactive services, and what volume of information is required to be transferred, subscribers face the prospect of a delay before any request they make can be executed. As the number of subscribers to the system grows, so does the potential delay.

Because of these delays and infringements of privacy, and the desire not to be dependent on STOAT, the British looked to a more sophisticated way of getting both the television and the two-way services to subscribers. The model favoured is called a star-switched network. This operates in much the same way as a telephone network. Using the same analogy as before, in a star-switched network blood would stop at the joint in your foot and your toe would then decide what components it wanted. In this system, then, the switching is done at a local exchange at the request of the householder, rather than in the converter on top of the television set. This means that the costs inside the home are considerably reduced (although the total system is more expensive), and the interactive potential is much greater. With a star-switched system it is also possible for households to communicate with each other in the same way as you do by using a telephone, making the telecommunications potential of the cable network much greater.

There has been little debate in Australia about measuring up the promises of cable against what it is capable of delivering, and even less about the inequality it could bring with it. If cable television is allowed to proceed in the hands of a few big companies, it is reasonable to assume that the more affluent areas of Australia will receive cable television first. People living in poorer suburbs, or country areas are less likely to have access to either the entertainment or the two-way services that cable eventually promises, creating an information rich élite and an information poor majority. David Jones felt that this was unlikely to happen in Australia because most people would be able to afford cable. But others, including some would-be operators, believe that less affluent areas will only receive cable television if the government subsidizes the operator. In Britain, Lord Hunt conceded that this disparity would exist, based on the ability to pay, but it was not something he 'felt uncomfortable with'. 'This was not an inquiry into inequality,' he said. Inequality is likely to be further entrenched, however, if the recommendations are accepted.

The only way to prevent inequality is to look to a common carrier model for cable television in the same way as there is a telecommunications common carrier. This could ensure that everyone has the same access to the tools of the Information Age, and that the profits in one area could be used to offset the costs in another in the same way that cross-subsidization has worked in telecommunications. This is recognized by all but the most tunnel-visioned profiteers. John D'Arcy, a senior executive with Queensland Newspapers in Brisbane, a company which is interested in operating cable systems said, 'I don't have any great love of Telecom, it is too bloody big, but we have to be practical about it.' Being practical about it for D'Arcy meant working out a deal with Telecom so that his company could operate a system which was owned and installed by Telecom.

In a country of only fifteen million people, where it is estimated that the cost of installing cable systems would range between $1,000 and $3,000 million, a common carrier system owned by Telecom is the only way of ensuring that everyone has equal access.

The common carrier model, apart from ensuring that most Australians have access to cable television, would also mean that the programming offered and the behaviour of the operator would be more accountable to the public. The tribunal recommended that a cable operator should have a fifteen-year licence (with ten-year renewals) during which time it would be difficult to enforce the promises that operators made. It would be unacceptable politically to remove the licence of a cable television operator who had spent $300 million to build up a system in Sydney or Melbourne, if licence conditions were not upheld. As the system and the licence would be literally 'concreted in', subscribers would have no option but to choose to buy the service or choose not to buy it. The absence of any competition on a network, apart from the competition between channels, (which would be determined by the owner) would mean, in effect, that the organization which owned the system controlled the content.

If, on the other hand, the system ownership was separated from the licensed operation of it, cable television could be much more acceptable. Although Myer and a couple of the other very big companies which are still interested in cable television have made it clear that they would not want to operate a system they did not own, there are many other smaller companies which would be much happier to operate a system owned and maintained by Telecom, at the direction of the operating company.

The question of separating ownership of the network and the licence has been strongly argued for and against since cable television first showed some of its promise. Although the broadcasting tribunal said that separation of ownership and operation should be 'neither mandatory not prohibited', this view was shared by only a handful of organizations. The regulatory problems and absence of separations stored up are immense, especially for governments committed to deregulation. In the United States, a great deal of lip-service was paid to the merit of separating the network from the licence, but much of this is now ignored as the politics of the free market predominate. In 1978, Henry Geller, the first director of the National Telecommunications and Information Administration, proposed that cable systems be restricted by law to operate as common carriers, with programme providers getting on to the system on a first-come first-served basis. Cable operators, he said should be prohibited from making any programme decisions; those who control the technology must be divorced from the message it conveys, 'I'm very strong on this issue,' Henry Geller said. 'If we don't separate the owner from the broadcast, we will have to have regulation. When the structure is right and working for you, then you don't need the governments involved, and that's desirable.'

Geller's interest in regulation, even if only to ensure fairness and balance, is now regarded as unacceptable by the deregulators at the FCC in Washington – an FCC which believes that there should not be an FCC, is how one observer described the present incumbents. Despite vast differences between Australia and the United States, these messages of deregulation are now being accepted as articles of faith by Australian businessmen and conservative politicians. In applying the principles of deregulation and market forces, concepts of the national interest, maximum good, equity, access, imagination and national integrity are quickly dismissed.

With only a little more imagination on the part of those recommending policies to the government, Australians could now be debating a very different cable television proposal. It would have been one which would be available to everyone, would enhance the local production industry, and could be used as the basis for developing high-technology industries in Australia. It could have been a system which incorporated financing commitments to ensure that access, educational, children's and community programmes were creative, innovative and watchable. It could have been a system which guaranteed the privacy of subscribers, which ensured that information gained about them was not abused by the operator or anyone else and which was able to deliver the two-way services it promises. In short, Australians could now be discussing a cable system which put people before the selling of goods and services.

Instead, the debate, such as it is, has dealt with a proposal for a cable system which will not be available to everyone, which will make the gaps between the information rich and information poor even greater, which will rely on foreign programming, which will undermine the local production industry, which will rely on the Same Tired Old American Technology, which will ensure that access, children's, community and educational programming is hampered by an absence of funds and facilities, which will not safeguard the privacy of subscribers, which will deny access for the ABC and the Special Broadcasting Service, and will certainly put profits a long way ahead of considerations about the public good.

Chapter Eight
Calling the Operator

A few years ago, Telecom telephonists used to joke wryly, if Subscriber Trunk Dialling (STD) had not been introduced every man, woman and child in Australia would have had to become a telephonist. As the number of long-distance calls has increased from 34 million operator connected calls in 1960 to 785 million (with only 6 per cent operator connected) in 1982 the joke had its elements of truth. But the laugh, unfortunately, was on the telephonists. Not only did the advent of STD prevent every man, woman and child in Australia from becoming telephonists, but it has virtually guaranteed that most of the jobs of today's telephonists will die with them.

Rather than singing the praises of STD lowering their work loads, many telephonists now regard the introduction of the operator surcharge for manually connected long-distance calls as a confidence trick they fell for. It took the telephonists a while to realize that the surcharge did not exist for any technical reason – that it was a surcharge on their jobs. This charge, which is currently $1, and is quite often more than the cost of the call itself, has had the effect of encouraging people to dial direct themselves. Between 1970 and 1977, the number of operator-connected calls had fallen from 114 million to sixty-seven million a year. Telecom estimates that by 1985, when almost everyone has STD access, this will be down to forty million.

STD calling symbolizes for many telephonists what they see as Telecom's unsatisfactory trade-off: opting for technology and profits at the expense of service and jobs.

About a decade ago 13,000 telephonists were employed by

the PMG. Now, according to internal documents, Telecom plans to need no more than 5,000 telephonists by 1985, despite predictions of a growth of 8 per cent. Now even if Telecom remains intact, the chances are that by the end of this decade telephonists will be a rare group at the commission. Suggestions that telephonists be retained to provide more personalized services, such as answering services and appointment calls, have received scant attention inside the commission.

The reality of this destruction of jobs is overwhelming on the fourth floor of the Dalley Street Exchange, at the windy end of Sydney City, not far from the tourist and commuter meccas of The Rocks and Circular Quay. The Dalley Street Exchange is an anonymous building in an inauspicious street. It has an overwhelming feeling of 1950s greyness, a relic of a bygone era of Australia, when life was simpler and operated at a slower pace, when floors were covered with linoleum and telephone exchanges still had windows.

Built in 1950, Dalley was for many years the hub of the New South Wales and Sydney telephone network. On its floors are exchanges. Now Telecom plans to empty the building, gut it and turn it into the hub of the network in ten years time.

Despite its greyness, Dalley is regarded fondly by most of the people who have worked there – perhaps because it has windows. In November 1982, 300 telephonists gathered at the Masonic Club at the other end of the city for a dinner to celebrate the exchange's twenty-fifth anniversary and the end of an era.

The exchange where most of the telephonists work is on the fourth floor. It is a room about the size of a football field. The room is criss-crossed with twenty-seven benches, each with places for eight telephonists. When Ruth Dalliston first started working at Dalley twelve years ago, about 900 telephonists worked there. 'It was so crowded,' she recalled, 'you'd come back from your break, and they'd send you away again on another one, because there was nowhere for you to sit.' That is no longer a problem facing the supervisors at Dalley. It is a rare shift in which more than thirty-five people work in the vast room. Now at the western end of the fourth-floor exchange, several rows are occupied with people tied to their work stations by black headsets and coaxial cords. With about twenty-four rows empty in between, another dozen huddle at the eastern end booking wake up and reminder calls.

In between, near where the pneumatic tubes spit out dockets for pricing, is a lonely poster, which is headed 'New Technology and You'. It announces that it is the first in a series of joint union management information bulletins to smooth the way for the introduction of new technology.

For those who work as telephonists at Dalley, this is all a bit hollow and a bit late. That the poster is on the wall of the pricing section is particularly ironic. The pricing section deals with dockets filled in by the operators with all the details of the call, it collates and collects the pieces of paper and works out the amount to charge the subscriber. It is the pricing section and its paper which the new technology set out to eliminate. 'The Docketless Operation', was sought by management. An internal document described the new computerized system: 'This eliminates the pricing, clerical and data processing staff requirement.'

Operators working the new computerized exchanges in one action switch and connect the call, and collate and collect call and price details. Those at Dalley who have not yet worked at a computerized exchange have friends who have, and not many of them like it. Meanwhile, the jobs go on disappearing. The federal president of the Australian Telephone and Phonogram Officers' Association (ATPOA), Marilyn Brown, said: 'Everyone knows at least one person who has been retrenched or made redundant.'

In the autumn of 1982, on eleven country radio stations around New South Wales, the banter of chat shows and the beat of country and western music was interrupted spasmodically by the harsh tones of a telephone ringing. What followed was a warning to the local community that Telecom was about to make them even more isolated, by re-directing manual assistance calls - emergency, directory assistance, service faults, trunks - away from the town. The calls would be answered 'hundreds of kilometres distant' if Telecom was allowed to get away with it. Sixteen MACs in New South Wales and four in Victoria were under threat. More than 200 jobs in the drought and recession affected country towns were about to disappear.

The radio advertisements were all different, but they reiterated the theme: the telephonists were looking after the townspeople and Telecom was trying to make things worse. At Young, in central western New South Wales, the commercial started with the screech of car tyres and culminated with a calm telephonist reassuring an hysterical passenger that she knew where she was 'on the highway near the old road' and would notify the police, ambulance and hospital. The message was clear: local telephonists help save lives.

Other commercials like the one in Cooma told the story and suggested that the local MP be contacted, and then gave his telephone number.

Over the four weeks of the MAC campaign, it was given prominent treatment by the media in the country and the city. The 'telephone girls' became local media personalities, and more than 25,000 people signed petitions demanding that the MACs be retained. By spring, four MACs in New South Wales, including the one in Cooma, had been saved. All four in Victoria were also saved.

Despite the victory, Telecom's longer term plans had not been altered, just slightly reorganized.

The MAC campaign went to the heart of telephonists' key concern about Telecom: the trade-off of service for profit. It also highlighted, once again, the political power of country people in Australia. After Telecom revised its MAC campaign at the direction of the then minister, and deputy leader of the National Country Party, Ian Sinclair, it came up with a recommendation which favoured the conservative parties. All the MACs saved in New South Wales were in Liberal or National Country Party electorates. In Hamilton, Victoria, telephonists lobbied their local member - the prime minister, Malcolm Fraser - directly. Not surprisingly, the Hamilton MAC received a stay of execution. Two days before Fraser was to see another Hamilton deputation, the Department of Communications rushed a three-paragraph letter to the minister, Neil Brown, for him to sign before sending it to Fraser. Its last sentence read: 'I am sure you will be pleased to know that the revised plan provides for the retention of the Manual Assistance Centre at Hamilton.'

The relative success of this campaign confirmed the belief of Marilyn Brown that although telephonists lack direct, strong industrial strength, they had plenty of political influence:

> One of the things you can't underestimate is telephonists' mouths. They will talk to anyone – they do in their jobs. Although they are generally a bit wary of speaking in person, they soon get over that. In Lithgow they found out that Sinclair was about to visit, they tried to get an appointment, but couldn't. So they saw him when they could – down a mine.

By 1985, Telecom's MAC plan called for only eighty-seven centres – a reduction of twenty-three MACs over five years. Under this plan, it was proposed that country centres be closed and all calls routed via a computerized exchange. These exchanges would be in Sydney, Canberra, Brisbane, Melbourne, Hobart. From there, the calls would be re-routed to the next available operator in the state. This could mean that a subscriber in Cooma would dial 013 to find a local number and the call would be routed via Sydney and then to the next operator who could be in Armidale, Orange or Wollongong. The association suggested that rather than calls being re-routed at random, they come back to the nearest possible operator. Telecom rejected this suggestion. Similarly, the ATPOA raised the concerns of subscribers about emergency calls. Would someone in another place be able to help as well as a local telephonist? Would the subscriber be assured of getting through, especially when the network was congested? If the computer failed, would the subscriber still be able to get through?

For telephonists anxious to help people, these are real dilemmas. For Telecom management under government and commercial pressure, the answer was reasonably straightforward: hand the emergency advice over to the state government; let the police handle the emergency calls themselves.

Telecom's plans were simple. Developments in telecommunications technology made it possible for calls to be answered many hundreds of kilometres away. As Australia's telecommunications network developed, it gained an international reputation for the extent and quality of its service. Initially, this was based on a vast network of country exchanges and manual assistance centres. Over the years many of these country exchanges were closed as the network was upgraded from manual to automatic. The next step of routing all calls to a central exchange became technologically possible in the late 1960s. The art of capitalizing on the technological possibilities built Telecom Australia's international reputation. Re-directing calls centrally also made economic sense.

As a bright young engineer in the PMG, Roger Banks helped make many of the decisions which equip Telecom today: plans for the national STD network and selection of International Telephone and Telegraph to supply computerized exchanges were two key projects. Roger Banks became the director for business development in 1980. As one of the most senior engineers in Telecom, he accepts responsibility for the MAC plan, although he did not devise it. To him, doing away with rural centres and replacing them with centralized assistance was the best possible balance between 'bottom-line economics', 'security of the system' and a 'diversity of operational centres':

If we just let telephone technology take its course, we would eliminate every MAC except those in Sydney and Melbourne. All the work could be eventually centralized in those two MACs. But that is just not on for social reasons; we couldn't place the lasses we displace in the country with jobs in the city; it just wouldn't be on. We decentralize to put positions nearer to where people live; it is just not on to have everything in the downtown city centre; for one thing it is not safe for the lasses walking home in the night when the downtown areas are deserted.

The ATPOA remains cynical about Telecom's commitment to decentralization. 'Decentralization means centralizing somewhere other than Sydney,' is the opinion of New South Wales vice-president, Julie Milligan.

Although the MAC campaign was the most successful the ATPOA had organized, it was not its first on the issue of closing country exchanges. In 1978, a campaign was organized to save the jobs of telephonists working in manual exchanges which were about to become automatic.

Val Foster, at the time of this campaign, was one of twenty-five telephonists at Walgett in New South Wales' dry central west. Although she had worked as a telephonist for six years, like most telephonists at that time, the determined but softly spoken Val had not been actively involved in the association. She recalls that one day, completely out of the blue, this changed:

We got a call from the union which was a real surprise, because in the country you never have anything to do with a union.

Of the twenty-five girls at Walgett, only two were willing to do the campaign to try and save the Walgett exchange. We really had to brainwash them that if they didn't change their attitude, their jobs would be lost. In the country you don't get involved with the union. The girls think of their reputation and what her friends will think of her, and they don't want to get involved with the union.

But Val Foster and a friend decided to go ahead and organize the campaign to stop Telecom closing the Walgett Exchange. The enormity of the task is difficult to comprehend without an understanding of the insularity of country towns and the feeling of control from the capital cities. As an Aboriginal, Val faced an extra problem. She recalls:

The girls at the exchange used to go on about the blacks on the missions, and I'd take them on, and they'd say, but you're not one of them, you're one of us, you're different. It is easy for people to accept individuals, but groups are much harder for them to accept.

When she decided to start organizing the campaign in Walgett,

Val and the others she managed to convince it was important, started door knocking:

The attitude was at first that Telecom had won, and there was no point fighting a battle that was already lost, so we had to fight just to get them to sign the petition, but we did. Then another problem started because we started at one end of the town saying that things would be really bad when they closed down the exchange, and at the other end of town the technicians were going around telling subscribers it would be better to have automatic phones, so we were fighting our own department.

I think that some of the techs thought that it would be great without us there because they wouldn't have to fix up switchboards and that it would be easy sailing for them. It took a while before they realized that they would too be put out of work by the technology they were installing.

The campaign to save the Walgett exchange was not won by Val Foster and her supporters, but it did in Val's words 'show Telecom we could fight'.

As a direct result of this campaign, the ATPOA, with other Telecom unions, was able to negotiate a redundancy agreement. The agreement directed Telecom to give permanent officers up to five years' notice before it closed an exchange, to continue paying the person for up to twelve months, and included retraining and relocation provisions. Val Foster believes that Telecom management was surprised by the fight:

Managers had to come out from Tamworth by plane to talk to the townspeople; one manager came from Armidale, but he didn't know anything. Telecom had not been notifying people before it went automatic. Afterwards that changed and also we got redundancy award provisions which included priority for jobs in other places, though that isn't much good if you are a married woman in a country town.

To people accustomed to picking up a telephone and calling anywhere in Australia or the world by just dialling a number, to people in a hurry, to people with secretaries and answering machines, the battle to save a manual exchange in a small country town may seem of marginal value. But they are all part of a speedier way of life than that which exists in rural Australia. The 'telephone girls' in country towns have long fulfilled the role of the town receptionist: locating missing people, re-directing calls to the number you would be next at, telling callers where you could be contacted if you did not answer the phone. Some people may have recoiled at the thought of a 'telephone girl' knowing so much about their life, but the services they provided free now have to be bought.

Val Foster recalls a Walgett man who was always bad tempered, blaming the telephonists when he couldn't speak to the people he wanted to, angrily denouncing 'the girls' as lazy, nosy, no hopers. One day he was invited into the exchange to see just what they did. He was so contrite later that he bought them all a Chinese meal.

When Jim Doyle talks, the sense of loss of a slower world becomes very real. Jim Doyle started as a boy telephonist in 1941 and is now the manager of the international exchange in Sydney. For seventeen years, before moving sideways to his present position, he was the manager of Sydney's national exchange.

Doyle talks of telephonists as 'a special people', the 'best people I know' and is obviously deeply committed to those he calls 'my girls'. His commitment, which was once regarded as paternalistic, is now probably more often thought of as patronizing.

Jim Doyle grew up in the working-class suburb of Zetland. Several of his mates worked for the PMG as mail boys, and he decided to sit for the telephonists exam:

It was quite something in those days to be a permanent officer at the PMG, really quite something. So when I started to get a job, I sat for the telephonists exam, not really knowing what a telephonist was. On the day of the exam, I walked into the city and realized I had left my pen at home, so I ran all the way home and back again to get it. Then I sat for the exam, along with 600 others – things like English, geography, spelling – and I topped the class. Only twenty-seven passed – some of them have been lifelong mates as a result.

Jim Doyle was among the last intake of 'dear little boy telephonists' during World War II. Up until the war years, although most telephonists were then as they are today, women, men worked the night shifts. As Jim Doyle remembers, that changed during the war:

The girls worked all night during the war and then afterwards again it reverted to men.

The night the subs raided Sydney Harbour, I was on the all nighter. It was quite dramatic, I put the call through from Garden Island [naval yards] to Richmond Aerodrome [army air strip]. I was a timid little fellow and didn't know what the hell was going on – but that is how much things have changed.

Doyle, like many telephonists of his vintage, talks fondly about the days when individual ability and initiative counted for more than it does today. To book a call from one place to another may have involved using circuits which took the call through far away places – like a call from Sydney to Lismore via Brisbane and Coffs Harbour:

It seems to have lost something, this new technology. Telephonists tell that you can't give the service they used to, once you start speaking into the processor you have lost all contact. It is a problem because the work is less satisfying. Mind you, if I owned Telecom, I'd do the same thing; it's not a criticism but a statement of fact that the work is less satisfying. Our days as telephonists are really numbered. If I was Mr Telecom, I suppose I'd do the same things, but maybe it is necessary to sacrifice a bit of profit for a bit of service; it can't be all one way, whichever way it is.

The introduction of new technology in the telephone exchanges has had a profound effect on telephonists. Not only will their jobs and skills disappear, but their work has become less satisfying. As a result, many for the first time have questioned authority and their 'traditional female role' of serving.

The impact of this has been two-fold. In the exchanges, the telephonists have rebelled against paternalistic and patronizing management practices. The ATPOA has also changed from being a part-time association, essentially run by and for supervisors, to being a union for telephonists. Its members have started to fight back. Over this period, almost exactly the lifespan of Telecom Australia, the percentage of telephonists who are members of the association has increased from 56 per cent to 91 per cent.

In the exchanges, tensions started to build up when married women were allowed to keep their jobs. Before 1965, only single women and men could work as telephonists. This bred a very hierarchical organization on top of a very big base: eight or ten senior positions and 3,500 staff with a disproportionate number of men in the most senior positions. The older single women who ran many exchanges were not well regarded by married women returning to work and the growing number of men in the exchanges.

Marilyn Brown is still appalled by the schoolroom environment, but concedes that it is changing:

A lot of men have become telephonists in recent years; there is a very big gay group. They tend to be people who have suffered enough and are very outspoken and the most militant. They have got acceptance and not very many are hassled. As well mature married women with responsibilities started returning, they weren't prepared to accept things.

It is just a part of the general change in society outside, but inside Telecom things have been a bit slow to catch up.

With those tensions developing at work, the ATPOA also changed quite dramatically over a few years. New South Wales was the first state to go through the metamorphosis. Although changes had been set in motion in 1975 when the association appointed its first full-time secretary, the turning point occurred a few years later, led by the telephonists working in Pitt Street computerized 10C exchange in Sydney.

The 10C exchange is so called because it was the third model of the tenth exchange system developed by International Telephone and Telegraph (ITT). The 10C system was selected by Roger Banks and a small team as the best available system after assessing exchanges produced by the big tele-communications companies. Its ability to cope with switching enormous quantities of telephone calls around the country and the world is not in dispute. But the conditions it imposed on the people working it caused considerable distress.

The telephonists hated it. Going from the dilapidated but homely GPO, with its plug boards and cords, to 10C, with its artificial lights and computer terminals, was a shock, quite apart from the change in the nature of the work. Even Roger Banks described the exchange as 'a tomb'.

During a technicians' wage dispute in 1978, the 10C exchange broke down. As is accepted practice when such computer failures occur, the 300 telephonists trooped across Pitt Street to the GPO to put the calls through with the old plug and cord gear which is still used as a back stop.

Julie Milligan was working at the 10C national exchange at that time. It is a place she recalls with horror: 'The job was stultifyingly boring, and the building was never designed for people.'

When the operators got out of the building, they decided that they would not return until certain concessions were obtained, and facilities improved. It was a spontaneous response to intolerable working conditions. After several weeks out of the new exchange, Telecom relented: improvements were made in lighting, the chairs were recovered with fabric, and telephonists no longer had to ask a monitor before taking a toilet break.

For telephonists to apply black bans and hold out for improvements was utterly unheard of. One woman recalls that at the time it was suggested that when telephonists joined Telecom they gave up their right to strike. They had not, of course, but the shock was as profound and fundamental as if they had. By this stage, however, it was too late to put windows in the tomb-like room.

Since its inception in 1924, ATPOA was representative of the people who chose to work as telephonists and supervisors. Telephonists have traditionally been women who were attracted to service jobs – often the only slightly unusual job a young woman could find in a country town was as a telephonist, and it was a job which disappeared on her wedding day until 1965.

The service nature of the job led, not surprisingly, to the ATPOA being a very conservative union. It came as something of a surprise to Mary Cox when she joined Telecom in 1975, after working for electronics manufacturer Plessey for some years. Mary Cox had always been an active unionist. Her involvement, she said, contributed to the breakdown of her marriage. At the time she joined Telecom, Mary Cox vowed she would stay out of union affairs to give her marriage another chance: 'I didn't want to be in a situation where I felt the blame because I was always going to a meeting or something.' So she distanced herself from the ATPOA for a couple of years:

Bah, it was definitely a supervisor's union then. They didn't want to know about telephonists. If you raised something, they'd say they'd look into it and wave their hands in the air and say 'next'. And they'd never look into it. It was a long time before a telephonist got onto the branch council; you had to be a six or an acting six [the classification of senior supervisors]. I had vowed not to become involved in the union, though I thought with 460 people at Pitt directory there should be a rep. I tried to get someone else to stand, then at the last minute I let myself be nominated.

The walkout at Pitt 10C was the trigger for change in the New South Wales branch of the union. Within months, rank and file groups were springing up all around the state, and health and working conditions were the organizing bases. A questionnaire organized with the assistance of the Workers' Health Centre was sent out to telephonists all over the state. The survey showed appalling work related illnesses, from stress to severe hearing difficulties.

Although the Pitt 10C walkout triggered increased participation in the ATPOA, the trend had started a couple of years earlier. In 1975, the conservative state council appointed Marilyn Brown as state secretary.

Marilyn Brown was an oddity in the history of the ATPOA.

She was the first full-time official in New South Wales. When she graduated with an economics degree and a Diploma of Education from Sydney University in 1972, she decided not to teach.

As a young woman, she didn't feel equipped for her chosen profession, and when she applied for research positions in major companies for which her economics background qualified her, she was not offered jobs, for a range of sexist reasons. As a result, she was unemployed for a year. After this she returned to the GPO international manual exchange in Sydney where she had worked during her university vacations. After twenty-four months in the job, she was appointed to the position of state secretary in New South Wales by the state branch council.

One of her colleagues recalls that at the time, although the council was not confident about her politics, it was impressed by the status of her university education. At the same time as the state secretary job was offered to her she was about to take up a job as a clerical officer in Telecom. 'So I knocked back the clerk position to work here and get ulcers,' she said.

Since Marilyn Brown became the secretary, the ATPOA has completely changed, and similar changes have started affecting the other states. Marilyn Brown recalls that in her first two years in the job those who contacted the association were generally reluctant to leave their names. The fact that the ATPOA had been dominated by supervisors for so long meant that supervisors took a dim view of the association stepping in to defend telephonists often against supervisors. Marilyn Brown and her supporters were characterized as the telephonists who were taking on the supervisors – until they finally won in 1980. (A rebel group of supervisors attempted to form a separate union but were not allowed to do so by the industrial commission which claimed that there were already enough unions available to cover supervisory telephonists in Telecom.)

Marilyn Brown became federal president in 1978, and similar changes to those which shook New South Wales are underway in the other states in the eighties. In all these branches, the activism of the general members has increased enormously: initially in response to the tremendous workload, and then because they gained results.

One activist observed:

Initially the rise of rank and file groups was in response to a plea that there was too much work to do, then it became more and more that if the rank and file groups didn't do the work, it didn't happen.

One of the issues which has galvanized this dissatisfaction has been the telephone shrieks, a result in part of Telecom's initial reluctance to investigate the 'spurious noises emanating from the telephone network' seriously. Instead, Telecom put the complaints down to 'mass hysteria' and the paranoia of 'hysterical', 'menopausal women'. That characterization has now been dropped, partly because men have now experienced the shrieks and more importantly, because they have now been reported in every state. The volume in decibels of the shrieks are much higher than the safe noise level of 85 decibels that Telecom accepts for continuous noise exposure. Shrieks have reached 135 decibels and some have reached as high as 143 decibels. Jet engines, steel rivetting and exposure nail guns register over 135 decibels but none of these noises is fed directly into the ear as the shriek is when a telephonist hears it, at random and unexpectedly, through her headset.

The first shrieks were reported in Adelaide's local service centre exchange in August 1980. The effects on the telephonist receiving the loud shriek through her headset were severe: she developed acute vertigo, noises in the ear and deafness. She ultimately underwent surgery that confirmed that the noise had resulted in physical damage to structures of her inner ear. Within the next twelve months, another 340 shrieks were reported in Adelaide alone. Nine women underwent surgery following exposure to them; one woman has a total and permanent hearing loss in the affected ear and in ninety-nine cases, the telephonist required at least one day's absence from work.

By July 1982, there had been 4,964 reports of shrieks from telephonists around Australia, and the number of subscriber complaints had also grown considerably. Although Telecom had undertaken some preliminary investigations into the causes, it was not until the ATPOA banned positions that had shrieks – which meant that in some exchanges a large number of telephonists were standing around doing nothing – that Telecom began to take the matter more seriously. The general secretary of the ATPOA, Sylvia Hall, believes that the shrieks are caused by connecting old 'cross-bar exchanges with stored programme [computer] controlled switching technologies, such as those used in the 10C trunk network and the ARE 11 local exchanges'. Others believe that digitally controlled switching is causing problems which are affecting the whole network. This argument is given extra weight by the occurrence of shrieks throughout the world, but Telecom, at the end of 1982, was still not ready to commit itself to an explanation of the causes. Instead, it drew up a list of four possible causes including incorrect operation of switching equipment, allowing multi-frequency code intrusion or connection to other network tones; incorrect transmission levels; faults on subscribers' lines and equipment, including high-level tones connected to telephone answering machines and faulty arcing switching contacts. To reduce the effects of the shrieks, Telecom has installed volume limiters on the headsets worn by telephonists. Although this reduces the impact, it does not solve the problem. Sylvia Hall commented:

I think they've reached the conclusion after two years that this problem is going to be with them forever, so the only thing they can do is install volume limiters. They say the network is a very complex matter and they've got to live with it.

Mary Cox is one of the women who has suffered from the shrieks. At one stage she said that the shrieks were happening at the rate of four or five a day:

As the volume of the work has got greater so has the number of shrieks increased. When one comes through, we pull off our headsets and hold it out at arm's length so that the next person can hear it and be our witness. Where I work at DAS/C [computerized directory assistance exchange], we had the newer light headsets where a little nipple sits right inside the ear; although they are just as easy to pull off, it seems worse because the sound comes straight into your head. As a result of the shrieks I've had, I've got damaged nerves in my ear. A specialist told me it was like mild shell shock the damage that has been done. It causes terrible neuralgia. Sometimes my eye feels like it has been punched, and there is a swelling here on my neck behind my ear which is sore to touch all the time. As a result I have ultra-sensitive hearing: the noise of a motor of a car starting starts my neuralgia. As a result, I can't use my headset on my left ear.

The shrieks are not the only cause of hearing-related problems, although they are possibly the most extreme. The 1978 health survey, organized with the support of the Workers' Health Centre, showed the disproportionate rate of hearing-related problems telephonists have; some ear specialists have even developed a name for it: 'telephonists' ear' they call it.

Hearing-related health problems are not the only ones telephonists suffer; the introduction of the new technology in exchanges is exacerbating other stress-related illnesses. The experience of telephonists who are transferred to the new computer based exchanges seems to follow a pattern similar to other jobs in which new technology is introduced.

This could be described as the new toy syndrome. When people first start playing with the visual display terminal, they attempt to beat it, to see just how many calls can be handled in a day, an hour, a minute; it is all so nice and neat and clean and quiet. You sit there at your station and a call flashes up on the screen and a voice in your ear asks for a call to Perth. You ask for the caller's number, the number sought, person-to-person details, keying information onto the screen and connecting the two parties before dispatching the call to the electronic rubbish bin, from whence it will only be retrieved under special circumstances, before being printed out and checked by the production control division a few days later.

In the exchanges, a supervisor can listen to telephonists' calls at any time, make comments, criticisms or reprimands about the way the call is being handled without the subscriber hearing a thing. The supervisor can also call up any operator's screen at any time, which is very different from the wandering around approach to supervising adopted in the plug and cord exchanges.

Many telephonists find this work mind dullingly boring, as they follow exactly the same formula with each call that drops into the headset or onto the screen.

Although Roger Banks talks with an engineer's respect for machinery, saying that people cannot be expected to work with equipment they cannot trust, his perspective on the new technology is drastically at odds with that of those who use it:

The automation of a lot of routine tasks can either be seen as deskilling or leaving the person free to concentrate on other aspects of the job to create a better job, to take the drudgery out of things, and makes the person deliver a better service. That's how I see it.

The tedium of the work which many telephonists now feel is made worse by the increased pressure of higher targets. In Australia, this has been kept under control by not collecting statistics about individual workers. Collecting individual statistics on how long each function took, how many queries were asked, how many screens were perused, and so on, is built into the technology. It is part of its surveillance and control function. The effect on people working with that surveillance and control can be devastating.

Mary Cox was one of the first Sydney operators to work on the computerized directory assistance system, DAS/C. She remembers how she and everyone else were clamouring to get onto the new system. Then individual statistics started to appear:

I was taken aside one day and told that although I was averaging thirty-nine seconds a call, which was no problem, there was a problem with the time it took from a call dropping in to when I started keying in. I was taking sixteen seconds, and they wanted me to get it down to ten seconds. I was relatively fast, but I slowly started feeling hassled and quite upset. I'd had a relatively hard life with five kids and had obviously been suffering stress without it surfacing.

But I started getting nauseous and having migranes and getting sick. I realized it one day when I was giving a subscriber a number and had to repeat it five times, and I realized I was subconsciously screwing the subscriber's neck.

But at that time I didn't realize how sick I was. After terrible headaches for a couple of months, I went to Sydney Hospital one night, and they said nothing was wrong with me, I was just play acting, and then I got into the car and burst into tears. I was so ill. The following Saturday I woke up and vomited and vomited and vomited. I went to my doctor and I just couldn't stop vomitting all over the doctor's surgery, until he gave me an injection to stop.

I was then given a month off for stress. It was just the pressure of the job trying to beat yesterday's stats.

Mary Cox left the directory assistance exchange a few months later and went to working on the old plug and cord boards. Before she left she set herself a task of seeing how many calls she could cope with in an hour if she really pulled out the stops. She found 135 numbers in an hour: 'At that rate you are literally going around the bend. No one could keep it up.' On paper records, the average call took one minute to handle. With the aid of a computer, a hundred an hour are expected.

Despite a 42 per cent productivity improvement, a million directory assistance calls go unanswered each year.

Perhaps the conflict between providing a public service and working for an organization which needs to make large profits each year is best seen in the people who place the trunk calls booked by subscribers.

Ruth Dailliston has worked at the Dalley trunk exchange for twelve years. She believes that people should have the choice between dialling directly themselves or going through the operator who can obtain a particular person, call back later, give a ring back price, and so on:

A lot of people don't realize when they call the operator that the rates are higher and they get charged a surcharge for using the operator. Sometimes when the call costs 50 cents it is less than the surcharge of a dollar. We've got to ban the surcharge.

It is a very big dilemma though. Do you tell people that they can get the call far cheaper by doing it themselves? To use the operator it can cost four times as much. It is a very big dilemma, because if we tell people we do ourselves out of jobs.

What Ruth Dailliston and her colleagues at the manual exchanges do is use their discretion. If the person making the call sounds like 'a little old lady' or an 'ordinary person', they will charge them at the cheaper rate. Such consideration and generosity does not extend to businessmen or people calling from fancy city hotels. That discretion is not possible with the computerized exchanges.

The charging dilemma manifests itself in other ways, too, besides deciding 'who to rip off'. As subscribers become more rushed and frazzled by the pace of life, so they take out their frustration on telephonists. Most telephonists agree that people have become more impatient over the last decade. They have also grown less tolerant of Telecom according to a *Choice* survey.

For telephonists who, like technicians and installation people, are the front line of Telecom, this intolerance and dislike of Telecom is a problem. Val Foster said:

Telecom's policies make us look bad. We are struggling to give a decent service; we are the meat in the sandwich between the public and Telecom. We are not Telecom, we are only responsible for the good things, not the bad things, though that's how Telecom wants it to look.

We've got to get the public on our side. The public can control Telecom. Even when people are rude and don't realize the pressure we are under, I say I'm going to give a good service because I want them on our side.

But it is very hard to show that your policy is not bad like Telecom's.

Chapter Nine
Taking on the Techs

If you had suggested in the 1960s that within a decade the Postal and Telecommunications Technicians' Association would one day be as feared in corporate boardrooms as the powerful unions which represent builders, metalworkers, wharfies, miners or printers, you would have been laughed out of the room. The Postal and Telecommunications Technicians' Association was at that stage a very tame association. But with a name change to the Australian Telecommunications Employees' Association (ATEA), a restructured employer, an injection of younger officials and a less complacent membership came a new stature in the trade union movement. From obscurity a few years earlier, the ATEA became one of the most influential unions in Australia. Because of it, the government set up committees of inquiry, the shorter working week became an acceptable work unit, and the wage indexation system which had operated under duress since 1975 finally collapsed.

In 1976, the ATEA became one of the first unions in Australia to negotiate a working week of thirty-six and three-quarters hours, organized as a nine-day fortnight, in exchange for productivity increases. Then as a direct result of the ATEA's dispute in 1978 over maintenance arrangements for the introduction of new technology the government established a Committee of Inquiry into Technological Change in Australia, and co-opted the association's federal secretary, Bill Mansfield, to represent the unions on it. Similarly, it was the dispute over wage parity for technicians employed by Telecom Australia which, in 1981, was finally the catalyst for ending wage indexation.

The ATEA officially acknowledges its responsibility for all of these landmarks, although officials modestly say that if it hadn't been the ATEA, another union would have achieved the same results sooner or later.

It was scarcely surprising, then, that when the government announced that it would set up the Davidson inquiry into telecommunications services some people decided that this was another legacy of the ATEA's new-found activism. Only a few months after the ATEA's pay dispute, which severely disrupted the telecommunications network, the government formed a committee to determine the extent of private-sector participation in the industry. These people, many of whom were in Telecom's management ranks, and in the companies which were hoping to compete with Telecom, proclaimed that the union had brought the wrath of the government down on itself and Australian telecommunications in general. 'You went too far this time,' they admonished.

But for the ATEA, the matter was not so clear-cut. The officials of the union disclaimed any responsibility for the establishment of the Davidson inquiry. If it was the ATEA's fault that the government had formed the committee, why was the same pattern occurring in other countries?

By no stretch of the imagination is Bill Mansfield, the ATEA's federal secretary, a militant. Mansfield is a reasonable man, a man who studied at night school to matriculate, and then went on over seven years to complete a law degree at Melbourne university, part time. A full-time trade union official since he was twenty-one, Mansfield is a man who believes in the social democratic system, a man who listens carefully to all sides before coming to his decision. He gives listeners the feeling that if there were the slightest possibility of the ATEA being to blame for the assault on Telecom, he would accept it, unwillingly possibly, but with good grace. So it is a little surprising to hear his trenchant defence of his organization, when asked if the ATEA should accept responsibility for the establishment of the inquiry into private-sector participation in telecommunications:

None at all. I don't accept any responsibility for Davidson being set up. Look at other countries, the UK, US and some European countries. What is happening in Australia is happening in those countries as well, where the unions have been very meek and mild, where they haven't fought at all, and the same thing is happening. It is just a desire on the part of profit-motivated ideologues to get into communications and make money out of it. I don't accept any responsibility. Neither do I blame what is happening on Telecom management. It is the federal government and those close to it who are responsible.

Telecom managers were quick to publicly blame the union for the establishment of the Davidson inquiry. 'They gave the vultures the chance to pounce,' according to director of business development, Roger Banks. But in more considered moments, Banks and other senior managers conceded that it was not the fault of the union. 'We were ready,' Banks said on another occasion, 'we saw it coming at least a year before; there aren't many surprises in our game if you study it.' Jim Smith, Telecom's deputy chief general manager, said that as 'a great watcher of other telecoms', the commission was not caught by surprise when the Davidson committee was established. 'Davidson was just another event in a whole chain of happenings,' Smith observed:

Some people, including the union, think they can stop the trend [towards competition]. I don't believe they can or should. We were not caught unawares. By 1979, there were significant public addresses by top management on the way we were going – statements that competition was both desirable and inevitable.

Both the ATEA and management were able to point to the rest of the world, and illustrate a global trend to introduce competition into the profitable areas of telecommunications. Management was able to analyse and learn from the strong campaigns organized by AT&T in the United States and British Telecom to protect their enterprises. But for the Telecom unions, there were relatively few international examples to copy - except for some Canadian and Japanese unions - of defence of the public-sector telecommunications network. In most countries, the communications unions have remained a fairly conservative, acquiescent group. In 1981, ATEA officials travelled to Tokyo, Japan, for a meeting of the international umbrella organization of communications unions, the Postal, Telegraphic and Telephone International. They hoped to pick up some tips on how to fight the issue, but they came away dissatisfied. 'The high point,' one delegate recalled, 'was when the Communications Workers of America donned their hats and picked up placards and marched around the conference room singing the union song.'

For the ATEA, the fight was clear-cut. The battle over Davidson and private-sector competition was to be the fight of its short life. If it lost this one, it might as well give up. Not only was the ATEA (and the other unions in Telecom) fighting for the jobs which stood to be lost by any private-sector incursion, but they saw themselves waging a campaign on behalf of all Australian telephone subscribers. The ATEA tried to prepare itself well for this battle, employing research assistants, consultants and publicists to do the job professionally and allocating $200,000 to the fight. For the first really significant time, the ATEA, with 26,000 members, joined with nine other unions representing most of Telecom's other 90,000 employees to ensure that the empire was defended.

It was not the first time that the ATEA had waged a campaign which assumed the characteristics of a national crusade. In 1978, it organized the first and only major new technology dispute in Australia to gain mass popular support. Although the 1978 dispute had its origins in promotional opportunities and staff structures, it quickly became known as the 'new technology dispute'.

The ATEA won the dispute over staff structures, and in the process forced Telecom to formally discuss plans to introduce new technology with the union before implementing it and to formally consider the maintenance arrangement proposed by the union for the new electronic ARE 11 exchanges. It was a victory which was described in the association's monthly magazine, *Teletech*, as being won as a result of a 'combination of logic and industrial muscle'. The dispute surprised Telecom and the Australian public and to a lesser degree the members of the ATEA, by bringing the telecommunications network to a virtual standstill for the first time. This alientated business and government, but won the support of some ordinary telephone subscribers who were able to make free STD and ISD calls because the ATEA was not repairing pricing equipment.

Assessing the victory, *Teletech* commented:

Logic alone will not win an issue; this has been proven in the technical staff structure because the Association has been putting the same logical argument to Telecom Australia for years. It was not until that logic was coupled with industrial muscle that our objective has been substantially achieved. The lesson we must learn is that in the future the combination of these two ingredients must be of the right mix and not fall for the trap of thinking that either one of those factors is sufficient in all situations.

The issue of new technology was a difficult one for the ATEA. Telecommunications has always been technology driven; it has improved with advances in the technology which have generally been installed and implemented with the considerable skill of the technicians. Technicians regarded themselves as artisans, craftsmen who could make the telephone system work. But with the decision by Telecom in 1976 to convert to electronic exchanges, technicians, for the first time, saw that the exchanges and technology they installed could make them redundant. Their skills would be made obsolete, the system would run on a series of circuit boards, and when they broke down it would be cheaper to throw them out than to repair them.

Engineers who had participated in the selection of the new exchanges accepted that the equipment would deskill the technicians but felt that this would be more than compensated for by increased job satisfaction from other (unspecified) aspects of the work. One senior engineer commented:

Have you ever seen technicians in an exchange? They can walk in and hear the clickety clack, clickety clack and hear it miss a beat and know that something is wrong, and then know how to fix it. Now the system has a nervous breakdown when something goes wrong and spits out a print-out that tells them what it is.

During the 1978 dispute, the technicians could see what was happening to their jobs in the booming industry of telecommunications, and as unemployment in Australia topped 7 per cent that year, they started to worry about people employed in other industries which were not growing. Although the potential existed for the ATEA to be the toughest and most important union in the Information Age in Australia, it was of little consolation if everyone around them was out of work, if their kids could not get jobs, and if their skills died with them.

The ATEA started to agitate for a national inquiry into the impact of technological change. In the same month as it won its fight with Telecom, *Teletech* featured an editorial saying:

The ATEA believes that a broadly based public enquiry should be established to examine all aspects of the introduction of new technology . . . Members of the ATEA are concerned about the future. Their jobs are changing, disappearing in some cases; costs were to be imposed on individuals and new training to be undertaken. Telecommunications is at the forefront of changing technology. We can see how the computerised technology is capable of deskilling work and eliminating jobs. We read of the potential it has for causing massive reductions in the need for labor in the service industries such as banking and insurance. We cannot see that any attention is being given to the problems by the most powerful representatives of the community – the Federal Government. The only thing the government has done to date is to establish a committee of public servants to examine in private a problem affecting workers over the length and breadth of Australia . . . It is not good enough . . . There should be an open and broadly based enquiry into all aspects of new technology.

Within three months, Prime Minister Fraser had announced the terms of reference for a committee to investigate the impact of technological change (CITCA). In December 1978, in the same month as he was elected to the position of federal secretary, Bill Mansfield was appointed as the union representative on this committee.

Not everyone on the ATEA executive was convinced that Mansfield should accept the position. According to meeting records of the time, the decision was only taken 'following direct representations to the ATEA by the Australian Council of Trade Unions'. Behind this statement was pressure from the ACTU president of the time, Bob Hawke. Hawke wanted Mansfield on the committee, and when it looked as though the ATEA executive was wavering, concerned that the absence of the new federal secretary would be detrimental to the association, Hawke suggested that the other possible trade union representative was John Maynes, president of the Federated Clerks' Union and a prominent National Civic Council member. Although the members of Maynes's union were being seriously affected by the introduction of the new technology, the Federated Clerks' Union, as a very conservative union, was doing relatively little at that time to impose terms and conditions on its introduction. The suggestion that someone with such radically different views from theirs would be the union representative on the committee it had argued so strongly for convinced the ATEA executive, somewhat reluctantly, to allow the new secretary to serve on it. For the next eighteen months, Mansfield spent one week in four on CITCA business.

Mansfield now says that if he had his time over he would not agree to sit on the committee.

It is very difficult to take on a CITCA type role, spend eighteen months in thorough study of an issue, listening and examining a whole range of evidence, which is not considered by others in your organization, and then present a conclusion, and explain that to others who have not gone through the same experience. If I was making the judgement now about my ability to maintain my position in this organization politically, I would not go on CITCA; in fact I have turned down offers to sit on other committees of the Australian Science and Technology Council because of that.

The report presented by the committee to the government in 1980 urged that technological advance not be hindered. It discounted the effects of new technology on the skills and jobs of the Australian workforce, arguing that innovation was essential for economic progress. The report failed to satisfy either the ATEA or the trade union movement in general. Employers and government were only slightly happier with it than the unions were, and the four volumes were unceremoniously pigeon-holed shortly afterwards. Members of the ATEA were not pleased with what some of them saw as the duplicitious role of their federal secretary. Mansfield himself conceded that his views on technological changes had altered over the two years since the 1978 dispute, although he remained committed to the principles involved in it.

It was not until the Davidson committee finally presented its report to the government in October 1982 that Mansfield adopted a cynical attitude towards committees of inquiry. When Mansfield, the federal president, Col Cooper, the federal vice-president, Ian McLean, and the industrial officer, Peter Green, sat in the ALP lounge in the Senate where they had set up a temporary office, and read the embargoed copy of Davidson's report, Mansfield's face fell. His worst fears had been confirmed. The committee had delivered a political document, not an objective assessment of the facts presented to it. 'Why do we even bother putting in submissions when they ignore us?' he asked his colleagues. Later that day, as the group of ATEA officials walked towards the car-park behind Parliament House, Mansfield turned to them and said, 'I now know how you blokes felt when CITCA came out.' It was the first time Mansfield had joked about CITCA. Later he said he hoped Davidson would get the same treatment that CITCA received.

The shock that Davidson's committee had presented a political document rather than an objective assessment of 'how private enterprise could best participate in the provision of telecommunications services in Australia' was not shared by Col Cooper. As the federal president and the secretary of the ATEA's largest state branch, New South Wales, Cooper had been predicting for months that the report would be a political document. Cooper did not have as much faith as Mansfield in the process of government-sponsored inquiries. This was not surprising, because Cooper, a shrewd and cunning trade union official, who had been elected in 1966, represented the ATEA's most militant state. It was not in his make-up to be surprised by events in the political process. The differences in perspective between federal and New South Wales officials have been of long standing and have occasionally erupted in conflict within the union. This reached a peak at the end of 1970, when the federal office launched an investigation into the New South Wales branch of the union.

After the investigation of the New South Wales branch failed, the New South Wales-federal office tensions remained dormant, and only erupted occasionally. Ten years later, in 1981, a dispute, involving technicians employed at the Haymarket telex exchange at the southern end of Sydney City, brought the tensions to a head again (although not on the earlier scale). The telex dispute over staffing levels was far from the easy battle that ATEA members, euphoric following their earlier pay victory over the government, anticipated. A few months earlier, extra staff had been assigned to the trunk exchange and the technicians employed at Haymarket believed that their case was so clear-cut that the extra staff would be provided quite quickly.

The dispute dragged on for a month. In the last few weeks, the telex network in New South Wales came to a virtual standstill, for all but the most minimal traffic. Although Col Cooper now concedes that the criticism of the handling of the dispute by other members of the ATEA executive may be justified, this, he believes, was happening at the time:

Telecom management initially wanted to take us on. They thought that if they were going to smash the ATEA they would need to kick New South Wales in the guts. After a while, they realized there was something in our case, but by that time they were locked in, the government was breathing down their necks.

When the settlement was finally negotiated, the number of

technicians in the exchange had grown from thirty-six to fifty-seven, but the New South Wales branch found itself without payroll deductions of union dues. The annual dues to the New South Wales branch of the ATEA top $1 million, and provide more than one-third of the funds for the federal office. The removal of payroll deductions placed considerable strain on the entire organization.

The tensions between the federal office and the New South Wales branch had been building up during 1981. Earlier that year, when the unanimous decision of federal executive was reached to set deadlines for industrial action if the pay parity dispute was not settled, some branches felt that New South Wales and Queensland were dragging them into another strike. The 1981 pay increase finally came through after extensive research into parity, after more than a year of negotiations, and finally twelve days of intense industrial action, which again brought the telephone network to a virtual halt.

The 1981 pay negotiations had elements of a calculated gamble by Telecom management to break away from the control of the government and the co-ordinating committee. The committee operated in the background, relaying government policy to Telecom. It had a right of veto in negotiations. But it was a gamble that Telecom management lost. During the negotiations, Telecom management conceded that the technicians it employed were paid less than other people with comparable jobs in other industries. In conceding this, management hoped to obtain productivity improvements as a trade-off for a pay increase. This concession did not fit, however, into the rigid wage indexation guidelines which then determined wages in Australia. On 10 June 1981, the Conciliation and Arbitration Commission refused to ratify the agreement between Telecom and the ATEA saying:

In our view Telecom is attempting to shelter behind this commission by requiring us to indicate an attitude to the agreement before it will be implemented, notwithstanding the fact that the agreement was not made subject to the ratification of this commission ... It is our prima facie view that the agreement is contrary to the passage of the

National Wage Case decision which indicated that settlements reached by collective bargaining, no less than by arbitration, must be made within the principles if the system is to survive. For those reasons we are not prepared to ratify the agreement.

The commission's president, Sir John Moore, did go on to say that as an agreement had been reached it would be bad faith on the part of Telecom if it did not honour it.

As Sir John concluded his determination, Jim Smith turned to Col Cooper and said, 'Well that's it.' Telecom had lost the gamble. The following day, 11 June 1981, after twenty-four hours' deliberation, the federal cabinet approved the agreement, and on the same day the managing director, Jack Curtis, resigned.

The pay increases were a considerable victory for the ATEA, placing technicians in a comparatively better position than other groups in the public service, but the cost was also high. Kevin Fothergill, the secretary of the Victorian branch of the ATEA, feared that the union had gone too far:

Sir John Moore is a clever bloke, he's not called Sir God for nothing. But nonetheless I wonder if we would have got the same with less industrial action. Management co-operated as far as it could, but the union was seen to go too far and the crabs were attracted. It gave the government the chance to find scapegoats. As soon as the employers concurred, they were done anyway, so why did we need the dispute, we would have got much the same result anyway.

Fothergill's concern was not shared by most of the association. Although he was elected on a left-wing ticket in Victoria, and still regards himself as a member of the ATEA's left-wing faction, his criticism was directed particularly at the other two key left-wing states: New South Wales and Queensland. Members in both these states were dissatisfied with the pay settlement and voted against it, convinced the union could do even better. The settlement was finally accepted nationally, but the divisions within the association were more clearly drawn.

As the biggest state branch, New South Wales has always presented problems for the federal organization. From his position on the eleventh floor of an office tower above Flinders Street in Melbourne, Bill Mansfield sees the occasional conflicts with the New South Wales branch in these terms:

It is one large branch which tends to take the view that its attitudes should prevail. The attitude that if it is not satisfied with the federal position it will settle matters with its own resources is an attitude that still prevails in New South Wales.

It is scarcely surprising that the New South Wales branch regards itself as the pace-setter for the ATEA. With nearly 9,000 of the association's 26,300 members, the New South Wales branch first embarked on the massive changes in attitude and organization which democratized the ATEA and made it what it is today. Until the late 1960s, the New South Wales branch was like all the other branches at that time – very conservative. Col Cooper recalls that in the 1950s and 1960s the New South Wales branch was 'in the hands of the Masons'. In the other states, and at a federal level, the right-wing National Civic Council was the dominant political faction, although by the early 1960s the Communist Party's Eureka Youth League was attracting considerable numbers of younger members. Throughout the 1960s there was growing discontent over pay disparities between public- and private-sector employees which led to a general $70 catch up for public-sector workers at the end of the decade. At the same time, concern about the apparent absence of democracy in the association was growing. But the real turning point for the New South Wales branch, and ultimately the entire association, occurred after the Redfern Mail Exchange was commissioned in 1966. The Mail Exchange was conceived in the 1950s as the answer to New South Wales's mail distribution problems. It was the bright idea of engineers and planners working for the PMG's department, at a time when centralization was the catchword of business efficiency and organization. The massive six-storey building, occupying an entire inner-city block, was where the ATEA learnt its early industrial lessons.

Ken 'Waldo' Walton is now an ATEA assistant federal secretary, but in 1966 he worked for Country Installations Number Three, the long-range desert patrol. For seven years he had worked with the patrol, installing long-line broadband equipment in the desert areas of New South Wales west of Dubbo. Waldo was in the second group of technicians to come to Sydney to work for the Mail Exchange. He volunteered to leave the bush and come back to Sydney, and there he had his first contact with industrial conflict. The first group of technicians to staff the Mail Exchange were not volunteers. Waldo said:

People were shanghaied from all over the state, but by the time I joined in 1967 we were all volunteers. It was the biggest location of techs all in one spot. The postal engineers thought they would be able to staff the place with 50 electrical tradesmen, but they weren't trained to do the work, and in the end they needed 500 technical workers.

Jack Kreger worked in the training section at the Mail Exchange in the early days:

People didn't want to go there. They were working side by side with the rather militant postal workers in a factory-type environment, which was a real industrial jungle compared to the small exchanges most of them came from. There was continuous industrial disputation about everything from the working conditions to the shifts; the disputes were never ending, although even the technicians weren't totally militant; at that stage, they certainly weren't walking out the door.

The turning point for the technicians at the Mail Exchange came during a postal workers' strike in 1967. As the dispute moved into its final week, the technicians were directed by the federal executive to work with the students and others who had been given pre-Christmas, strike-breaking jobs in the Mail Exchange by the Gorton government, which was anxious to settle the dispute. The debate about whether they should work with scabs split the Mail Exchange sub-branch and was only very bitterly accepted. Jack Kreger remembers the federal decision with distress:

It was a very traumatic point for the union. Unfortunately, we did work with them [the scabs], but from that point on our members at the Mail Exchange, technicians and technicians' assistants, would walk out at the drop of a hat – issues like the numbers on a shift, demarcation disputes, manning disputes – they were all symptoms of what was going on.

'The Mail Exchange demonstrated we could take action and have an impact,' Waldo said:

Before that there had been an underlying belief that the machines would work for everyone, but this showed we could disrupt a valuable service; it demonstrated that we could be effective. The manager at the time used to say that there were two unions in the exchange, both of them could stop the mail, the Australian Postal Workers' Union and the Postal and Telecommunications Technicians' Association. He said that the APWU made thirty-six threats to stop the mail in one year and did four times, and the PTTA made eighteen threats and walked out twenty-nine times.

This uncharacteristic action by the technicians had ramifications throughout the association. Many of the full-time officials of the ATEA today came up through the 'industrial jungle' of the Mail Exchange. Other members of the association tended to regard the people working at the Mail Exchange as 'rat bags' and 'all bloody mad', but the action was a very serious threat to the power and authority of the federal office. Up until 1968, a national plebiscite instigated by the federal office had to be held before any industrial action could be taken. This subsequently changed to no industrial action being allowed without the approval of the federal executive. The Mail Exchange and the New South Wales branch threatened the authority of the federal office. At the federal council meeting in Perth in October 1970 it was decided to set up an inquiry into the administration of the New South Wales branch with a view to expelling it. The decision to proceed with a formal investigation was taken on the basis of legal opinion which held that it would not be possible to expel a branch without first investigating it. A four-man committee was appointed to examine the written and verbal complaints of members in New South Wales and elsewhere. The committee consisted of the federal president, Dick Griffiths, the South Australian president, Bill Glass, the Victorian president, Stan Cassidy, and the New South Wales president, Jack Kreger.

The committee had hardly begun its deliberations when the New South Wales branch received a direction from the federal office to disband the Mail Exchange sub-branch. Knowing that the New South Wales branch would refuse to comply with this direction, the federal office had expected to gain additional ammunition for the expulsion of the branch. But before the direction could be implemented, it needed the support of mass meetings in every state. In New South Wales, although many members found it difficult to accept what those at the Mail Exchange were doing, according to Kreger, they 'closed ranks and would not agree to the sub-branch being expelled'. The New South Wales branch then dispatched Ken Walton to speak to meetings in Brisbane and Melbourne and put the case for the Mail Exchange. The Queensland meeting ratified the federal directive, and the final vote hinged on the Victorian meeting. The New South Wales branch lined up three speakers at the Melbourne meeting to counter the attack from the federal office which was led by Bill Mansfield. It was a very close vote in Victoria against disbanding the sub-branch. Because of the federal structure of the ATEA, New South Wales and Victoria, with most of the members between them, hold the right of veto.

After this, the inquiry into the New South Wales branch lost some of its steam. When it finally presented its report, exonerating the branch and criticizing the federal office, to the 1971 federal conference in Adelaide, it was simply noted and received. Jack Kreger said, 'It was simply tabled. Things had changed so much that no action was recommended and punitive action wasn't even considered.'

More than ten years later, the events of that summer are still emotive for those who lived through it. 'The federal office could see the New South Wales branch setting the pattern and power starting to slip away from the executive,' Kreger believes. For Bill Mansfield, who had moved from his position as the Victorian branch's assistant secretary to the federal office in 1966, the explanation has a slightly different twist:

The greatest dissension with the federal office was between 1967 and 1973-74. At that stage, the federal office was held in some awe by most of the branch officials. Up until the early 1960s, most of the branches still only had part-time officials, so they were very dependent on the full-time officers for guidance and advice. The NCC influenced the association from the mid 1950s through to the mid 1960s, and the full-time officials were basically very, very conservative. With the New South Wales situation, it was growing pains as much as anything else. The New South Wales branch was ahead of the federal body and the organization in terms of attitudes and objectives at that time.

It was after the abortive attempts to expel the New South Wales branch that moves to democratize the union got underway seriously. This coincided with a change of leadership in Victoria, so that the two biggest states, with one other state's support (often Queensland), were able to push changes through the federal council. The trigger for the move to democratize the union came after an agreement negotiated by the then general secretary, Ken Turbet. Known as Determination 138, it effectively reclassified technicians as telecommunications tradesmen. Although this was sweetened by a pay increase, it effectively removed promotional opportunities for tradesmen who did work comparable to that of technicians but earned up to $1,000 a year less. In a move which would be totally unacceptable today, and which outraged the membership then, Turbet went to Canberra in 1970 armed with the imprimatur of the federal council, to negotiate the staff restructure to a conclusion. This was done without ever referring it back to either the council or the membership. For a membership which was becoming increasingly active, this was utterly unacceptable, and the sub-branch structure began operating effectively for the first time. Although it took until 1978 to reverse Determination 138, it is still regarded by many as 'Ken Turbet's legacy'. Turbet left the general secretary's chair in 1978, just a couple of months before the technology dispute got underway. When he went to a seat on the Conciliation and Arbitration Commission, the transformation of the ATEA was nearly complete.

In each state, the things which sparked the increased activity by the membership varied from recap tyres, air conditioning in vehicles, travelling allowance, recall phones and the closure of country exchanges to Melbourne Cup Day holidays. The only constant was outrage at Determination 138 and enthusiasm for moves to democratize the union.

During the 1970s, the structure of the ATEA changed significantly. Sub-branches, although they went under different names in various states, were introduced and given the ability to negotiate directly with the district telecommunications manager. Federal officers were elected for the first time and the rules changed so that decisions could not be made without referring them back to the membership for ratification or rejection. During 1977, the ATEA also relinquished its position on the board of Telecom, seeing it as a conflict of interest.

These changes were all a direct result of the changing age structure of the union, and the general changes in the national psyche, which made it possible for a Labor government to be elected for the first time in twenty-three years. In the late 1950s and early 1960s, the APO had taken on hundreds of apprentices every year, and by the middle of the 1960s, a new breed of officials was being drawn from their ranks and was starting to have an effect on the expectations of the association. By the time Telecom Australia took over from the PMG's department, the ATEA had changed and was prepared for changes in its employer as well.

Col Cooper, like Jack Kreger and Marilyn Brown, believes that Telecom did the industrializing and politicizing of the workforce for the union. 'The technology made us militant, from the Mail Exchange on,' Cooper said.

During the earlier years, technicians had been reluctant to take industrial action, largely because they had a sneaking suspicion that they weren't really needed. Many thought that the exchanges would run without them. Although they prized their skills, they believed in the machines, as people who work with machines every day, must. Technician folklore had elevated a story of a long strike in the United States in the early 1960s which had severely weakened the Communications Workers of America. During the dispute, AT&T discovered that rather than engaging in preventative maintenance, with pieces of equipment routinely removed for service as it had done, all that was needed was repairs when something broke down, corrective maintenance. In Australia, a system of qualitative maintenance applied. Somewhere between corrective and preventative maintenance, qualitative maintenance meant that repairs were made when needed, following indications by fault maintenance monitors. The technicians feared that if they took industrial action the equipment may not need repairs and they would find themselves out of jobs.

The Mail Exchange changed this, and technicians realized that machines did break down, and if repairs were not made, the service could be interrupted. As the move from step-by-step to cross-bar and then electronic switching equipment was made, the technicians became aware of their increased industrial power. Now that they have discovered their power, debates centre around when and how to use it.

The formation of Telecom Australia was supported by the technicians, who saw a rosy future for themselves if they were no longer 'dragged down' by 'the deadwood of postal'. They saw the chances of maintaining their skills and being paid more for them as higher in a commission concerned solely with telecommunications, free of Public Service Board intervention, than in a two-headed department of state. But they were not prepared for the change of management style that the new commission developed as it emerged from the department of state. When Telecom started balancing service with productivity increases and profits, many technicians, as well as other Telecom workers, started to feel under pressure.

Jack Kreger worked for the PMG's department and Telecom for most of his adult life. Before retiring he worked in Telecom's training division, while being active in the ATEA. He has observed huge changes in attitudes over the past decade:

It was remarkable, since Vesting Day, the changes which occurred. The PMG had been staffed by people who were a product of the depression, wrapped in the flag. A large proportion were if not for God, Queen and the country, at least knew that they had a job for life, a good job, and were quite prepared to accept paternalistic management. There was no real reason to rock the boat. Then there started to be a change in society, with young people who were better educated and more independent. They were brought up in a different world, and rightly so; they didn't owe anyone anything and wouldn't take the things that my age group would. When in the 1970s we started getting involved in disputes, it pained many of them; they were upset to see what was happening; they were very loyal and were pained that the young people had none of their loyalties.

But then, as time progressed, Telecom did things with total disregard for human beings and the older men started to hate Telecom, and all the more so because they were trapped because of their age. Where could they go? Older people and lower skilled techs were more militant than the younger ones. They lived Telecom, and then Telecom dropped its paternalistic nature and started sending people anywhere, with no consideration to the problems it caused. It failed to retrain people and adopted a gung-ho style of management, assuming that good management in the private sector just walked all over people.

Good technicians were castigated and denigrated for not becoming senior technical officers, when they were quite happy doing a good job; then all of a sudden they were run down because they didn't want to be something else, which just discounted and disregarded the contribution they had made to the system. The old and faithful people were overshadowed by the honeybees dodging all over the place. It's doubtful that they contribute anything of lasting value. Previously, there was a strong bond between the staff; they would support each other, and there was a bond between the staff and middle management, but that doesn't happen any more – that sort of bond doesn't come out of management training schools.

It was after this fundamental change in the attitude of the people working for Telecom occurred that the suggestion of the workforce defending the organization against a private-sector onslaught was raised. Officials in all the Telecom unions recognized early that the fight would be a life and death struggle to save jobs and keep the telecommunications network in the public sector. Although the network had been built up by the people working for Telecom and the APO, officials feared it would be difficult to convince people who had grown to hate Telecom to fight to save it. This contradiction was highlighted by the apparent reluctance of Telecom's management to publicly defend the commission or the people working for it.

The decision by Telecom's most senior management to quietly fight Davidson, and all he represented, using the back door to people and politicians with power and influence, was one which left many people working for Telecom confused and angry. The management decision was not unanimous. Some of the most senior people, including the deputy chief general manager, Jim Smith, felt that it was necessary to say that Telecom was worth fighting for, and to say so loudly and often, but Smith and his associates did not have the numbers, and the back-door approach was adopted by Telecom in defence of itself. In October 1982, Smith said:

The difference of opinion has had an effect on the unease of the people working for Telecom. They aren't sure where top management stands. It is all very well to put the case to meetings and seminars and in face-to-face discussions, but it is not the same if people can't read it in the *Financial Review*. They don't believe it unless you are prepared to go public with it. I see *Teletech* is saying that it is about time management started defending Telecom instead of just leaving it to the unions. I understand very well what they are on about.

This left the unions, and particularly the ATEA, as the loudest defenders of Telecom. The nature of the campaign varied from state to state. In Victoria, an active joint unions campaign began shortly after the trends became apparent. The Victorian campaign, and those in the other states, had two aims, one to inform the members of the unions of the nature of the threats and to canvass methods of opposition, and the second to inform members of the public and politicians. This meant that the complex issues needed to be broken down into simple concepts. The ATEA had had some experience in organizing political campaigns in marginal electorates which stood to be detrimentally affected by the domestic satellite but had never embarked on anything so far ranging.

The catch phrase of an educative, political, public and industrial campaign was adopted. Although many debates centred around when and how to use industrial action, many ATEA members and officials expected the political campaign to be easier. Both the ATEA and APTU are affiliated with the Australian Labor Party and expected political support for their crusade. But when at the beginning of 1982 they read the submission that Senator John Button, the ALP's shadow minister for communications, had given to the Davidson committee, they realized it would be an uphill battle.

Button's submission, far from re-stating a commitment to a public monopoly telecommunications network, had accepted the concept of competition. On 25 February 1982, George Slater, the general secretary and treasurer of the APTU, dashed off a furious telex to Button, accusing him of contradicting ALP policy. The ten-paragraph criticism was littered with words like, 'grave concern', 'absolutely contrary', 'amazed', 'serious situation'. It read in part:

In our view you should immediately withdraw your submission as the general line you are advocating would have a very demoralising effect on the Telecom workforce as a whole who are currently facing, and experiencing, the savage effects of the Razor Gang proposals. If your submission stands there will be no other alternative open but for the union to attack it in the strongest terms in public hearings of the inquiry. Quite frankly, if this report is the best that you can do you should turn the game up. Your submission ignores the absolutely basic right of all Telecom employees to their jobs.

As we understand the party platform, the rights of workers to a safe and secure job at a reasonable living wage is paramount. Yet you are recommending procedures which would lead to the loss of thousands of jobs of APTU and ATEA members.

I personally think it is tragic that a Labor Shadow Minister should support the dismantling of a vital and important asset owned by the Australian people. This is in total opposition to what the Labor Party stands for, and if you want to take that line, then you should sit on the other side of the Senate.

George Slater was, for many years, a very powerful operator in the centre unity faction of the Victorian ALP, and at the time of his telex to Button, Button's preselection for the Victorian Senate ticket was under consideration. The left in Victoria had no love for Button, and the combination of factions could have meant that the leader of the opposition in the Senate lost his preselection. He did not, but he did prepare a supplementary submission to the Davidson inquiry. Three-and-a-half pages long, the letter placed a condition of upholding the national interest and of requiring any competitor to offer a complete national service.

The dissatisfaction with Button was not kept exclusively between him and the unions. When the Queensland branch of the ATEA saw the submission, it wrote to every member of the federal ALP caucus demanding Button's resignation from the shadow ministry. Button then attended a meeting of the Queensland branch council, at which he put his case and listened to the position of the ATEA. The previous lack of consultation had been one of the things which infuriated George Slater. In his telex he wrote:

We are amazed that you did not see fit to take the time or the trouble to meet with the Telecom unions to discuss the nature of your submissions so that an opportunity would have been available to study a draft copy and thus avoid the serious situation which has now arisen.

After he spoke to the Queensland branches, Button asked the state secretary, Ian McLean, to write to the caucus secretary, indicating that the differences had been patched up. McLean wrote saying that they now 'understood' each other's position better and 'appreciated' the visit. Trust and confidence were still lacking.

The rocky relationship with Button continued into the year.

Although the unions were confident of the support of the former ALP leader, Bill Hayden, and the caucus, they felt that if Button became the minister they would 'have to knock on his door every ten minutes; I'd want to be bloody close to him', said Ian McLean. At the ALP's federal conference in June 1982, policy statements were debated and determined. Some months earlier, the Telecom unions had drafted a proposed communications policy, but the policy proposed by Button was a watered-down version of the original. An amendment to bring it back to the original was proposed and shown to Button, who was initially reluctant to accept it. 'Don't you trust me mate?' he asked one delegate. Evidently the delegates did not, and half an hour before the policy was to be debated, Button was told that he no longer had 'the numbers' to get his proposal up, if it went to a vote. Ever the consummate politician, Button then moved the amendment himself, and the ALP was committed to a publicly owned single telecommunications authority.

Chapter Ten
Banging the Drum

In journalism, a phone call from a public relations company to invite one to lunch is not unusual. It means that the company has a client who wishes to have a story placed in a newspaper or magazine or on radio or television. The polite fiction of a personal chat and lunch is maintained as the public relations people pitch their story and the journalist weighs it up. Seldom do these briefings prove a source of direct quotes, and it is rare for major stories to emerge from such lunch table meetings. It is only when there is a degree of urgency about the luncheon invitation that the journalist can assume that a good story may be involved. That urgency occurs far too seldom in most journalists' working lives.

A phone call early in 1982 from a Sydney public relations man called Ian Nicholas, who ran a company called Concise Communications, requested a lunch time appointment as soon as possible. Nicholas was retained by Business Telecommunications Services Pty Ltd (BTS), which represented a group of companies established to challenge Telecom's monopoly in Australia. Since its formation in 1980, it had generated great publicity in its demands for changes to the Australian telecommunications system to allow private companies to compete with Telecom. But it was not so much a formal announcement that Nicholas sought to promote over lunch. He had a tale straight from the pages of a spy novel. The previous weekend, the offices of BTS in Castlereagh Street, Sydney, were burgled. Two alarms had been put out of action, and it appeared that only the BTS offices on the seventh floor of Medibank House had been broken into. A small amount of

179

petty cash was missing, but more significantly from Nicholas's point of view, it appeared that one and possibly two copies of the company's submission to the Davidson inquiry were missing. None of the submissions was public knowledge because their release had still not been authorized by the committee investigating Australian telecommunications.

Who could possibly have stolen such pedestrian material as a submission to a government inquiry? Nicholas did not proffer a list of suspects, although the conclusion one was invited to draw focused attention on the ATEA. One could scarcely envisage the solid citizens of Telecom senior management organizing so audacious a raid. On closer questioning, however, there appeared to be doubts about the number of copies taken or, indeed if one had 'slipped down behind a filing cabinet', in Nicholas's words. A report had evidently been made to the police, who regarded it all as a professional job, no matter what the motive. As a story, there were too many doubts to justify going to print. That was also the opinion of a fellow journalist on the *Australian Financial Review*, who was offered the story but decided it would not stand up to the scrutiny of the lawyers.

That such a luncheon conversation could take place indicated that life in the telecommunications industry had moved into hitherto unexplored territory. BTS's appearance on the Australian scene in September 1980 changed the rules of the game, not only in the public relations tactics it employed but also in the level and credibility of information it dispersed about communications. From the outset, when BTS declared itself a research organization, it represented its constituent companies in a fashion foreign to Australian business. It relied heavily on its high-public profile and its ability to package complex issues into slick, US-style slogans about the efficacy of concepts such as competition. In general, it had an uncritical press, helped by the lack of specialized knowledge about telecommunications among journalists who attended the many BTS press conferences. The company also maintained an oblique attack on Telecom, claiming to represent the public face of an upsurge of dissatisfaction among Australian business telecommunications users. BTS represented itself as the forerunner of a new wave in communications. The words it used to announce its existence made that clear: 'The emergence of BTS shows the increasing significance of telecommunications to business as the much-reported communications revolution gathers momentum.'

The press release which signalled BTS's formation was signed by Peter Holmes a'Court, a name which caused some confusion in business circles because of the activities of a Perth-based entrepreneur with the same surname. Peter Holmes a'Court, however, had been known in some of Australia's largest companies, first selling computers for IBM Australia Ltd and later as a member of its board. He was variously reported to have resigned from the IBM board, where he was director of corporate relations, or to have taken leave of absence. His new title was general manager of BTS, of which his former company was a member. The members of the BTS consortium were collectively powerful enough to direct a substantial section of the Australian economy. As they scanned the list of large companies which were members of BTS, senior executives of Telecom saw for the first time how serious were the intentions of big business. The group's members included some of Telecom's largest customers and one of its major suppliers. BTS's early participants were joined by others, to make up one of the most formidable collection of companies in Australia.

The list was headed by Amalgamated Wireless (Australasia) Ltd (AWA), one of the two largest suppliers of telecommunications equipment to Telecom and the only one which was based in Australia. It ran a diversified empire which embraced radio and television broadcasting, micro-electronics and components, data processing and office equipment. Its mainstay was telecommunications and, with the ITT subsidiary in Australia, Standard Telephones and Cables, it was the largest supplier of telephone handsets to Telecom. The largest of the Australian-owned petroleum suppliers, Ampol Petroleum Limited, was also announced as a member of BTS. Although not directly involved in the communications industry, Ampol was a large user of Telecom facilities. Australian Consolidated Industries Limited (ACI) was also a large communications user, as the manufacturer of containers, glassware and other products. ACI ran a commercial data processing bureau and the Ausinet information retrieval network, both of which required use of Telecom-leased lines for data transmission. As an example of a diversified user of a range of Telecom services, ACI was one of the best big business case studies available. Australian Mutual Provident Society (AMP), one of the country's largest insurance companies and institutional investors, was also a member. Its communications needs were typical of many large commercial companies, with large offices in each state and a network of branches throughout the continent.

The largest Australian company, Broken Hill Proprietary Company Ltd (BHP), was also a BTS member, and its presence, more than anything else, convinced Telecom that this was no mere research organization. The mining and resources giant, CRA Limited, was also a member, as was one of its competitors, CSR Limited. Some companies, such as AWA, were fully Australian owned, and others, such as CRA Limited, were subsidiaries of groups based in other countries. Some, such as IBM Australia Limited, were fully owned by their overseas principals. With a lower market share in computers in Australia than almost any other country in the western developed economies, IBM was nevertheless an influential company in Australian business. It had introduced many large Australian organizations to computing and, in some cases, the man who sold them the systems was Peter Holmes a'Court. James Hardie, another large and diversified Australian manufacturing company, was a big user of communications, as was the largest transport company, Thomas Nationwide Transport, a transnational in its own right.

The final two members of BTS were Kerry Packer's Publishing and Broadcasting Limited and the Myer Emporium Limited. The Packer organization had been responsible for reopening discussions about an Australian satellite which led to the establishment of Aussat Pty Ltd. In its submission to the inquiries held by the government into satellite communications, Publishing and Broadcasting had also revealed an interest in telecommunications. Myer was the large and relatively staid Melbourne-based retailer which had entered communications as a spin-off of its normal operations. It had one of the largest computer centres in Australia and a leased-line network which transferred sales and stock details from its many stores back to corporate headquarters. The company had formed a division to explore information technology and, using a Canadian system, was planning a videotex service it called Videonet.

Each of the dozen partners put up initially $100,000 to finance BTS's operations and, later, requests for further funds were made. In the two years from September 1980, BTS was estimated to have spent more than $2 million of its shareholders' funds. In public, it called itself a research company. In practice, it was organized as a lobbying group which was designed to influence and persuade the Australian business community that the time had come for Telecom's monopoly over telecommunications to end. For its staff, the company raided some of the institutions it sought to change. One early recruit was Ross Abbott, from commercial services at Telecom headquarters, a man who only months before had been arguing in the press that Telecom be allowed to pursue aggressive marketing policies in the sale of terminals. He was replying to criticism from terminal suppliers' trade associations that Telecom sought to dominate the market. Abbott took a back-seat role in BTS's public relations activities. His defection aroused hostility from former Telecom colleagues. One Telecom executive was still saying privately that Abbott would never be re-employed by the organization, two years after he had left. BTS's interest was less in terminals than in networks, particularly along the model provided by SBS in the US.

Not all the executives hired by BTS stayed with the company. Its first operations director resigned in early 1981. His replacement was a consultant then working with the British-based PA Consultants, Ted Sandeman, who took up his post in April 1981 but had departed by July 1982. The reason for his resignation was a serious disagreement with Holmes a'Court about the viability of a competitive common carrier to Telecom. Sandeman maintained that the best business option for BTS was to establish itself as a carrier which competed on major inter-city routes but which did not attempt to provide a national service. The competitive option was an SBS-style system which offered a complete communications service to large organizations, allowing them to use satellites to transmit in bulk both voice and data. It was an important argument, because the difference between the two options was crucial to at least some BTS members. The carrier question was BTS's major motive for pressing for the Davidson inquiry into telecommunications, a fact which was to emerge later. Sandeman's opinion was that Australia was not ready for an SBS system and the market was, in any case, not big enough. Studies of Australian communications demand showed that the SBS option was not viable, according to Sandeman. He backed a different US model, offered by the Bell System's primary microwave competitor, MCI. It competed on selective inter-city routes and had become a company with a turnover of $1 thousand million within a decade of being formed in the early 1970s.

Apart from Holmes a'Court, who was an assiduous public promoter of BTS's cause, the two most prominent executives were Bob Jones, who was called director of public relations, and Neil Tuckwell, called director of finance. Jones described himself as a union man to the hardened industrial disputants of the ATEA, based on his experience with what is known as a 'house union'. Jones was seconded to BTS from his usual employer, AMP. He had taken an active role in AMP's house union some years earlier. Unions not affiliated to the Australian Council of Trade Unions are rare enough, but house unions do not operate independently from their employers, and there is no record of them going on strike. Behind Jones's back, the Telecom unions joked about having a comrade in the ranks of BTS. Jones's colleague Tuckwell played the role of cool front man for BTS. Tuckwell was impressively qualified. He had a master's degree in economics and a diploma of financial management; and he had worked with Bell Canada and the International Wool Secretariat until he joined OTC and rose to become director of planning. He used a vocabulary which exactly mirrored the language used in BTS's submission to the Davidson inquiry. Tuckwell led the BTS evidence at the committee's public hearings, while Holmes a'Court sat beside him, making only occasional contributions.

It was Tuckwell who was the main author of the BTS submission to Davidson, although Holmes a'Court conducted many media interviews and made most of the set speeches. Holmes a'Court occasionally slipped into an evangelical style at press conferences as he pressed home BTS's message. He was, confessed Bob Jones to the authors at a cocktail party, frankly ideological in his attitude to telecommunications. Of the nationalized sectors of the Australian economy, only telecommunications offered significant return on investment. Hence, ran Holmes a'Court's logic, it should be transferred to the private sector, the proper repository for profitable activity. Jones said Holmes a'Court had a sense of mission about rolling back nationalization and public ownership in telecommunications. Holmes a'Court saw the unions, and not Telecom management, as the major obstacle to achieving that aim, according to Jones.

Face to face with the Telecom unions and the organization's senior management, the BTS executives sought common ground. They played down differences and declared that little separated the BTS attitude from Telecom, a view shared neither by senior Telecom management nor the unions. Senior Telecom managers said it was simply wrong for BTS to claim consensus when it did not exist. They were under no illusions that the longer term aims of the consortium conflicted with the notion of a publicly owned telecommunications monopoly.

While BTS waited for the decision of the Lynch Razor Gang to set up an inquiry into telecommunications, it watched anxiously over a separate investigation into the terminal market conducted by Malcolm King. A member of the Davidson committee, which was announced before he had completed his inquiry, King had been deputy general manager of CSR Limited, a BTS consortium partner. BTS argued that the real inquiry needed to be conducted into Telecom's network monopoly, not just the equipment which was allowed to attach to its network. BTS's own preparatory work for Davidson included a survey of telecommunications needs and attitudes among major business users of telecommunications and an investigation of the requirements of their own members.

For $100,000 a head, the companies which joined BTS were assured of an analysis of their communications. For some of them, it was the first detailed examination by an outside organization of the efficiency of one of their largest operating costs. On the basis of the work done by BTS, some of its members were claimed to have saved large sums through more efficient use of the communications facilities available to them. In return, BTS was receiving useful information to enable it to reach a decision about its future direction. By acting as adviser and consultant to its member companies, it was collecting, at their cost, information which was sought by telecommunications carriers around the world. The marketing division of AT&T, for example, had devised a whole strategy to collect the information that BTS was gathering.

The marketing strategies of AT&T since the mid 1970s have been guided by former IBM executives who introduced a sales approach devised by their ex-employers. IBM's tactic in selling its large mainframe computers was based on convincing top management in target companies of the need to buy IBM, encouraging them to take corporate decisions, rather than to leave purchasing to middle managers. Once IBM was adopted as the company's computer supplier, expanding the range of products sold to corporate clients entrenched the IBM presence. Companies found themselves committed to using IBM equipment to such an extent that a whole secondary industry arose as new companies sold equipment which worked with IBM computers. These suppliers accepted the decision of many companies to buy IBM and simply sold computers and terminals which could work with the equipment which was already installed. So successful was the IBM approach that the new company formed after the divestiture of AT&T's local operating companies in January

1982 adopted the same strategy. American Bell, as the company was called when its formation was announced in June that year, promoted itself as an organization involved not in telecommunications but in the 'knowledge business'.

American Bell aimed to approach the 500 or so largest US corporations with the suggestion that their communications needs and expenditure warranted examination. The best way to do this, it was suggested, was to invite Bell to sit in on meetings and to get to know the company from the inside. This was an extension of a marketing technique that AT&T has used for some years with large corporate customers. At its most effective, this involved Bell's placing one of its staff within the client company to oversee communications. His salary and expenses were paid by Bell, but for most other purposes, he was regarded as a senior executive in the organization in which he operated. The aim of creating this insider's view was to investigate information flows, identify bottlenecks and suggest organizational and technological solutions. It depended for its success on the quality of information acquired in the process.

The resemblance to BTS's tack in Australia is clear, but its antecedents came from within IBM, not from AT&T. Although it is true that the member companies of the consortium were given advice about their communications, the benefits for BTS were incalculable. If an organization had set itself to gather the relevant market data to establish what sort of telecommunications alternatives to Telecom were economically viable, no more effective mechanism could have been devised.

The information led to BTS shelving for the time being its objective to re-create the SBS satellite model in Australia and instead to concentrate on the possibility of a competitive long-distance carrier, such as MCI in the United States. A mistake in choosing between those options would have cost many millions of dollars.

The BTS submission to the Davidson inquiry was couched in the language employed by IBM. One had to read carefully to unpack the implications of phrases which on first reading appeared bland and unexceptional. The recommendations actually amounted to a radical demand for the dismantling of Australian telecommunications. Its underpinning assumptions and arguments were taken from a particular interpretation of events in North America.

A distinction which had currency in US discussions about deregulation of telecommunications was between 'basic and enhanced services', a phrase used by the Federal Communications Commission in its 1980 decision, known as Computer 11. The commission sought to distinguish between services which had been the traditional province of telecommunications carriers and newer services more closely associated with the computer industry. The first group of activities should be regulated like telecommunications and the second should not be, like computing, asserted the commission. In a transplant of the distinction, BTS argued in its submission to the Davidson committee that Telecom Australia should have its monopoly confined to basic services, consisting of the carriage of voice traffic. Telecom's monopoly should be retained over local and trunk traffic, provision of telegrams and public telephones, in 'kerbside' locations, and installation of the first cable into customer's premises. The same division of function was also urged on OTC, although the Davidson committee had excluded it from investigation. BTS's determination to disregard that restriction sprang from its recognition that access was required to international communications links and not just to the local network. In attempting to open up an area already ruled out of court by the committee, BTS pursued the interests of international corporations in deregulating gateway points in and out of countries.

BTS urged that enhanced services, all those additional to the list of basic facilities marked down for the Telecom monopoly, should be open to competition. Data services, telex, electronic mail, message switching, store and forward voice facilities, videotex, information retrieval, electronic funds transfer – all the high growth areas of communications – should be open to private suppliers. And Telecom should not have monopoly over any segment of the terminal market, so that private companies could compete. The range of terminals embraced the domestic telephone handset, premium telephones with added features, such as memory dialling and automatic recall. But it also included newer generation electronic PABXs, facsimile machines, telephone answering units and a whole range of devices used for entering data, right up to micro- and mini-computers. Telecom should not be excluded from providing enhanced services and terminals, but it should compete on what the private sector regarded as equal terms. BTS suggested that a subsidiary, providing more than basic services, should be called Telecom Enhanced.

The term it used to describe the subsidiary, 'arm's length subsidiary', was borrowed from the same Federal Communications Commission's decision, which was the source of the basic and enhanced distinction. The reason for those terms in the United States environment was the commission's insistence that AT&T establish a separate subsidiary to market enhanced services and terminals. The subsidiary came to be referred to as Baby Bell. It would compete against other companies offering similar services, most notably IBM. Whatever the merits of the distinctions in the United States, there was, before the formation of BTS, virtually no demand for a similar separation in Australia. And what BTS was suggesting was no more than IBM and other anti-Bell forces had pressed for in the United States.

The value of the basic network to corporate users, however, was its ability to connect them to millions of other points across the country. No private investor would be willing to make the investment required to provide that network which, in Australia, had a capital worth of more than $8.5 thousand million in 1982. According to BTS, the network should be available for lease or sale to private communications carriers. Telecom, and OTC for that matter, should become what are referred to in the United States as 'carriers' carriers', providing facilities with which competitors could come in and construct their own networks. The Australian satellite system, which some years earlier IBM had suggested should be run by a consortium of private interests, including IBM, was treated similarly. Aussat should provide satellite circuits which could be sold or leased by private carriers. The emphasis on a particular interpretation of US telecommunications developments dictated BTS's version of events in the rest of the world. Canada, for example, was depicted by BTS as a country in a fervour of deregulation. In fact, the decisions of its regulatory body, the Canadian Radio and Television Commission, on liberalization had to be balanced against a strengthening of its intervention in other areas. Similarly, an administrative committee decision in Japan, which mooted deregulation, had to be weighed against fierce opposition encountered by Japanese suppliers in the United States. Decisions such as US federal government directions that Japanese companies be passed over for telecommunications contracts they had won in open competition with US suppliers will be reflected in Japanese decisions on deregulation. The Japanese recognize that the beneficiaries of US-style deregulation of telecommunications are large US-based companies, not indigenous common carriers and suppliers. It was overly optimistic for the supporters of deregulation to posit Japan as an open, competitive market, in either network services of terminals.

One of the main claims of BTS was that the Telecom monopoly in Australia had inhibited the introduction of new services and technologies. The charge depended for its force on a simplistic equation between innovation and efficiency in telecommunications. In fact, there was little evidence of delays which disadvantaged users to a serious degree. There was, however, evidence that Telecom's cautious attitude to the introduction of new technology was the correct policy. The secret of success in telecommunications was more often than not in the selection of the appropriate technology, rather than simply the latest. Telecom's decision to delay the introduction of newer signalling systems for the network in order to wait for the pulse signalling system, which it uses, is one example of caution proving the best policy. In other areas, customer demand in the very much larger US market did not justify earlier introduction of services in Australia. An instance is the facility known as INWATS, or inward wide area calling, which allows companies to offer free phone calling to prospective customers.

In other areas where BTS claimed delays were causing difficulty to business users of telecommunications, such as Telecom installation of modems, the reality of regulatory changes was ignored. Before the Davidson committee had reported, Telecom began a progressive liberalization of the use of modems, the devices which allow computer traffic to be carried on telephone lines. As long as they met technical standards, modems could be installed by private companies in their own premises. Beginning with the cheaper modems, which allowed lower speed transmission of data, Telecom ceded the exclusive right of installation and supply and was progressively extending the policy to higher speed modems. Delays in providing leased lines had been reduced by Telecom within the previous two years, taking much of the force out of another BTS complaint. The question of delays in the provision of service also served to focus attention on how BTS might improve matters.

The most publicized areas of Telecom connection delays to domestic subscribers in the newer out-lying suburbs of the major cities would not be improved by the sort of solutions proffered by BTS. The competitive common carriers it had in mind would not be challenging Telecom's role in installing telephone handsets in less profitable areas, such as the outer suburbs. Similarly, delays in providing services to outback areas, another source of complaint against Telecom, would not be shortened by the intervention of private competitors. Those rural services were provided at a loss. The newcomers evinced litle interest in non-profit making activities. The word 'profit' did not appear in this context in the BTS submission to the Davidson inquiry. Services were termed 'commercial' where they had money-producing possibilities for private entrepreneurs. Where they did not, the word 'basic' was used.

By careful wording, the submission sometimes disguised its intentions. Trunk calling, for instance, was ceded to Telecom, despite business voice traffic between the major capital cities being a major revenue earner. But BTS said Telecom should have control over trunk traffic only on a 'call-by-call' basis, that is, for long-distance calls dialled up through the public network. This demarcation did not exclude independent network providers from offering voice facilities on trunk calls, for the traffic would be diverted from the public network and on to leased lines. Similarly, the cautiously phrased section on terminals provided for a break in the Telecom monopoly supply of telephone handsets, a suggestion later adopted by the Davidson committee. The resemblance between the report and the BTS submission also showed where the committee had gleaned some of its terms. BTS insisted in its submission that there should be 'non-discriminatory interconnection' by Telecom of the networks of other operators. Davidson used the same phrase, which was drawn, as were many others, directly from the US deregulatory discussion.

An appendix to the BTS submission canvassed the 'MCI option' for competing common carriers. MCI was the US company established to use microwave links in competition with the Bell System. It had moved into profit within four years of coming into operation and its initial float on the New York stock exchange had been swamped by investors. The internal disagreement within BTS which led to the departure of Ted Sandeman concerned the appropriateness of an MCI-type carrier in Australia. After insisting that the original strategy be followed, and an SBS system be the consortium's aim, Holmes a'Court had abandoned this more ambitious project, in the short term. Because of the restricted size of the Australian market, an MCI operation was now favoured, but only as an interim solution. At the first seminar to be held after the report was released, Malcolm King told an audience of business executives that the recommendation approving the establishment of independent networks had been misinterpreted. King said that the only networks the committee had in mind were specialized arrangements where Telecom could not provide a service, and he cited a microwave network used in Bass Strait by oil companies. That was far from the SBS option initially favoured by BTS.

In the weeks after the release of the Davidson report, BTS

confined itself to cryptic quotes welcoming it. Then its publicity machine went into operation, calling press conferences and dispatching representatives to a series of seminars and conferences held to evaluate the likely effect of the report. While welcoming the results, although offering mild criticisms of the recommendations, BTS nevertheless claimed its due share of the credit for the inquiry. Neil Tuckwell began an address to the first post-Davidson seminar in this way:

The very existence of BTS testifies to the mood for change in telecommunications in Australia. The recommendations of the Davidson inquiry indicate that the committee has also recognized the changes occurring in our society which require that telecommunications must be fundamentally restructured if we are to fully exploit opportunities now within sight.

Despite some reservations about it, the report constituted a 'blueprint for the future', Tuckwell said. The more immediate future for BTS was its own existence and Tuckwell was also tacitly addressing that question.

While the Davidson committee was sitting, defections from BTS reduced its number to five companies. Among the first to drop out was AWA, the only locally owned telecommunications company rivalling in size the international competitors operating in Australia. One of the few of those which pulled out of BTS to comment on its move, AWA said it perceived a conflict of interest between its role as a Telecom supplier and its participation in BTS. The others to defect were Ampol, BHP and its resources compatriots CRA and CSR Limited, James Hardie and Thomas Nationwide Transport. The remaining members' convergent interests revealed the shape of BTS as a prospective common carrier. True, members such as AMP had no record of high-technology involvement to compare with other consortium members such as IBM and Publishing and Broadcasting. But AMP had seconded Bob Jones to BTS, and it was a large communications user. ACI remained in the group, consistent with possible business opportunities through the expansion of its computer bureau network and its Ausinet information retrieval system. The remaining member was The Myer Emporium. Its information technology project, called Videonet, continued to operate, seeking commercial opportunities for videotex.

Some of the five companies which remained suffered downturns in business as the recession began to hit in late 1982. Myer, with a huge interest bill and a lack of success in disposing of some of its substantial property holdings, did not look the ambitious communications entrant it had appeared when BTS was formed. As a large manufacturer, ACI also suffered a drop in profit, reducing the chances of a major expansion requiring large capital investment in communications. The Packer organization's troubles were highlighted in November 1982 with the announcement that its publishing flagship, *The Australian Women's Weekly*, was to appear monthly. Its magazine division, Murray's, was also sold off to a suburban newspaper group owned jointly by Packer and Fairfax. Retrenchment of staff, including more than 400 printers at John Sands, which printed the *Weekly*, focused media attention on the group's financial standing. AMP looked healthy enough, but its participation in a communications project of the sort envisaged by BTS would involve a drastic change of corporate direction. At the centre of the group, the company which had started the ball rolling, IBM Australia, was in good shape. Under its belt it had the results of the most comprehensive large corporate investigation of telecommunications needs and a report from a government inquiry which eminently suited its ends.

BTS continued to represent itself as the agent of change. Tuckwell outlined the future for his audience at a seminar in late November. Supporting his contention that the Davidson report pointed the way in which communications would follow in Australia, he said:

Day by day, these forces are growing in strength. To reach any other conclusion than that far-reaching structural change is needed would seem to us to be absurd. It is necessary to build for the future, to position the industry so that it may take advantage of new opportunities and innovations as they occur, and to improve its efficiency.

Nowhere was there mention of what the commercial objectives of BTS were in all this. It was simply a research company, assessing investment opportunities for its participants. In fact, the BTS presence had dominated the debate. 'We speak for business', Tuckwell told another conference in November in Brisbane organized by the Telecom unions. BTS at that stage spoke for five large companies, one of which, IBM, was potentially the most formidable force in world communications outside AT&T. The claim to be speaking on behalf of a wider, but silent group of interests peppered BTS announcements. Tuckwell again:

What all of us must acknowledge – and must bring others to acknowledge – is that the present arrangements have become inappropriate. That does not, and should not, mean that Telecom has been negligent in its responsibilities. It simply recognizes that there are forces at work which are driving us inexorably down the road to change.

The 'forces' could be clearly identified by the alert observer of BTS's campaign.

In selling its message to the business community and politicians, BTS adopted tactics which were unfamiliar in Australian public debate. It adopted a technique of holding separate press conferences for different sections of the media. To one session would be invited the daily papers and radio and television. To another, the trade, business and technical press would be invited. The sole aim of duplicating the significant expense involved in holding a series of press conferences appeared to be to avoid the more informed and aggressive questioning to which BTS representatives were subject from the business and trade press. Its message was easier to sell to the reporters from television and tabloids, who had neither the time nor the expertise to master the real issues at stake behind BTS's pronouncements. The BTS approach sometimes also involved failing to invite to press conferences journalists who would interfere with the message they intended to convey.

In other areas, BTS applied pressure tactics in its dealings. The British consulting company, Logica Pty Ltd, which had conducted research for BTS, undertook a project for the main Telecom union, the ATEA, which showed that there would be a significant siphoning off of revenue from Telecom trunk routes if private competition were permitted. As part of the BTS position had been that no significant revenues would be lost to Telecom from competition, the Logica survey was damaging. Soon after the study was released, Holmes a'Court wrote to the managing director of Logica about the study undertaken for the union. In his letter he said that the publication of the study's conclusions in mid September 1982 had had an effect on public discussion:

They provide significant reinforcement of the line of argument that they [the ATEA] have adopted as a defence against what they identify as 'attacks' upon Telecom by private enterprise organizations.

It pointed out that BTS had been a client of Logica and it advocated the contrary position, adding:

We have developed considerable expertise in this field and the conclusions that we have reached are in strong conflict with those contained in your report. We have thoroughly reviewed the Logica study itself . . . and we find no reason to amend our conclusions. It is our belief that the report produced by your organisation contains fundamental flaws which substantially reduce its worth.

The brunt of BTS's demand was that Logica should disown its study for the ATEA in view of tariff changes which had been announced after the survey had been completed. Holmes a'Court said, in the least subtle of language:

We have no wish to embarrass you nor damage your company's reputation, however, you will appreciate that as the conclusions Logica have reached have been placed before the public in a highly politicised manner, as could have been expected, we have no option but to counter them in that forum.

A terse reply from Logica's managing director told Holmes a'Court:

Apart from the question of outdated tariffs, the residual asserted shortcomings appear either to derive directly from the terms of reference or to have a substantial subjective content.

Rather than letting the matter rest, BTS produced its own rebuttal, which it sent to the media with a covering letter. It said in part:

BTS believes that there are serious flaws in the assumptions underlying the study and we have discussed these at length with Logica, who now fully appreciate why our conclusions differ so significantly from theirs.

According to the man who conducted the Logica study, Peter Saalmans, there was no such implied agreement to accept the BTS view of the report; quite the contrary.

The approach adopted by BTS also annoyed the senior executives of Telecom, for whom the world of media and public relations promotion was unfamiliar territory. Telecom's director of business development, Roger Banks, who headed the commission's task force for the Davidson inquiry, and led the writing of its submission and response, gave this assessment of BTS's role:

What disturbs me about interest groups and pressure groups lobbying, quite apart from the techniques used, is that they have shrouded their true motivation in a rationale which is less than candid. The rationale has been purely and simply to get into lucrative areas of communications for private benefit, at the expense of the entire nation. Telecom is merely a reflection of the way the nation mobilizes its resources to deliver telecommunications to itself. The only way to proceed in a balanced way was to give one organization responsibility for building the infrastructure, so that the profits could fund the loss areas. The pricing structures reflect the need to deliver to Alice Springs, and the Top End and wherever else. If you put in a system to deliver to Sydney, Melbourne and Canberra, it would cost a lot less and make a handsome profit. But this would create no new wealth, just siphon to others the profits and leave the nation to make good the difference from somewhere else.

These lobby groups have advanced plausible, but misleading arguments. Even in the light of what has happened in the US, it is bordering on mischievous. They say they only want special or data services, that is using a sprat to catch a mackerel, trading on the gullibility, naivety and innocence of the Australian people to make a fast buck. SBS started the same way in the US, but found you can't make money out of data, so they got the right kind of permissions and found out they can't make a buck. Then when the political commitment is beyond the point of no return, the government has to give them permission to open up telephone services. But they knew before they started that this is what they would do.

Having completed its response to the Davidson report, two more defections from BTS occurred in January 1983. IBM Australia Limited, employer of Peter Holmes a'Court, and AMP, Bob Jones's boss, withdrew, wishing luck to the three survivors, ACI, Myer and Publishing and Broadcasting. The lobby group's job was done. It was time for an Australian version of MCI to emerge.

Chapter Eleven
Davidson Reports

Jim Davidson, a sharp-faced man with thick spectacles dressed in the dark grey suits of old-style Australian business, became the central figure in Australian telecommunications from September 1981. Whenever the future of Telecom was raised, it was the figure of Davidson which hung over the discussion. He became the embodiment of the threat and the promise. The unions regarded him with the same mixture of dislike and discomfort as they would a member of the Fraser cabinet. For Telecom management, he was the arbitrator; albeit one they feared from the outset. In the telecommunications industry boardrooms, he was the agent of change. If he got it right, they would applaud him, perhaps in public, but more importantly in the private circles in which politicians mix. If he got it wrong, the knives were already sharpened.

How did Davidson come to shrug off the relative obscurity of chairman of Commonwealth Industrial Gases, a large but unglamorous manufacturing company, to enter the public arena of the government's inquiry into telecommunications? Davidson, the most reticent of men, offered no explanation. He gave no press interviews and sent out one standard press photograph of himself looking suitably respectable and alert. Not until the day before it was tabled in Parliament did the report's content leak, and then not through Davidson. In a country where even details of the federal budget leak, it was a comment on Davidson's caution and reticence.

In the public hearings of the committee he chaired, Davidson exuded purposefulness, asked no unnecessary questions, and became involved in no unseemly differences of opinion.

Occasionally, he diverted or silenced his more long-winded colleagues. Davidson sat centre stage, with the other members of the inquiry arranged to left and right. From the outset, those who appeared before the committee had no doubts that it was Davidson they were talking to.

He and his fellows, assisted by a small secretariat and research staff, were charged with examining the prospects for turning telecommunications in Australia away from the principles written into its charter only six years before. The announcement by the government that a committee of inquiry would be established to examine Telecom was made as part of the report of the review of commonwealth services carried out by a cabinet committee. Through its chairmanship by Sir Phillip Lynch, the federal minister for commerce and industry, it became known as the Lynch committee. And then, as its intentions became clear, it was dubbed by the press, Lynch's Razor Gang. The tag stuck.

If Telecom management was interested in omens, Lynch provided one. In addition to recommending that a committee of inquiry be set up into Telecom, Lynch insisted on an immediate cut in its staff of 2,000 despite the numbers employed by Telecom remaining static since 1975. In the meantime, the volume of its business increased enormously. Although there was little public evidence from Telecom management that they recognized it, this was to be a very different inquiry from the one chaired by Sir James Vernon.

Telecom's management only had to put the terms of reference of the two inquiries side by side to detect the change in tone and intent. Vernon's letters patent began with the formal preamble required for royal commissions and then asked him to examine:

In the public interest, what changes, if any, should be made in the organisation, administration and operations of postal and telecommunications services (including overseas services) provided in Australia, including inter alia, changes in relation to . . .

Vernon's terms of reference went on to list the matters it was asked to investigate. They included the range of services which should be offered to the public; finance, management and staff relations: the role of OTC; urban and regional development; Australian industry; and the place of contract work.

Although some of those headings were later taken by the Davidson inquiry as reference points on which to structure its report, the terms of reference differed sharply from Vernon's.

The preamble of Davidson's terms of reference read:

Having regard to the continuing need to provide adequate telecommunications services throughout Australia as efficiently and economically as possible and the significant technological advances which are now occurring in the telecommunications field both in Australia and overseas, the committee is requested to examine and report to the minister for communications on ...

At this point, the terms diverge widely from Vernon and must be read with an understanding of their genesis in the recommendations of the Lynch Razor Gang.

The committee was asked to report on:

(a) the extent to which the private sector could be more widely involved in the provision of existing or proposed telecommunications services in Australia either alone, in competition with or in conjunction with the Australian Telecommunications Commission; (b) what consequential changes may be necessary in the statutory functions, duties, financial objectives and monopoly provisions of the Commission; and (c) the effectiveness of the Commission's operational policies and organisational arrangements.

About the only organizations involved in telecommunications which were free to say that the terms were biased, loaded and politically motivated were the trade unions, and they did. Although the same conclusion was reached by some senior Telecom managers, they offered no hint of protest. From the outset, it was clear they would play by the rules set by the government, no matter how dubious they regarded them.

The primary objection to the terms of reference was to their assumption that there was a role for private-sector participation in telecommunications. 'The extent to which the private sector could be more closely involved . . .' brooked little argument about whether telecommunications should be a public-sector activity. It would take an independently minded and determined committee to interpret the question of public/private-sector participation in all its permutations. The government's selection of committee members appeared to militate against that.

Davidson was virtually unknown outside senior Australian business circles, although federal government ministers were certainly aware of his existence. Ian Sinclair, the minister of communications who established the inquiry, opened a new CIG plant in the New South Wales town of Tamworth in mid 1981, before the Davidson inquiry was set up. That would have been an event which passed unnoticed as one of the minister's normal duties, for Tamworth was part of his electorate, had it not been for Sinclair's speech. He used the opening of the plant to put forward the possibility of Telecom using contracted labour for its capital works programmes. When Telecom was contacted by the press for comment on the minister's proposal, it was compelled to reply that it was the first the commission had heard of it. Davidson was certainly aware of the government's views on the future of Telecom before he was appointed to head the inquiry.

Of Davidson's fellow committee members, Malcolm King had most claim to seniority based on business experience. In appearance, he and Davidson could have been taken for brothers. They are both from the old school of Australian business and King, recently retired as deputy general manager of one of the largest Australian companies, CSR Ltd, sat shoulder to shoulder with his chairman throughout the public hearings. King's claim to membership of the committee was at least direct. He had been conducting an inquiry of his own into the terminal equipment market when the government announced it would be superseded by Davidson.

King had not been given the chance to publish his report on terminals, but the Telecom staff he came in contact with certainly thought that he was in favour of private-sector competition. There had also been informal discussions about how

Telecom could compete, through an 'arm's length subsidiary' which prevented it subsidizing its marketing efforts with profits from the network. King's former connection with CSR was clearly not regarded by the government as an impediment either to his own inquiry or to his membership of the Davidson committee. Yet one of the members of the BTS consortium was CSR. King proved a loyal lieutenant to Davidson, siding with him in the committee's only major disagreement, whether Telecom's terminal company was to be a subsidiary or fully separated.

The least known member of the committee was W. A. Dick, accountant and chairman of Pacific Carpets. Dick had no previous connection with telecommunications but proved an enthusiastic questioner in public hearings, not always incurring the pleasure of his chairman.

Tony Karbowiak, a professor of communications in electrical engineering at the University of New South Wales and the fourth member of the committee, had a background in telecommunications. In addition to his academic work, he had acted as a consultant for Telecom on some important projects. The one which brought him some public attention was when he was asked to evaluate the trial maintenance arrangements adopted by Telecom and its technicians' union as part of the settlement of their 1978 new-technology dispute. Karbowiak produced a document which declined to be bound by the either/or alternatives posed by the joint trial. Instead, he emphasized the virtues of group working, which was opposed by the union.

There were signs that the roles of Karbowiak and Dick in compiling the final report were less important than those of Davidson and King. In the final few weeks before the report was expected to be completed, Karbowiak was listed as a speaker at a conference on telecommunications held at Sydney's Wentworth Hotel. It was apparent that in the crucial final stages not all the members of the committee were involved. Even some members of the servicing secretariat of the inquiry found themselves excluded from the process of putting the report together. One member of the secretariat who was not shut out was Helen Vallier, a former staff member of Tony Staley's when he was minister of post and telecommunications. Vallier had left Staley's staff to work for Australian Associated Press, the news agency which was the co-ordinating body for BTS's rival lobby group, based on the Fairfax and Herald and Weekly Times groups. She was influential in forming the group's policy on telecommunications technology. Her value to the committee was recognized. At the beginning of August 1982, she was promoted from her post of senior policy analyst to the Davidson inquiry, to the position of assistant secretary.

The committee was given just a year by Ian Sinclair to make its report, requiring it to call for submissions by mid December 1981. To those parties who protested at the timetable, principally the unions, Peter Holmes a'Court, general manager of BTS, said that everybody had expected the inquiry so complaints about the time allowed were ill founded. The unions responded that he might have had forewarning, but they had not been so privileged.

The total number of submissions received by the committee has not been revealed. It heard 143 'public' submissions but also accepted a number of submissions it classified as confidential. The identities of those who submitted them, let alone their content, was not made public by the committee. The inquiry also refused to divulge with whom it held private discussions, which were again classified as confidential. This led the ATEA to declare that it was a secret inquiry. Public hearings were held in some capital cities, principally in Sydney and Melbourne, and in some country centres in New South Wales and the Northern Territory. Although reported by the media, the hearings were seldom given more than cursory press treatment.

The three key submissions came from Telecom, BTS and the unions, and the other 140 contributions could be measured against them. In their appearances before the committee, the three main contestants offered contrasting styles. Telecom and the ATEA presented the same line-up they would wheel out for a major industrial confrontation. It was a rare sight to see Bill Pollock, Jim Smith and Roger Banks lined shoulder to shoulder with their colleagues. The ATEA similarly presented Bill Mansfield, the federal president, Col Cooper, and the deputy general secretary, Mick Musemici, and the union's research staff. BTS's presentation was not headed as expected by the general manager, Peter Holmes a'Court, but by Neil Tuckwell, the company's finance director and a former executive of OTC. Tuckwell played the role of opening BTS's submission, taking almost all the committee's questions, with Holmes a'Court adding comments from his side. The audience for BTS's appearance contained many senior figures in the Australian telecommunications industry, including Alan Deegan, head of Standard Telephones and Cables and Bruce Goddard, chief of Plessey.

All three parties made weighty submissions and had sessions of more than an hour before the committee. But it was in the committee's confidential hearings that the real interrogation took place, at least for BTS, Telecom and some others. The ATEA was not accorded the privilege of a private hearing. On ten central points before the inquiry, the three had different views, which contrasted in varying degrees with the content of the committee's report.

The existence of the cross-subsidy Telecom operated between its profitable and loss-making activities received close attention from the three key submissions. Telecom argued that it ought to be maintained, estimating that profits from areas such as trunk routes provided a cross-subsidy of $290 million a year, most of which was used to cushion country subscribers. BTS attempted to persuade the committee of its distinction between 'basic' and 'enhanced' services, described by the unions as distinguishing between services which made money and those which did not. BTS said the latter should remain with Telecom and the former should be put out to competition in the private sector. If any activity needed subsidizing, it should be done directly to the subscriber by the government. The ATEA urged that the cross-subsidy, far from being weakened, should be bolstered by Telecom. Its dilution, according to the union would lead to higher charges for country subscribers.

The question of common carrier competition, while addressed by most submissions, had about it an air of unreality. While the Davidson committee was supposedly deliberating the issues of carrier competition, Aussat Pty Ltd was announcing a satellite contract with Hughes Aircraft and earth station contracts with Mitsubishi. Aussat, the company established by the government to handle satellite communications, was inevitably going to become a competitor to Telecom for long-distance traffic as soon as its first spacecraft was launched in mid 1985. Telecom argued that there was no need for another carrier, pointing out that it already supplied 400,000 leased lines, 44,000 data services and 140,000 private lines. OTC was an independent carrier which connected to Telecom's network but did not compete for traffic. BTS promoted the view that the entry of a number of competitive common carriers would be reflected in prices for long-distance traffic. It sketched how those competitors would evolve, using Telecom leased lines first and then switching traffic to the domestic satellite. The ATEA disputed the claim that competition either stimulated market growth or brought down tariffs; the US experience showed that prices were set by the number one carrier and followed by its competitors.

On regulation, Telecom pointed out it was already responsible to some degree to five bodies, the departments of transport and communications, Aussat Pty Ltd, the Australian Broadcasting Tribunal and OTC. It wanted to retain control over tariffs and interconnection by other parties to the network, a suggestion directly opposed by BTS. The lobby group had made great play in public discussion about the alleged anomaly involved in Telecom's being both a supplier and regulator of terminals and services. Instead of Telecom approving terminals and licensing carriers, the function should be performed by the Department of Communications. BTS argued that Telecom's tariff-setting should be overseen by the Trade Practices Commission. The ATEA asked whether there was evidence that Telecom had abused its dual roles of approving terminals and determining tariffs. The union concluded that there were no grounds to support allegations of a conflict of interests. It was also concerned that the hiving off of technical standards to an outside body could lead to damage being caused to the network through the connection of faulty equipment.

Telecom had chaffed under restrictions on its ability to borrow on loan markets, particularly overseas, since the late 1970s. The Davidson inquiry gave it an opportunity to state its case in public – the only other protest it had made was a series of mild rebukes to the government in its annual reports. Internal financing of its capital spending programme exceeded 80 per cent when the use of superannuation funds was taken into account, but Telecom was obliged by its charter to provide only a minimum of 50 per cent from internal sources. In addition, the refusal of the government to allow it to use special leasing techniques meant that it had to find an extra $120 million from other sources. BTS was uncharacteristically quiet on these restrictions, which would be unacceptable to any private-sector company. Instead of recommending that Telecom be given a freer hand, BTS said only that as a government organization its borrowing policies were dictated by political priorities. The ATEA pointed out to the inquiry that a report into Telecom, prepared by the international consultants McKinsey, recommended that Telecom be given greater freedom to borrow. It in fact advocated a lift in capital spending. The union said that the companies which supplied Telecom with goods, equipment and services from the private sector were the losers as a result of those cut-backs.

Industrial relations, a relatively peaceful area of telecommunications until a national dispute between Telecom and the ATEA in 1978 over new technology, was high on the list for all three main parties. Telecom suggested that interference, exercised through the co-ordinating committee which transmitted government policy in disputes, meant that settlements were prolonged. It quoted figures to show that Telecom's average number of hours lost each year from disputes was much lower than the national average in the private sector. Telecom urged that restrictions imposed by adherence to Public Service Board service and conditions guidelines should be removed. BTS, which had used Telecom's highly publicized disputes in 1978 and 1980 as examples of the unreliability of a monopoly common carrier, had little to say about improving industrial relations. It had previously described its interest in disputes in terms of market strategy. One of its main selling points was that business communications users should have an alternative path for traffic during industrial disputes. The ATEA shared Telecom's dissatisfaction with the co-ordinating committee, which drew its members from the departments of communications and industrial relations. It urged that Telecom and the unions be permitted to negotiate settlements without government intervention.

The unique relationship between Telecom and the industry which supplies it was brought under closer scrutiny by submissions to the Davidson inquiry. Unlike any other major industry, electronics and telecommunications is crucially dependent on the purchasing policies of the government, whether through agents such as Telecom, or directly through the defence department. In the financial year 1981-82, Telecom had bought $570 million of telecommunications production from local industry, and Telecom argued that any competitor should not be permitted simply to import its equipment. According to BTS, preference for products with local content should not be exercised by Telecom. That was a matter for government policy – besides competition would allow Australian manufacturers to export their goods. The fact that six out of seven of the main suppliers were the subsidiaries of international companies, which manufactured in Australia directly as a result of Telecom policy, evaded BTS. The ATEA criticized the failure of local manufacturing to lead to Australian ownership of the companies involved. It also suggested that impetus be given to Telecom's research and development activities and that its workshops be expanded into the manufacturing area. In particular, an indigenous electronics manufacturing industry could only be established under Telecom's umbrella role as the major customer for goods produced locally.

All three submissions made comparisons between Telecom and telecommunications authorities or companies overseas, from which they drew different conclusions. Some differences between Australia and the rest of the world could be accounted for by size, as Telecom pointed out. Australia had only 2 per cent of the world's telephones, although it had a high penetration rate of fifty-three telephone services for every hundred in the population. The United States had 38 per cent of the world's telephone services alone, said Telecom, and urged the committee to beware of distortions in comparing the United States and Australia. The US experience in telecommunications was a preoccupation for BTS, and most of its arguments were drawn from the United States.

A BTS member, IBM Australia Limited, had a direct conduit for information about markets available to common carriers through the IBM-backed Satellite Business Systems. For two years SBS had argued its case before the Federal Communications Commission in the United States to be allowed to operate as an independent common carrier using satellites. The ATEA disagreed that direct comparisons could be drawn with the United States and dismissed the government-sponsored Beesley report in Britain as shallow and inaccurate. It steered the committee's attention towards Europe, where publicly owned telecommunications carriers had been strengthened. In many other countries, the pressure for deregulation was negligible said the union.

The role of the minister for communications became relevant because of the direct intervention which had occurred in Telecom's affairs since Tony Staley banned it from the under fifty-line PABX market in 1979. As diplomatically as it thought prudent, Telecom recalled the days when it existed as a government department, saying it was not subject then to the direct veto the minister could now exercise. No restriction was put on the size of Telecom contracts, for example, but the minister, since 1975, had been able to refuse to approve contracts greater than $500,000. This power was used in the PABX case and in preventing Telecom from establishing a public videotex service. Telecom's suggested ceiling on contracts which required ministerial approval was $10 million. Contrary to that view of a diminished role for the minister, BTS wanted greater ministerial powers, for example, to approve joint ventures between Telecom and the private sector. The ATEA position was that ministerial intervention in Telecom's affairs was contrary to the spirit of the charter which set it up as an independent commission. It cited as an example the announcement of Ian Sinclair's ministerial initiative on sub-contracting at the opening of the factory belonging to CIG in Tamworth.

The area on which Telecom was prepared to give most ground, the supply of terminal equipment on a competitive basis, was one in which there were sharp differences between management and its unions. In return for a PABX market in which it could compete freely, Telecom would concede private suppliers rights to operate in former closed markets, such as supplying government departments with PABXs. Telecom denied that it unduly restricted terminal attachments, saying it granted 1,000 permits each year and that the total of 7,000 approved attachments demonstrated its relaxed policy. According to BTS, if terminals were to be sold by Telecom, they should not be marketed by the existing organization but by a subsidiary. If that arrangement was not made, Telecom could subsidize its terminal activities with profits from the lucrative long-line routes. The ATEA's outright opposition to private suppliers intruding on Telecom areas was based not only on the potential loss of its members but also on the danger to the network of sub-standard terminal installation and maintenance. If the privately owned suppliers were to be allowed into markets occupied by Telecom, they should demonstrate an ability to provide service Australia-wide. Otherwise, the ATEA argued, they would concentrate simply on the profitable urban areas, leaving Telecom to pick up the country districts.

The missing party in all the inquiry's deliberations was the

OTC. It had been specifically excluded by the Davidson committee at the outset. Similarly, the position of Aussat, the satellite operator, was not regarded as central to the committee's investigations. Telecom maintained that the satellite may not be economic, as claimed by the government, for telecommunications in the outback area. It should not be allowed to lease transponders to potential common carriers or set up in business as one itself. OTC was not pardoned from the BTS split between 'basic' and 'enhanced' services, and it should also be split accordingly said the lobby group, at least maintaining its consistency. The ATEA's position on OTC harked back to the split vote on the Vernon commission in 1974 which resulted in overseas telecommunications remaining outside Telecom's control. Now was the time to roll that decision back it urged. It prescribed similar medicine for Aussat, saying it should be disbanded and the satellite brought into Telecom's operations.

In the face of these and competing voices, the Davidson committee was confronted with three choices. Either it could leave Telecom alone, it could recommend that telecommunications be handed over to the private sector, or it could opt for a solution which attempted to satisfy all parties. The third alternative was clearly the most difficult, for some of the desires of the major parties were contradictory. Even if there were a middle path which could, with care, have been taken by the committee, it would take time. And time was pressing on the inquiry's members because its chairman had undertaken to meet Ian Sinclair's deadline of twelve months from start to finish. In any case, the inquiry did not have the resources to search for a solution which would be acceptable to all parties. It had a small secretariat by the standards of recent Australian government inquiries with a budget of $600,000 compared, for example, to the $1.5 million for the Myers inquiry into technological change. The second alternative, leaving Telecom's monopoly position alone and accepting the argument that the national interest demanded a universal, cheap telephone service before private profit, was untenable. Only the most courageous interpretation of the inquiry's terms of reference would allow it the option of leaving well enough alone. The terms of reference determined that only the second and third alternatives were possible, failing the intervention of a determined and independently minded committee. So the committee opted for a thorough-going restructure of telecommunications, handing virtually every profit-making aspect of Telecom's activities to unspecified entrepreneurs. Telecom would be left to salvage what it could from the inquiry by back-door negotiation and attempts to steer the federal bureaucracy away from the most damaging recommendations. As for the unions, for all the notice the committee took of their submissions, they may as well not have bothered.

When the minister for communications, Neil Brown, handed down the report in Parliament in October, the reaction of the unions was immediate. Instead of Brown's announcement dominating the evening television news, it was the union's reaction which was the top story. Brown later accused them of a knee-jerk reaction to his announcement, but they had had three hours to study its recommendations before holding a press conference and it was enough to tell them what they needed to know. Bill Mansfield declared the report a disaster, and said that a three-week study of the report by the unions would not have resulted in a different assessment.

Davidson had produced a report of some complexity, organized in a haphazard fashion and containing 103 recommendations, some of them so ambiguous that one had to look for clues in the text for their meaning.

Telecom immediately set up a head office task force. The day after the report, it had produced a summary of the recommendations which was sent to its 90,000 employees. The reaction of Telecom management was wary and neutral. Roger Banks was appointed head of the task force, and twenty-four hours after the report had been tabled, he admitted wearily that there was a lot of work to be done. By the Friday afternoon after the report's release, he had not slept. He and other senior Telecom executives had been studying the report all night and producing their response to it. There were cautious words from BTS; it was not until a month later that the lobby group began to hold a series of what it called briefings for journalists. The group's representatives declined to answer the most popular question from the journalists: – what was BTS's future?

The report was in three volumes, but its recommendations were contained in thirteen chapters of volume one. Compared to the Vernon commission, Davidson had produced a report couched in often vague and sometimes laboured prose. Assumptions were adopted and not argued for, and factual support was sometimes thin and occasionally non-existent. The committee had begun its task by adopting a series of general principles which it then pursued in a straight line, no matter what the difficulties encountered.

Its first general principle was that in the organization of any economy, private sector was good and public sector was to be avoided. This led to a number of subsidiary principles, one of which asserted that where profits were to be gained in an area of economic activity, that area should be vacated by the public sector to allow private entrepreneurs to flourish. The converse principle also applied: if there was no money to make, the public sector should accept responsibility for the activity. The adoption of that primary principle and its two subsidiaries became the basis for a number of the committee's decisions. Telecom was to have exclusive rights to operate the local telephone network, where some telephone services returned profits and others losses, but the latter was out-weighed by the former. Because it was a non-profit, public-sector activity, the private-sector principles of competition did not apply.

As a result, a recommendation by the Australian Broadcasting Tribunal's cable television report, that telecommunications services be offered by carriers using Telecom's ducts, was rejected by Davidson. Competing in the non-profit areas was unrealistic, reasoned Davidson; there was no prospect of private companies participating without the promise of profit.

There were areas of Telecom's activities which were profitable, principally the provision of trunk routes and network services, and these were to be opened to competition.

Although Telecom made no net profit on providing terminals, including the standard handset, there were areas of that market which were profitable; PABXs were the prime example. Telecom managed to spread the profits and losses of its various activities by charging tariffs which were not always a direct reflection of cost. Davidson saw that if it was to disassemble the mix of services it must dismantle the cross-subsidy on which the whole structure was based. To do that the report insisted that prices for services should reflect their cost to Telecom. Where that resulted in severe anomalies, such as the price that country telephone subscribers were forced to pay, the solution was a direct subsidy. The government should make direct grants or allow tax rebates to compensate those disadvantaged by the destruction of Telecom's cross-subsidy arrangements.

As for the profitable areas, in particular the carriage of business voice, data, telex and facsimile traffic over long distances, Telecom would be just another competitor. The difference between Telecom and its rivals is that the telecommunications authority had a network. Davidson solved that by giving unrestricted access to the network to competitors using leased lines or constructing a network of their own. It was not quite unrestricted, ministerial approval would have to be given, but that was not seen as a problem by the potential competitors, and it had to be said their confidence was well founded in view of recent Australian telecommunications policy making. There were restrictions on what Telecom could carry on its own network. Services such as videotex, for instance, could not be cross-subsidized so that they could be provided in rural as well as metropolitan areas. Again, direct subsidy was proffered as the solution. Davidson's unpacking of the cross-subsidy, was selective; it did not suggest there should be competition for telephone services in the profitable middle-class suburban areas.

The fragmentation of Telecom was taken a step further with the recommendation to establish a private company which the committee dubbed 'Telequip'. It would compete in the profit-making areas of terminal equipment supply but without any of the benefits of size which being part of Telecom had given it. To allow private companies into the wiring of premises for telecommunications services, Telequip was relegated to the role of terminal supplier, with a capital structure which allowed it be handed completely to the private sector.

In short, the Davidson committee approached Telecom as if it were a business opportunity. Its approach was as calculated as that of any property developer who sub-divided, strata titled and priced parcels of land on a potential site. Where the developer walked away with the profit, Davidson handed it back to the various private-sector claimants. The committee justified its actions by asserting that it was acting in the national interest. Only if one regarded Australian society as Australia Ltd, a company which was run by a private sector board of directors, could Davidson be said to have identified the national interest.

The first set of Davidson's recommendations concerned networks, and its proposals were radical. Whereas Telecom had power to decide who hooked into its network and what equipment they used, the committee transferred the first right to the minister and removed the second. Telecom could no longer determine the prices it charged, for they should be non-discriminatory. They could not be used to impede the growth of independent networks or those constructed of leased lines. There were some in Telecom management who saw this as an obligation to not just tolerate a parasite on the body corporate, but to guarantee its sustenance. Despite the committee's desire for 'equitable competition', no procedures or regulatory bodies were proposed. Permission to interconnect with Telecom's network rested with the politicians, and rights of redress for those with grievances could be assumed to reside also with them. Aussat Pty Ltd could connect with Telecom's network because it competed for long-distance traffic, but it could not set up a local network, because that would be competing in a non profit-making sector. Cable television operators were treated similarly, with approval for licences to operate systems providing telecommunications vested again with the minister, despite the established role in broadcasting regulation of the broadcasting tribunal.

The result of these arrangements for Telecom were easy to predict. Forced to compete for long-distance business traffic with independent networks, Telecom could not respond effectively. It would not have the power which a private-sector quasi-monopoly such as Broken Hill Proprietary Ltd would, to bring real commercial pressure on prospective competitors.

It could expect reduced market share and less revenue. Because Telecom was also forced to allow the lease and resale of its lines to organizations which wanted to carry their own and other's traffic, revenue which would otherwise have gone to Telecom would be siphoned off to the private sector. The committee's anticipation of these consequences was to maintain that an increased market, fuelled by the competition, would give Telecom a greater chance of pitching for larger stakes than it had. But Telecom was expected to compete with one hand bound behind its back and its shoelaces tied together.

Telecom's dominant position in the supply of terminals meant that technical standards and installation and maintenance practices had to be prised away. Control of such matters was regarded as anti-competitive by Davidson. More correctly, it gave Telecom an advantage over private-sector participants. Standards were, therefore, hived off to the Standards Association of Australia, a worthy body with limited resources and no particular expertise in telecommunications, as it readily admitted. Instead of Telecom technicians, who were all members of the ATEA, carrying out installation and maintenance, particularly in the PABX area, a new breed of installers ought to be created, according to the Davidson committee. Called 'telectricians', they needed only to show they had installed telecommunications equipment before, to be licensed by a new authority. And to remove Telecom's advantages of size, the committee recommended that a new and separate company be established, using long-terms debts to the government as its equity. Telequip was the company's suggested name.

The committee's recommendations, which flowed from

their adoption of general principles, came hard up against some inconvenient facts. Far from straining at the leash to conduct their own installation and maintenance, two of the seven PABX suppliers had sub-contracted Telecom to do their installation, although they were free to do it themselves. There was also not a universal demand to be allowed free range in the small PABX market, defined as under fifty lines. The approved suppliers were not keen to incur the cost of supplying small PABXs to country centres and had virtually ceded that area of the market to Telecom, which supplied equipment on request. Where Davidson argued it would allow Telequip to compete in areas it was previously excluded from in return for the private sector being allowed into Telecom territory, its sums were wrong. Instead of there being an equitable exchange of similar-sized markets, Telecom was asked to relinquish areas with an annual turnover of $350 million for markets worth a tenth of that. Prime among the areas it lost exclusivity over was the provision of handsets, worth $60 million a year. Not even the Thatcher government in the UK had taken that step.

The notion of direct subsidy was used heavily in the Davidson report because it was the only substitute available to shore up the inequalities created by destroying Telecom's cross-subsidy. The Davidson committee made clear that its report was not concerned with issues of social justice. If people such as country subscribers were disadvantaged by its recommendations, it was not the committee's concern. Social issues rested with the government, not its utilities. The range of matters on which it was thus committed to direct subsidies became wide. Videotex, because it was a service which could be cross-subsidized to allow it to penetrate the city and the country, should be provided in areas where it was not self-supporting, by direct subsidy. The telex service should be similarly treated, as should facsimile, data lines, recorded information about the time, weather and entertainment, and the clutch of services under the heading of telemetry: automatic reading of gas, electricity and water meters and the provision of burglar, fire and safety alarms. For good measure,

Redphones, originally bought by Telecom from the private sector, were to be handed back, and the exclusive right of Telecom to provide public telephones was to be ended. Neither public phones, nor telegrams, which were handed to Australia Post, were money makers. But Davidson's desire to strip Telecom of all but the basic telephone network meant that they also had to be jettisoned.

The desire to restructure Telecom as if it were a private company was also behind Davidson's recommendation that local content not be a priority in the goods and services supplied for telecommunications in Australia. It was aware that an end to those local-preference policies would lead to more equipment being imported but insisted that the issue of whether Australia had a domestic high-technology manufacturing industry was a matter for the government. The conceptual neatness of that approach is rather ruined when the reaction of the private sector to a government demand that it manufacture locally is considered. Telecom could not be free to establish the system of industrial patronage which supported the Australian telecommunications industry. The new charter proposed by Davidson would oblige it to buy directly from overseas where goods were cheaper. Developing countries such as Taiwan, Hong Kong and Korea could import virtually duty free, and no local manufacturer could hope to compete with their low-wage economies for equipment such as handsets. The committee admitted it could not assess the effect of the changes it suggested for the Australian industry. In the absence of firm government directives on local manufacture, a flight of manufacturing companies could be anticipated. A parallel existed in the exodus of semiconductor suppliers from Australia in the early 1970s, when government preference, in the form of tariff barriers, were reduced. Imported components took the place of local production.

Although the Davidson committee was prepared to accept the simple if radical results of removing local preference, it attempted a similarly simplistic approach to Telecom pricing policies and strayed into a minefield. In order to dismantle the cross-subsidy, the Davidson inquiry had to find a different basis on which to structure Telecom tariffs. It was not an easy task, as the Vernon commission had found a few years earlier. Vernon and his fellow commissioners discovered the cross-subsidy issue was so complex that the costs of dismantling it outweighed any advantage. The Vernon report said:

It would be difficult if not unrealistic to attempt to quantify the permissible limit of cross-subsidisation within particular services. The commission believes that it can only state a general principle that the tariff structure not reflect a gross distortion in favour of some categories or classes of users of a service at the expense of the majority of customers ...

The Davidson committee was to be deterred by no such warnings, for it had to come up with a means of ensuring that Telecom did not support its unprofitable, although socially desirable, activities with revenue from money-making areas. Because it wanted to operate Telecom as if it were a company, it had to reject ministerial intervention in price setting. Its solution was the demand that each service be priced according to cost. If it cost more to install a telephone in the country, then it should be passed on to the consumer and not subsidized by Telecom. If charges for subscriber trunk dialling were returning revenue which was used to subsidize local calls, then local tariffs should be increased.

A difficulty Davidson did not concede in outlining this new approach was that it depended upon being able to identify costs accurately. The committee tacitly recognized the problems because it did not take its demand for the end to cross-subsidy to its logical limit. In metropolitan areas, there are profitable and unprofitable areas for telecommunications. In general, the inner-urban and middle-class suburbs sustain a profitable network, but the fringe areas, where population density is lower, tend not to. If the committee wanted to be consistent, it had to demand that subscribers in Vaucluse paid less for their telephone service than those in Campbelltown, on the far south west of Sydney. Similar differentials would have to be created in all Australia's major cities. The political ramifications of such a suggestion may have deterred the committee from taking its principles further than was convenient. But on an economic front, it would have proved a formidable, some would say impossible, task.

The effort had proved too much for the largest telecommunications supplier in the world, AT&T, which had grappled with the cross-subsidy problem for a decade. The Bell System which AT&T operated had been under pressure from the Federal Communications Commission to introduce what was known as 'functional accounting' to inhibit it from pricing competitors for long-distance traffic out of business. When the commission made its landmark 1980 decision, and insisted that Bell establish an operating subsidiary, AT&T abandoned the effort to relate prices to costs. Part of the complexity involved comes from the technology. Take a multiplexer, for example, a device which splits signals at either end of a communications path so that they can be directed to their intended recipients. How could one allocate costs and hence structure prices on the basis of assigning to each telephone call a proportion of the shared cost of the multiplexer. The same degree of difficulty attached to splitting costs on exchange equipment, cables, microwave towers and the myriad other equipment used in a telecommunications network. Davidson demonstrated the point. In a table of costs which it presented in its report as an example of how they would be allocated, there was a glaring ommission. The committee had failed to take into account the cost of maintaining state and head office administration in Telecom, one of the most obvious cost considerations which needed to be included when constructing tariff schedules in the way suggested by the committee.

The revenue denied the local network by competition for long distance traffic had to be made up somewhere, and Davidson saw timed local calls as a prime source of revenue. The committee estimated that by charging local calls by a unit of time, such as three minutes, Telecom could increase its revenue from the local network by 73 per cent. It was undeterred by the cost of introducing timing equipment – estimated by Telecom to be $150 million. Instead of admitting that the reason for timing calls was to gain more revenue, the committee attempted to argue that it was necessary because otherwise services such as videotex would not be introduced. Not only was this false, the price of $150 million was ludicrously high. The issue of timed local calls had been discussed by Telecom before but it had adopted a different strategy from that suggested by the committee. Instead of following the US model and charging for local calls, Telecom set a standard charge with unlimited time and extended the area over which the call could be made. In Australia's geographically dispersed major cities, it was possible to call for a standard charge across 50 kilometres. In the United States, that would count as a trunk call and the subscriber would be charged accordingly. Telecom maintained that below 175 kilometres it consistently priced its calls lower than the Americans, although US long-distance rates were cheaper.

The desire to strengthen Telecom's marketing was regarded as so important that it rated a separate chapter in the Davidson report. Lost revenues from the areas in which Davidson's committee recommended there be competition could be made up, thought its members, by increasing traffic on the network. This could be achieved by more aggressive marketing by Telecom and the encouragement of devices which recorded the cost of STD calls. Known as 'call charge recording' (CCR), this facility was a feature of the new digital exchanges which Telecom was in the process of installing. Nevertheless, they could be bought by subscribers and fitted as an attachment to their telephone or switchboard. A similar facility, designed for business houses, and called TIMS, meaning telephone information management system, could give a print-out of the costs incurred from each telephone extension. It gave details of the time calls were made, their duration, destination and the extension from which they were made. The same information could be provided by electronic PABXs, now quickly replacing mechanical systems in offices. STD bills showing individual call costs had proven politically popular; Tony Staley had suggested them to Telecom in 1979. When the cost was pointed out to him, his interest waned. The introduction of these systems raises serious questions of privacy.

What rights do people have to use the telephone without a record being kept by an employer, government department or company? Davidson ignored the issue.

The Davidson committee's adherence to the private-sector model of Telecom obliged it to accede to the demands of both Telecom and its unions that the government's exercise of industrial relations control through its co-ordinating committee be abolished. After all, no private company would accept that restriction on its autonomy to deal with its employees. Instead, said the report, if the minister has something to say to Telecom, it should be communicated directly to the board, not through a committee.

On the assumption that the government's instructions remain the same, no matter the conduit through which they are communicated, this represented little improvement for either government or unions. Davidson recommended that all the terms and conditions of Telecom employees should be transferred to the new company and also called for consultation on industrial relations matters. This did not inhibit it from dismantling the major piece of consultative machinery for Telecom and its unions, a committee on which both were repesented and which met twice a year.

Another area where Telecom had felt the presence of the government was in finance and the committee, in line with its private-sector vision of Telecom's future, recommended that borrowing restraints be lifted. Telecom should also be able to borrow overseas and engage in lease-back financing, Davidson recommended. In return, it had to be taxed like other businesses and had to tailor its investment policies to commercial principles. It should not invest in areas which would not show a profitable return. Nevertheless, the committee concluded that Telecom should lift its investment in the network by 50 per cent, a recommendation which needed to be read in the context of its desire to banish Telecom from involvement in the terminal market. About 22 per cent of its current capital spending was on terminals, and, the committee said that that should be diverted to the network to increase the rate of introduction of new technology. In particular, the

AXE exchange programme was to be speeded up, as was the conversion of manual exchanges to automatic in country districts.

While the committee was still deliberating, it was announced that eight manual exchanges would not be converted. The telephonists' vigorous campaign struck a chord with government members of Parliament, who saw the closures as electorally unpopular. Among the interventionists was Prime Minister Fraser, and the exchange at Hamilton in his electorate was saved.

Two paradoxes resulted from the Davidson recommendations that Telecom pay tax and depreciate its capital investment using current cost accounting. Using the depreciation methods advocated by the committee, Telecom's profit for 1980-81 would reduce from $232 million to just $4 million and because of its high level of capital spending it benefited from government taxation rebates. As a result, its profit, a source of embarrassment to Telecom, because its explanation that the figure represented a high rate of internal funding was never fully understood, would have been turned into a loss. Among other initiatives sought by Davidson were a partitioned telephone bill which distinguished between charges for wiring and for the handset. The border between the two represented a marketing distinction rather than one based on the technology. Similarly, a desire to hand what it could to the private sector led to the requirement that Telecom aim to contract out 50 per cent of work, such as terminal installation, cabling and the erection of microwave and radio towers. The end of the use of direct labour for all Telecom's requirements came in the 1960s but was re-instituted in 1973 because of the inefficiencies of private contracting. The report showed no evidence of having taken note of this in its attempt to reverse history.

The company which the committee came up with, called Telecom Ltd, was structured for a government sell off. With a minimum of legislative amendment, shares in the company could be offered to private investors. There was disagreement in the committee about how the terminal equipment company,

Telequip, should be structured. Davidson and King thought it should be a fully separated company while Dick and Karbowiak saw it as a subsidiary of Telecom itself. The chairman's view prevailed but not without creating some problems. The equity base for Telequip was to be part of the long-term debt owed to the government by Telecom. It was to be used to set up the new company. How the government was to recover the interest it was owed by Telecom on that debt was not explained by the committee. There was doubt in the longer term about Telequip's future. The report qualified its commitment to the continued existence of the company in the terminal market, leaving the question open.

Davidson's adherence to basic principles led to a quite arbitrary division between Telecom's activities. Although it rightly rejected the BTS division between basic and enhanced services because the technology of telecommunications would make the division redundant, it repeats BTS's mistake in distinguishing between networks and terminals. Integrated networks which carried both voice and data traffic indiscriminately as part of a single stream could not tell the difference between voice and other traffic. But there was no longer a clear distinction between what constituted a function of the network and what was performed by the terminal. Switching and billing which occurred in network exchanges could be carried out by office PABXs. And the humble telephone handset was beginning to take over functions from switching exchanges, whether they were located in the network or in a business office. Telephones with semiconductor components could store numbers for abbreviated dialling, they could be programmed to automatically re-call engaged numbers, and they would be programmed to divert calls to another number when the subscriber moved from one location to another. The technological distinction between network and terminal had begun to disappear, yet Davidson based its conclusions on the separation of the two.

Before the Davidson committee reported, rumours began to circulate that it had engaged the services of a lawyer skilled in drafting legislation, at a cost of $13,000. The fruits of his efforts were immediately apparent, for attached to the report was draft legislation which implemented most of the changes required for the adoption of the committee's recommendations. This was a departure for Australian government inquiries, which had generally considered their work done by gathering the facts and reporting them as well as they knew how. In addition to providing the government with a legislative programme, the committee urged immediate action. Standards decisions, for instance, should be transferred within a year to the authority suggested by the committee, and a licensing board for telectricians should be established with equal speed. A telecommunications advisory council, with non-existent terms of reference and a vaguely defined membership, was also to be established to advise the minister and to oversee the implementation of the report. And perhaps most provocative of all, the committee objected to its report going through the usual procedure of being studied by an inter-departmental committee. Instead, a task force was recommended and Davidson made it be known that he would be prepared to head it to guide his recommendations through to cabinet. The committee's objection to its report being handled by the bureacracy was that it represented a conflict of interest.

It fell to the minister, Neil Brown, to sell the report in public. He addressed the National Press Club in Canberra in late November but covered other more newsworthy topics such as the ABC, and the report was lost in most media coverage. It seemed that Davidson might defend the report from early criticism from the unions. He appeared on talk-back radio in Melbourne with the ATEA's federal secretary, Bill Mansfield, and attacked union opposition in uncompromising terms. He objected to the ABC news coverage of the release of the report in Sydney and was given equal time to reply. But two weeks after the report had been tabled, the structure of the inter-departmental committee had been decided in Canberra. Davidson was asked by the organizers on the first public conference on the report if he would speak at it. He declined and Karbowiak and King spoke instead. 'Mr Davidson,' a conference organiser said, 'seemed tired of it all.'

Chapter Twelve
Private versus Public

The debate about the future of telecommunications in Australia has been couched in terms of public versus private sector. The political debate over which sector of national economies generated growth goes back a good deal further than discussion about the future of telecommunications. Since the second half of the 1970s, a period which saw the election of the Fraser and Thatcher governments in Australia and Britain, the competing virtues of public- and private-sector economic activity have been pushed into prominence. Even in those countries where the monetarist economic philosophies most stridently expressed by the Thatcher government were less popular, anti-public sector forces emerged with renewed confidence. The rise of what has been described as the New Right in the United States, culminating in the Reagan administration, was based on a similar view of the public sector.

That view, in broad terms, is that the public sector is monopolistic, unresponsive to demand from consumers, inefficient in its work practices and more costly for the taxpayer to maintain than private-sector activity. By contrast, the private sector is painted as the repository for entrepreneurship, innovation, economic growth and efficiency born of competition. A commitment to that economic philosophy led the Thatcher government to wage war on the large public sector of the British economy. Cuts were instituted in the labour forces of nationalized enterprises such as steel, motor vehicle manufacture and ship building. In telecommunications, state participation in the previously government-controlled Cable and Wireless company was reduced. And in a much more radical move, the government announced its intention to sell off a majority interest in British Telecom to private investors. Spending cuts introduced by the Reagan administration hit welfare recipients and state and federally funded social programmes.

In Australia, the clearest expression of the monetarist approach was in the government's committee of review of commonwealth functions, dubbed the Lynch Razor Gang after its head, Sir Phillip Lynch, and its intention to slash public spending. The Razor Gang had a poor record in convincing the private sector it should take over areas such as government clothing factories. Some of its proposals, according to the committee's critics, led to a more expensive and less efficient service in areas such as government canteen operations. But for telecommunications, the Razor Gang's most significant recommendation was the establishment of a committee of inquiry into Telecom Australia. The terms of reference for that investigation could have passed as a brief statement of the monetarist position that the private sector could prima facie conduct telecommunications with greater efficiency.

It would be a mistake to underestimate the political nature of the debate over the merits of the public versus the private sector because it was an imperative for the Thatcher, Reagan and Fraser administrations to be seen to attack public spending. The appeal of a government committed to free enterprise, however that was interpreted, was to that sector of the electorate which most strongly supported conservative rule. The decision to establish a committee to 'deal with' Telecom Australia's monopoly and alleged inability to respond quickly to the needs of business was a political decision. It was designed to demonstrate to the government's business supporters that action was being taken to encourage the private sector. For the government, the move against the telecommunications monopoly was made easier by the fact that, unlike the railways or the supply of gas and electricity, Telecom could provide profits to private companies if it was fragmented successfully. Its inquiry into Australia Post showed up few potential areas for private profit, and pressure to sell the publicly owned domestic carrier, Trans Australia Airlines, diminished as aviation entered an economic slump. Telecom was a much riper plum, with the potential of large profits from segments of its operations.

The attack on the public sector was not couched in quite those terms by government and business proponents of monetrism. It focused, first in the airline industry and then in telecommunications in Australia, on regulation. Telecom, it was claimed, inhibited private sector economic activity through its role as a regulator of equipment which was attached to the national telecommunications network. In order to remove the regulatory hand of Telecom from private companies doing business in telecommunications, it was necessary to dismantle the national authority's powers to influence the market. In the process of presenting the argument for that action, promoters of the deregulation demand represented Telecom as a monopoly which was inflexible, lacked initiative and was unresponsive to demands for change. It also had, as the Davidson report was to say, 'a public service culture', a description not intended as a compliment.

Nowhere in the argument for public-sector telecommunications to be turned over to private interests was it explained satisfactorily why the shift was necessary. The obvious explanation, that technological convergence with computing made telecommunications strategically important and profitable, was not forthcoming. Instead, platitudes were substituted for rational discussion. Competition was the catchword of those who represented themselves as the agents of change. They argued that the fierce competitive environment of the marketplace had increased private sector efficiency which benefited both participants and their customers. Certainly, there were areas of economic activity, particularly in high-technology industries, such as computer manufacture, where companies competed and technological innovation kept them on their toes. But even there, the colossus of IBM had a quasi-monopoly, supplying about two-thirds of all computer capacity world-wide. Private-sector monopolies, by and large, escaped the criticism directed at public-sector monopolies.

The exception among the mostly publicly owned telecommunications authorities internationally was AT&T, an even more formidable private-sector quasi-monopoly than IBM. Among the major western economies, AT&T was the only fully privately owned telecommunications operator. It is true that in Spain there was mixed private and public ownership, as there was in Canada. And Hong Kong had a monopoly over internal telecommunications which was in private hands. The essential ingredient of competition which the proponents of deregulation of monopolies had demanded of telecommunications authorities was missing even in the private sector. Privately owned telecommunications operators had not built up their national telephone systems on the basis of competition.

In the United States, the combined effects of the 1934 *Communications Act* and the Federal Communications Commission resulted in little direct competition for the Bell System. Pressure from groups wishing to establish competing common carriers for certain services, such as long-line traffic, had been licensed since the late 1960s. But at the local level there were long-standing agreements designed to minimize competition. The *Rural Electrification Act*, passed in 1936, established most of the 1,400 independent companies which acted as local network carriers and connected to the Bell System. Without funding provisions under that act, rural dwellers in the United States would not have been serviced by Bell, which found those areas unprofitable. Little of the innovation which was introduced into telecommunications following the establishment of competing microwave carriers of long-distance traffic can be attributed directly to their presence. Satellites provided a new pathway for voice and data traffic, but Bell used satellites to supplement its terrestrial system just as quickly as its sompetitors.

Where telecommunications was part of the private sector, and those countries were in a minority, advancement could not be attributed to competition. In Canada, telecommunications companies at a local level did not compete for custom. Bell Canada, the privately owned carrier in the east of the country, did not compete for local traffic with BCTel, the subsidiary of the US transnational GTE, which dominated the Canadian west coast. In the middle, a mixture of carriers operated within defined areas. And some of them, such as Sasktel in Saskatchewan and MTS in Manitoba, were owned by the provincial governments. Certainly, there was competition between the two microwave and satellite services which carried traffic east-west across Canada through the string of cities north of the US border. But there were only two carriers, one operated by the railway companies and the other by Bell Canada. There were more examples of co-operation than competition. Telsat, Canada's national domestic satellite system, had all the carriers, publicly or privately owned, as shareholders.

In Britain, West Germany, France, Sweden and many other European countries, there was a similar lack of competition, and the telecommunications authorities were all in the public sector. Yet in North America, Europe and other parts of the world, including Australia, advanced and innovative telecommunications networks had evolved. Unlike the computer industry, that evolution was not accompanied by an absence of national and international standards, which meant that terminals from different suppliers were unable to communicate. Also unlike the computer industry, telecommunications had grown with regard to social needs in the societies they served, not just according to the profit motives of those who provided services. That was not achieved by 'market forces'; far from it. The private companies such as AT&T had to be legislated against to extend their services beyond the profit-making areas. The formidable technological, socially beneficial and efficient telephone services were built up with hardly a whisper of competition. Competition in many areas of telecommunications could be more accurately described as wasteful duplication.

The reasons why the forces of deregulation have achieved some success have been examined elsewhere in this book. What is undeniable is that they have managed to create, especially among their allies in business, acceptance of their case which goes beyond any support they can muster for their argument. The movement towards deregulation, against monopoly and the public sector is by no means universal. To redress the balance, consider the case for defending and in some cases extending the control over national telecommunications by monopoly state-owned authorities. It is a case which has been virtually lost amid the welter of public relations propaganda about deregulation.

Because of its reputation for probity, technical excellence and general efficiency, Telecom Australia presents a better case study than most in how an enhanced public monopoly might operate. The ideological underpinning for such an organization would be much different from the prevailing philosophies in the Fraser, Thatcher and Reagan governments. Its premise would be the provision of a low-cost, universal service, a requirement written into Telecom's charter and imposed on AT&T by legislation. A strengthened public monopoly would take that condition as its touchstone. One of the slogans used by the Telecom unions in their defence of the principle of a universal, low-cost service is 'Make the telephone a right, not a privilege.' In a sense, that does not go far enough; much more than the telephone is involved.

What is at stake in the struggle between monopoly telephone authorities, and the coalition of political and private-sector business interests which opposes them, is more than the retention of a basic telephone service. The telephone network can be used to carry a range of new services in addition to providing a pathway for voice traffic. As Telecom's attempts to introduce a national public videotex service showed, the new non-voice services are caught up in the argument. Ordinary citizens face not only the prospect of a more expensive telephone service but also the possibility that they would be shut out by price from new services such as videotex. Providers of telephone services will discriminate between their potential customers on the basis of price if the universal, low-cost principle is destroyed. New information services, which cost more to operate, will be sold only to those who can afford connection and usage charges. The economic gap between the small élite who exercise power through wealth and most people will be the basis for a new segregation. If ability to pay is the criterion for deciding who participates in what has been described as the new information order, access to new telecommunications services will be restricted. The demarcation between information rich and poor will become almost precisely that between the economically rich and poor. No better reason for that division has been advanced than that it is the wish of companies and individuals in the private sector to make money from information technology.

Instead of regarding the telephone network as an undug mine, an uncut forest or any other unexploited resource, telecommunications has a claim to be treated differently. The telecommunications networks which exist in most parts of the world have been established through the support as consumers and taxpayers of most people in society, not just a few. They are not natural resources to be plundered by the first private-sector group to be licensed to dig or to cut. There is a strong case for regarding them as national assets, not simply in a strategic sense, but for the good reason that they improve the way people live by making it easy for them to communicate. And if the desire of the private sector to make money from telecommunications is recognized as a legitimate ambition, how powerful is the claim of most people to continue to have a universal, low-cost telephone service? When the merits of the competing claims are weighed, the judgement of their worth is political.

The supporters of the notion of telephones being regarded as a benefit to be spread across society and not partitioned by one's capacity to pay have allowed the running to be made by their opponents. Consider the alternative.

The lifeline of a universal telephone service is the network into which Australia's 5.3 million telephones connect. That is of crucial importance to those business interests which want to bypass Telecom's network, using either leased lines, satellite circuits, or microwave networks of their own. The effect of the diversion of traffic from Telecom is to bring the cross-subsidy between profit and loss-making areas of the national network under pressure. The siphoning of revenue by private telecommunications carriers would not be confined to the high growth but still relatively small sector of data communications. If it ever really needed proving, Satellite Business Systems, the IBM-backed carrier competing with the Bell System in the United States, has shown that carrying data alone will provide insufficient revenue. The competing carriers also need to siphon voice traffic away from Telecom in order to make money. The part of the voice traffic they have set their sights on is clearly business traffic between the major capital cities in Australia.

Instead of sacrificing Telecom to private operators, there is an alternative. Telecom currently leases 200,000 private lines to business organizations and government departments on which they are permitted to carry their own traffic, but not anyone else's. The tariffs charged for those leased lines are somewhat higher than in some other countries, a factor influenced heavily by the distances between large cities in Australia and its small market. The charges are certainly not unreasonable and the economic benefit to their lessees depends on the amounts of traffic carried on them. That commercial judgement is left with the company or government department which leases the lines. The only restrictions imposed are that technical standards must be complied with and third-party traffic, over which Telecom has the monopoly under its charter, cannot be carried.

The disadvantage for lessors of Telecom lines are hard to pin-point. Certainly for some computer companies and large organizations with huge volumes of data flows between capital cities, there may be a desire to increase the speed at which data can be sent. Telecom, however, is providing alternative routes, through the Austpac packet-switched network which began operation in December 1982 and through its planned digital data network due to be implemented over the following two years. There have been some complaints that leased-line users are unable to use techniques which would effectively reduce the prices they would have to pay. One is known as interleaving, by which voice and data are sent along the same line in separate bursts of traffic, effectively turning a line leased for one purpose, carrying data, into one which also carries voice. Tie lines are also rented out by Telecom for voice traffic; for instance, between a company's factories and administrative offices. Higher quality lines are provided for data traffic because levels of distortion acceptable for conversation can render the data streams between computers unintelligible.

As a method of developing a coherent, technically compatible telecommunications network, the leased-line system works well. No applicant is unreasonably denied access to leased lines, and their purpose is well recognized. It is in the economic interest of organizations to lease lines rather than route traffic through the public-switched network. Telecom allows a degree of siphoning off of revenues which would otherwise flow to it and that is recognized in the tariffs it charges large communications users to circumvent the network.

The money that Telecom makes from leased lines and from trunk routes, the major component of which is business and government traffic, is not matched by revenues from the local network. It is the wish of deregulation supporters to have the local and trunk networks regarded separately. If they are regarded as distinct sources for profit, the trunk area clearly stands out against the local network. But the two segments are part of the whole of a national telecommunications system. The trunk routes alone would be as ineffective as the local network without access to trunks. The ordinary subscriber pays no less than business users for trunk calls and does not benefit on a cost per call basis by possessing the economies of scale to justify leasing lines. Business users pay a higher rental but then constant use makes their equipment more likely to require servicing and maintenance.

The pressure to prise control of telecommunications authorities away from the trunk network is not unique to Australia, where those efforts have already been more successful than in most other countries. When the major priority of the telephone provider is a universal low-cost service, the rationale for an Australian domestic satellite fades considerably. In the form presently suggested, Aussat Pty Ltd will become a direct competitor for Telecom's long-distance data and voice traffic when the first of its Hughes-built satellites is launched in mid 1985. Telecom's participation in the satellite project as a user has always been limited, confined to backing up new services, rather than creating new ones.

Telecom is able to use the satellite for extra capacity when it is carrying television traffic between the major cities, particularly for commercial broadcasters. That need for extra capacity may not be constant because it will fluctuate with programming needs. Major sporting events or ceremonial occasions mean there is more demand for Telecom circuits to transmit programmes. In industrial disputes between Telecom and its unions, the television broadcasters have had interruptions to programmes. This has prompted at least one, the Packer owned Publishing and Broadcasting, which operates Channel TCN9 in Sydney, to construct its own alternative. Using the outside broadcast frequency of 8/9 gigahertz, Channel TCN9 supplements its use of Telecom bearers between Sydney, Brisbane and Melbourne. Use of the frequency is virtually unsupervised by the Department of Communications, which grants approval for outside broadcasts in it to all television stations. The signal is picked up off air outside Sydney and transmitted via a series of microwave dishes erected on poles and towers located 50 kilometres or so apart on high points of the terrain to Brisbane and Melbourne.

As an example of haphazard and unregulated development of communications, the creation of networks such as that used by Channel TCN9 rivals the evolution of cable television in North America. The beginnings of cable networks in Canada can be traced back to small-business entrepreneurs who brought down US television signals as they came across the border and redistributed them by cables in local neighbourhoods. On a technical level, picture quality was poor and on the regulatory front, confusion abounded. One of the rationales for an Australian satellite was that it would give television broadcasters an alternative to Telecom microwave bearers as a route for their programmes, especially during industrial disputes. There is in fact no guarantee that any sector of the

Australian workforce can be used as a strike-breaking force during disputes. Certainly, the unions which would lay claim to members engaged in satellite signal distribution have not been immune from industrial conflict.

The other potential major user of the domestic satellite is the ABC, which has been an enthusiastic supporter of the project since its inception. The ABC's interest has not been so much directed at increasing capacity between capital cities than at serving country areas with programming picked up from satellites by community antennas. Its plans for rural programming would not be altered if ownership of the satellite remained in public hands. Those other supposed beneficiaries of the domestic satellite, outback dwellers who do not have a telephone, are unlikely to receive help from the satellite project to any marked degree, despite promises made to the contrary by politicians. Telecom has let a tender for the supply of sixty prototype ground stations, but they will not be its main weapon against the lack of telephony in remote outback areas. The Telecom Research Labs, together with Japanese component manufacturers, will extend rural telephony at lower cost than using satellites by the use of advanced radio techniques. Digital radio concentrators will enable telephones to be located in the outback using terrestrial means. The Department of Transport, another large user of the satellite, would be even less affected if it remained in the public sector. It competes for satellite capacity with commercial organizations, the representatives of which dominate the board of Aussat Pty Ltd.

The arguments for Aussat remaining a separate organization, whether controlled by majority private or public shareholdings, are flimsy. The satellite users who stand most to lose are those who see it as a competitor to Telecom, offering lower tariffs and less regulatory control. They are the same companies which currently use Telecom leased lines and realize that destruction of cross-subsidization would result in lower charges. Leasing capacity on Aussat, which does not have to support a local terrestrial network, achieves a similar end – to dismantle Telecom's cross-subsidy. The interests of other users would be well enough served by a reliable, technically efficient service, albeit with tariffs a little higher than they might prefer. That is the price they should be expected to pay for the creation of a national telecommunications system which is of substantial help in the running of their businesses. In some cases, their companies would cease to exist without a national network to facilitate the swift movement of information.

An Australian satellite system which was located within the public sector would also be less a prey to conflicting private interest groups, each seeking the most favourable use of it. And its shareholding mix could not be altered from majority publicly owned to privately owned simply by ministerial fiat. A national telecommunications system run according to the aim of providing universal service, and using the cross-subsidy to do so, is inconsistent with the creation of alternative common carriers. A more rational solution would be that the satellite, now contracts have been signed for it, be brought under the control of Telecom Australia. Satellites provide an alternative transmission path to copper and coaxial cables, fibre optics and microwave. All but satellites are currently used by Telecom which has the strongest claim to supervise their integration into the network. When communications traffic between the major cities outgrows the terrestrial capacity of cable and microwave, satellites can be brought into service.

Apart from preventing siphoning of Telecom long-distance revenues, there are positive benefits to the national carrier owning and operating the satellite. There are those handful of remote communities in the outback which can be provided with a telephone only by satellite. There are uses of the satellite for education and training purposes, which will remain unexplored if it is controlled by private interests bent on making the most profit. One of the real cultural gaps in Australian life exists between country and city dwellers because broadcast entertainment is directed, with few exceptions, at city dwellers. The educational needs of children on outback properties and in small hamlets not big enough for a school are currently provided by terrestrial radio services. The educational uses of School of the Air services have been inhibited by the technical clumsiness of the communications involved. Those problems range from pedal-driven radio sets to poor-quality voice channels and interference from unfavourable atmospheric conditions. Satellite broadcasting to remote areas, pioneered in countries such as Canada, will only be introduced with public-sector funding, because there is no profit to be made in them. Vocational training and adult-training courses can also be conducted by television, especially if there is some interactive capability, which can be provided best through a telephone circuit. Examples would be courses on the repair and maintenance of agricultural machinery, wood-working and craft courses, and programmes on theories of stock husbandry and agronomy.

The American Broadcasting Company has been given permission by the Federal Communications Commission in the United States to use off-peak hours to transmit scrambled signals to video cassette recorders. The cassette unit is pre-set to record the programmes, and the owner retains the video for up to a month, for a charge. Satellites are an efficient means of distributing such services, whether the cassettes are used for entertainment, education, vocational training or for professional and business information. If the aim of the national telecommunications system is equity in who is able to benefit from it, the needs of country dwellers would be taken seriously. Their role in public discussion about improved telecommunications has often been token. Sympathy towards their needs is mouthed rather than genuinely extended.

In commercial applications of a Telecom-owned and operated satellite, video conferencing and mobile telephony suggest themselves as services which could be provided. Telecom has video conferencing facilities between capital cities which have remained under-used for more than five years. If demand for that sort of service increases, and the evidence from the United States is that it will, satellite has sufficient capacity to handle it. A sharp rise in the level of video conferencing may, however, stretch Telecom's microwave capacity. Constraints on mobile telephony exist outside capital cities. A series of radio masts can provide coverage in cities with even the most rugged terrain, but outside metropolitan areas, mobile telephony and radio services are severely restricted. Temporary radio links, such as those used at mining and exploration sites in rural Australia, could also use satellite communications.

In countries where there has been a more rational use of satellites, their role has been recognized as more important than competitive levers by which private interests can exert pressure on the existing common carrier. The Scandinavian countries plan a satellite which will cover Iceland, Sweden, Finland and Norway, with each national administration paying part of the bill. France's Telecom 1 satellite, which like Australia's Aussat, is expected to be launched in the middle of the decade, will be operated by the public telephone and telegraph authority, not by the private sector. Canada's Telsat authority is not a threat to other domestic carriers. British Telecom has negotiated with Satellite Business Systems in the United States to operate a joint satellite venture which would carry transatlantic business communications. Outside the United States, only Australia has created a pale imitation of Satellite Business Systems' role in setting up in competition with the dominant carriers.

The Overseas Telecommunications Commission has had a different evolution from Telecom, but its present separate existence is owed to the Vernon commission into telecommunications which reported in 1974. The organization which was to become OTC was not then part of the same government department which embraced domestic telecommunications and the postal service. Its status as a separate commission dated from 1946, when the federal government took over external communications from Amalgamated Wireless (Australasia) Ltd. The members of the Vernon commission disagreed about the future of OTC and it was only on the insistence of the chairman, Sir James Vernon, that it retained its separate identity. OTC has head offices in Sydney's Martin Place, controls a number of international telephone exchanges and earth stations, and employs 2,000, compared to Telecom's staff of almost 90,000. An intense lobbying effort accompanied the decision of the Vernon commission to maintain OTC as a separate organization. It was led by the general manager, Harold White, later executive director of the Australian Telecommunications' Users' Group (ATUG).

The Vernon report described the disagreement between its chairman and his fellow commissioners in this way:

Commissioners Callinan and Kennedy see no justification for a separate corporation for overseas telecommunications and recommend a merger of the OTC with the ATC [Telecom]. They observe that so long as there are two separate authorities involved in the nation's telecommunications system, problems as to division of functions will arise. The director-general of posts and telegraphs considered that, notwithstanding the fact that the APO [post office] had responsibility for postal services as well as telecommunications services, the OTC could logically be joined to the APO. In public hearing the director-general was asked if he considered that the OTC should be merged with the APO. His reply was: 'I think it would be fairly hard to put up an argument that it should not become one.'

Sir James Vernon argued that once Telecom and Australia Post had been established, the question of OTC's status should be reviewed, saying:

When the ATC [Telecom] is fully established as a going concern, the relationship between the ATC and the OTC should be reviewed by the boards and managements of both corporations and by government and a decision then taken as to whether the dual operation should continue, whether some closer form of association should be developed, or whether the *Overseas Telecommunications Act* should be repealed and the OTC operations merged with those of the ATC.

No such review has ever occurred, and OTC was specifically excluded from the terms of the Davidson inquiry. The question posed by members of the Vernon committee is still, however, a live one, particularly in view of OTC's role in the development of an Australian satellite system. It was clear that the political appeal of the satellite to the government was in its potential usefulness as a weapon against Telecom. It had the added benefit of satisfying the demands of the large television networks and the aspirants to the role of competitive common carrier to Telecom on business routes. That much was certainly clear to senior management of OTC, who saw the satellite project as a means of strengthening the commission's role in dealings with Telecom. The largest single portion of OTC's operating costs relate to use of the Telecom network, and negotiations about the amount which should be paid each year are protracted affairs. It has been a complaint since 1975 by OTC that Telecom has obliged it to pay more than it considers fair for local network services. OTC's separate existence allowed the government, by entrusting the satellite project in its initial stages to OTC, to drive a wedge between the two commissions. Apart from OTC, the only repository of technical expertise on satellite communications which could be found in Australia was in Telecom. Had OTC and Telecom been part of the same organization that process would not have been possible.

Positive reasons exist for bringing OTC into the same organization as Telecom. In terms of return on investment, OTC is a very much more profitable organization than Telecom and is likely to become increasingly so. Growth rates for international telephone calls, telex traffic and data communications are much higher than for domestic traffic. Although a fraction of Telecom's annual turnover, OTC's sales each year have increased at a faster rate. Dividends are paid directly to the government from OTC and in recent years the rapacious demands of Treasury have squeezed the amount of retained profit OTC has been able to re-invest in the network. The government's financial assault against OTC, although involving smaller sums than the extra revenue it gains from restructuring Telecom's $4.5 thousand million long-term debt, has been equally determined. While Telecom has been unable to withstand the pressure exerted on it by the government, OTC is in an even more vulnerable position. In political terms, the usefulness of OTC to the government has passed. It undertook much of the heavy administrative and technical burden associated with acquiring a national satellite system. That included industry briefings, the writing of space and earth segment tender specifications, and the assessment of proposals. Only after that work was done was Aussat formed to take over responsibility for the project. OTC hopes of retaining the satellite system to operate in competition with Telecom were dashed. The minister for communications announced in October 1982 that he was considering selling off a majority interest in Aussat to the private sector.

OTC has been under attack on other fronts. It has been a matter of frustration to the commercial television networks that OTC is the exclusive broker for international traffic. As the Australian representative on the board of Intelsat, the international satellite authority, OTC can theoretically direct the course of all traffic in and out of Australia. Negotiations between Intelsat and the two largest commercial television networks, Channel TCN 9 and Channel ATN 7 in Sydney, led to direct agreements for the use of spare capacity on Intelsat satellites. Both networks took yearly leases on an Intelsat Pacific Ocean satellite in order to bring programmes into Australia from the west coast of the United States. Those programmes would normally be routed through an OTC earth station at Moree in north western New South Wales. Telecom bearers would then transmit the signals to TCN 9's Willoughby and ATN 7's Epping studios in Sydney, from where they would be relayed to associated stations. To avoid that, TCN 9 and ATN 7 were given permission by the minister for communications to construct their own satellite receiving stations located at their studios. These 18 metre diameter dishes, costing about $1.5 million each, receive programmes beamed via Intelsat satellite from studios both channels had established in Los Angeles. In the meantime, OTC was refused permission by the minister to build an earth station of its own at Doonside, on the outskirts of Sydney. That earth station would have overcome the commercial stations' objection to using the distant Moree satellite receiving station.

The vulnerability of OTC, because it is a separate entity, was increased by government demand for higher dividends and the effect of the removal of commercial television traffic from its annual revenues. In the light of the demand by the Davidson report that Telecom operate like a private company, the fate of OTC is not difficult to predict. If there is a single profitable sector of Australian telecommunications which the private sector could be expected to covet, it is international communications.

The advantages of integration have been demonstrated in Britain. There, British Telecom's control of international as well as domestic communications enabled it to ward off attempts by its common carrier rival, the Mercury project, for access to international circuits. That access would have allowed Mercury's customers to bypass British Telecom for international traffic. Mercury must now seek permission from Telecom for the use of international circuits, although it is free to connect to privately operated international satellite systems.

Cable television systems, although further removed as a threat to Telecom than either a satellite system or the international telecommunications carrier in private hands, represent a competitive challenge to Telecom's network. Even the Davidson inquiry, albeit for its own reasons, rejected the Australian Broadcasting Tribunal's recommendation that competitors be allowed access to Telecom's local distribution ducts. Without stating it in such positive terms, the Davidson report concludes that the most rational carrier of cable television programmes is Telecom. A licensing process which divorced the licensee from the owner of the network would allow more effective regulation of programme content by the broadcasting tribunal, despite its apparent reluctance to undertake the task. There are also reasons why Telecom is the natural heir to the development of interactive services on cable systems.

Cable television networks are being used in some parts of the world, principally in the United States and Canada, to provide information services such as videotex and teletext. Cable systems offer some advantages for a service such as teletext which in most other countries is provided over the air by television stations. Larger storage capacity and shorter response times can be achieved if teletext is transmitted by cable. But innovative uses of cable which have a greater social point than providing entertainment have also been developed. Manitoba Telephone System in Canada, a carrier owned by the provincial government, has an experimental project which explores some of the possibilities. The cable system is a two-way path, so it is able very simply to record activity in a remote location. The water, gas and electricity meter readings now carried out manually can be done over the cable. Linked to an automatic billing system, accounts can be generated directly from the cable system's readings. Fire and burglar alarms work similarly. A central data bank at the fire station can record the location of an alarm and provide information which can help in fighting the blaze. Among details held in the fire station's computer are the material used in the building's construction, the number of occupants, whether any are elderly or likely to require help and whether flammable goods are stored there. Burglar alarms can notify police stations immediately, and activate floodlighting and an external alarm as soon as an intruder is detected.

In the hands of private operators, such services will be provided only to those with the ability to pay. The questions of privacy raised by the storage of personal information in computer files may be inadequately policed by private-sector companies, if their record on such matters as consumer credit is a guide. There are examples of systems designed to protect elderly people using interactive technology, in both the public and private sectors. A number of retirement villages in Florida have a service which alerts social workers if an elderly occupant of an apartment does not follow his or her normal pattern of behaviour. Infra-red light rays stretched across doorways detect movement as the occupant walks from room to room. An elderly person who became bedridden would be detected by the system. A pendant suspended around the neck of the elderly resident can be pressed if illness strikes or its wearer has an accident. A less sophisticated service operates in Australia, run by a small private company now owned by the Swiss pharmaceutical giant Ciba Geigy. If an elderly person presses a button to alarm the system, an automatic call is placed by a mini-computer to two successive numbers, usually those of relatives. A recorded message tells the recipient of the call that the subscriber needs help. Where calls to relatives are unsuccessful, a nursing home is notified.

In Sweden, the state-owned administration, Televerket, is developing a system which provides help for the elderly but which aims to be universal and cheap. Using the economies of scale available to a publicly owned monopoly, alarm messages are automatically relayed to local welfare centres and help despatched. With the profits it made from cable television programmers, Telecom could easily cross-subsidize such services to ensure that they went to all subscribers, and not just to those who lived in wealthy suburbs or retirement communities. A Telecom Australia run exclusively according to business principles, as recommended by the Davidson report, would not develop any of those services on a universal basis.

A review of Telecom's future as an extended public-sector monopoly addresses one of the most fundamental problems facing Australia. With an economy dependent on agriculture and mining for the largest proportion of its exports, Australia's industrial base has atrophied for the last two decades. Now many industries, such as textiles, footwear, heavy engineering, ship-building and motor car manufacture, are in decline. With the exception of that segment of the electronics and telecommunications industry dependent on Telecom and the Department of Defence, Australia has no indigenous high-technology industries to speak of. A major recommendation of the Davidson report, that local preference be removed from Telecom purchasing policies, contains devastating implications for the local high-technology products that are manufactured in Australia. Imports from low-wage economies and developing countries, which by virtue of their preferred trading status can import virtually duty free, would replace local manufacture if the recommendation were implemented. Local manufacturers have conceded that on the terms suggested by Davidson they would be forced to transfer their manufacturing operations off-shore and retain only a marketing presence in Australia.

In that respect, they would resemble the computer companies operating in Australia, the world's eleventh largest importer of data-processing equipment. A handful of struggling local companies attempt to compete in the toughest computer market in the world. It would require great imagination to describe their combined activities as an industry. That is the future which awaits the Australian component electronics and telecommunications industry if Davidson's report is implemented.

The alternative, of Telecom being used as a base for Australian manufacture, has been put forward tentatively in a number of forms since World War II. The 1980s may be the time to revive that proposal. There are precious few alternatives for Australia's economy, blighted by government neglect and over-reliance on the mining sector. The decision to nourish an Australian telecommunications industry was taken immediately after the war, when it became apparent that Australia's reliance on imports of foreign technology was almost complete. The strategic results in war-time were obvious, but so were the peace-time weaknesses of a national industrial strategy which was so dependent on other countries. As a direct consequence of that policy decision, Telecom Australia became the largest single domestic customer for electronics and components manufacturers. That is not to overstate the indigenous nature of the industry. Almost all major companies are subsidiaries of foreign transnational groups. The possibility of lessening dependence on those companies has existed for some time.

In the early 1970s, Telecom developed what was at the time one of the world's first working digital telephone exchanges. It operated successfully for more than a year at the Windsor exchange in Melbourne, running in parallel with existing cross-bar equipment. In a speech made by the later Victorian general manager of Telecom, Rollo Brett, the suggestion was made that this Australian breakthrough be exploited by taking it a stage further and looking at the possibility of manufacturing it. Brett was speaking about the potential for joint ventures with private industry, but the reaction from telecommunications manufacturers was swift and harsh. All the major companies with international headquarters had plans of their own for digital exchanges, and the possibility that Telecom should become a competitor greatly alarmed them. The prototype digital switch was barely known, either outside or within Telecom, where the project's existence was unknown except among engineers. Few realized the potential contained in Brett's remarks, other than the manufacturers.

Televerket in Sweden and the Italian and French telecommunications authorities are deeply embedded in manufacture, either alone or in joint ventures with private suppliers. The role of AT&T as both the common carrier and the world's largest single telecommunications manufacturer, through Western Electric, remains undisturbed as a result of its divestiture agreement with the Department of Justice. The proponents of monetarist economics and deregulation have driven underground the argument for an indigenous industry based on Telecom. It is barely even discussed in Telecom Research Labs, which have a world-wide reputation for excellence. Davidson's report recommended that the laboratory arm of Telecom concentrate on applied rather than pure research, as if the two could be neatly separated in telecommunications. And Telecom's workshops have been reduced to the repair and rehabilitation of equipment. Whenever there have been signs that the workshops have been manufacturing equipment, even on a small scale, there is an immediate call from the private sector for them to desist.

The timidity of the government towards using Telecom's status as the dominant consumer of high-technology products as a launching pad for a domestic industry has not been shared in many other countries. Canada, with the world's most avaricious high-technology corporations on its doorstep, has encouraged local manufacture through government intervention in the economy. Without substantial funding and preferential purchasing by the Canadian Department of Communications, neither developments in communications satellites nor in videotex would have been possible. If the base for such industrial development is not Telecom Australia, it is difficult to see where else it can be. In the face of the question of where Australia's employment prospects will be in the last two decades of the century, a government inquiry has recommended the dismantling of one of the few industries with the potential of economic growth. And it suggests selling the more lucrative areas to speculators, many of whom have failed to do much more than repatriate profits from their Australian subsidiaries.

A new future for Telecom needs to be discussed in public debate, not in private hearings and back-room negotiations. The starting point should not be the perfection of the Telecom we have. There is some criticism of its cumbersome decision-making and monolithic approach to telecommunications which is justified. As an organization, its lack of responsiveness towards its employees has led to an alienation which will not easily be overcome. But the basis exists for the people who have determined Telecom's past – its technicians, telephonists, administrators, clerks and lines staff – to put the case for a new future. There is also the opportunity for consumers to become involved in policy making through consultative machinery set up to reflect their views. In the process of rejecting the future for Telecom mapped out by private-sector interests at home and abroad, there is an opportunity to raise the argument for something different. The case for turning Telecom into something better rests on the fundamental principle that the future of communications is too important to be determined at an auction sale where private corporations are the only bidders allowed.

Epilogue

Despite more than one hundred years of existence, only relatively recently has the telephone become a necessity of life. For most of the more than one century of its use, the telephone has existed in only a minority of households. In business, the telephone is so essential that many companies would cease to function without it. For most Australians, the connection of a telephone service has only recently lost the position of a status symbol. Yet so swift has the transition from luxury to necessity been that the revolution in telephone use has passed into the national consciousness with barely a comment. It was only a very few years ago that the telephone we now take for granted was installed in a minority of Australian homes.

From its invention, the telephone was seen as an aid to business. Its role in domestic life has been slower to evolve, although it usefulness was understood early. There was no doubting the wonder of the age when the *Australasian Sketcher* described the new Melbourne telephone exchange in its January 1881 issue as a 'palace of winged words'. The magazine published this description of the phenomenon of the telephone:

Of its utility there can be no two opinions. An invention which will enable a man sitting in his own office to ask his bank manager for an overdraft, order a coat from his tailor, and send his wife any reasonable excuse for his non-appearance at home at the usual hour, deserves a first class certificate in the direction of usefulness.

It was no slip by the author that the archetypal telephone

user was a man of some substance, communicating with his bank manager and tailor. Most ordinary people would not have been on such confident commercial terms with either the custodian of their money or the maker of their suits. The residual use of the telephone was for domestic purposes. Despite the stereotype of the telephone user being a man of secure economic status, who was engaged in business, and having a sexist attitude towards his wife, it remained an accurate profile for many years.

During 1983 the number of telephone services in Australia will surpass five and a half million, approaching 85 per cent of all households. Only twenty years ago, the number of services was 200,000 short of two million. In the almost hundred years of telecommunications in Australia to 1970, 2,700,000 telephone services had been installed. Thirteen years later, the number has more than doubled. The notion of the telephone as a universal, low-cost tool of communications is as recent as that.

Those telephone services have been provided by a monopoly state enterprise which, like many of its counterparts providing water, gas, electricity and other services, has gone about its work largely unnoticed and without praise. The true nature of some of its achievements have been outlined in this book. When the general media cover telecommunications, the standard story has consistently the same ingredients. There is an aggrieved consumer, a cumbersome state bureaucracy, an anomaly in a bill, a faulty telephone service, a delayed application or a wrong disconnection. So rare is serious coverage of one of the most important areas of national life that editors and journalists find difficulty breaking that formula. It is not a trait confined to Australia. Ralph Nader, the US consumer activist, has detected the same failing in the US mass media, saying: 'Perhaps the greatest single self-serving failure of the mass media has been their blackout of news about changes in telecommunications, which will further alter the balance of power in our democracy.'

What is proposed for Australia by a government inquiry is the reversal of the relatively recent trend for the telephone to become a service most people regard as a right rather than a privilege. The radicalism of the proposal has not been reflected in public discussion of the issues at stake. Consider the coverage that change on a similar scale would attract if it concerned the private rather than the public sector. Australia's largest private-sector organization is the steel maker Broken Hill Proprietary Ltd. Although it employs 30,000 less than Telecom's 90,000 staff, its sales and profits, in good years, have exceeded those of Telecom. The planned acquisition of General Electric's Utah subsidiary will push revenues and profits well beyond Telecom's. BHP's performance cannot be directly compared to Telecom's. Making steel (although not BHP's only activity) is currently a more depressed economic activity than telecommunications. But there are resemblances, in size and domination of the market: BHP's monopoly is enforced almost as rigorously in the private sector as Telecom's is in the public. BHP's recent history of steel production has been one of declining profits, depressed world markets and retrenchment of its employees in traditional steel manufacturing centres such as Newcastle and Wollongong. In Britain and France and some other countries, the making of steel is a nationalized activity. In Australia, that possibility is only raised when BHP begins to perform less profitably. If we construct the converse of what the Davidson inquiry proposes for Telecom, using BHP, it would go something like this.

In a period when BHP is making good profits, its annual sales are increasing and the industry which it dominates is predicted to grow even faster in the next few years, a proposal is made for it to be nationalized. The nearest example we have had to such a proposal in Australia is the attempted nationalization of the banks by the Labor government in the late 1940s. The furore that suggestion aroused, the virulence of the attacks by the business sector against the government, the propaganda mobilization of the banks, had never been seen in Australia before. It would not be unreasonable to assume the same reaction to the suggestion that a booming BHP be nationalized. To adhere to the analogy with Telecom – which will not be compensated for the loss of revenue and assets suggested by the Davidson inquiry – BHP would be national-ized without compensation.

Unlike the proposals facing Telecom, nationalization of BHP would become automatic front-page news in Australian newspapers. It would lead the television and radio bulletins and would be dissected in depth by the analysts. The editorial columns would thunder in unison and the virtues of monopoly business would be carefully explained to readers, viewers and listeners. By contrast, the fate of Telecom has aroused barely a flicker of interest.

How do we explain that difference in treatment, beyond the known biases of the mass media and, as Nader points out, the protection of their self-interest? In addition to its unfashion-able status as a public enterprise, Telecom has further diffi-culties in making its case. Unlike the directors of BHP, the management of Telecom is responsible to the government of the day. Also unlike the BHP directors, Telecom manage-ment's task of explaining the issues in telecommunications is considerably more difficult than those raised by the making of steel. There is also the nature of the relationship between Telecom as a public-sector organization and the elected parlia-mentary representatives of the Australian population.

Has not a conservative government the same rights to press for the transfer of profitable telecommunications to the private sector as a socialist government has to move the profits of banking or steel making into the public sector? The answer to that question depends on whether the interests of most Aus-tralians are best served in the process.

Whereas the nationalization of steel or banking may be con-tentious in its effect on the national economy – on prices for material and financial services – neither has the impact on most Australians of the proposed changes to telecommuni-cations. Implementation of the proposals of the Davidson inquiry means the end of the concept of providing the tele-phone as a universal, low-cost service. That was not a part of any political party's platform in recent federal elections but the course towards that aim has already been set.

In January 1983, advertisements placed by Telecom in

national newspapers gave details of tariff increases. Local telephone calls rose one cent to thirteen cents from 23 January. There was a rise of 8 per cent in fees for community calls and short-distance trunk calls. For long-distance calls, there were reductions in tariffs ranging from 10 to 20 per cent. On the most profitable routes, connecting Brisbane, Sydney, Melbourne and Adelaide, the reduction in fees reached 25 to 30 per cent. The adjustment of tariffs so that domestic subscribers paid more and business users paid less signalled that the process toward dismantling the provision of telephones on a universal, low-cost basis was already under way. Telecom was reacting to the political pressure it has been subject to for the last three years, culminating in the recommendations of the Davidson inquiry.

The attack on the concept of a universal telephone service at a price most people can afford has until quite recently been conducted by stealth, through the traditional mechanisms of political lobbying and influence. That assault is now out in the open. It concerns more than the ambitions of those who want to make money out of telecommunications. Anything which inhibits people's ability to communicate restricts their capacity to participate in the society in which they live. A feature of undemocratic societies is that they confine and monitor communications. Australia had a short taste of what that inability to communicate would be like during the 1978 Telecom dispute. It became difficult and sometimes impossible to make telephone calls between the major cities. Unlike the possibilty confronting Australia in the 1980s, as a result of the Davidson report, that interruption to communications was only temporary. Implementation of the Davidson proposals would lead to the permanent annexation of the means of communications provided by the telephone.

The use of telecommunications networks for the spread of ideas and the exchange of information is recognized in most modern states. That is why so many of them devote large budgets to internal security forces. A large part of their intelligence gathering operations are directed at tapping telephones, intercepting telex messages and tampering with the mail. So important is the telephone network for transmitting information that few of society's activities would be hidden from systematic surveillance of it. The US novelist, Sol Yurick, has taken that as the theme of his novel *Richard A*. His central character develops the skill of tapping into telephone conversations at will, using the Bell network. The practical possibilities of stripping privacy from every telephone conversation which traverses the public network have existed for many years.

The most effective means of restricting use of the telephone is to erect economic barriers which exclude much of the population. Expensive telephone services would shut out the poorest sections of society first. The diversion of funds away from domestic telephone subscribers would also lead to a deterioration in service which would further impede communications.

If the Information Society is not to be a stratified high-technology structure based on economic and hence information wealth, the role of the ordinary domestic telephone is central. Without the means to communicate cheaply, only the gullible would welcome the brave new Information Society. For without a universal, low-cost telephone service, the Information Society becomes a cynical coda for the segregation of those with knowledge from those without.

Further Reading

As in so many other technologically based areas, little has been published about communications which is not in the jargon of the technologists.

Books

Crough, Greg and Wheelwright, Ted, *Australia: A Client State*, Penguin, Melbourne, 1982.

Didsbury, Howard, *Communications and the Future*, World Future Society, Bethesda, MD, 1982.

Hindley, M. Patricia, Martin, Gail M. and McNutty, Jean, *The Tangled Net*, Douglas & McIntyre, Vancouver, 1977.

Godfrey, David and Parkhill, Douglas, *Gutenberg Two*, Press Porcepic, Toronto, 1980.

Jones, Barry, *Sleepers, Wake!*, Oxford University Press, Melbourne, 1982.

Kleinfield, Sonny, *The Biggest Company on Earth*, Holt, Rinehardt and Winston, New York, 1981.

Reinecke, Ian, *Micro Invaders*, Penguin, Melbourne, 1982.

Sampson, Anthony, *The Sovereign State*, Coronet, London, 1978.

Schiller, Dan, *Telematics and Government*, Ablex, Norwood, NJ, 1981.

Schiller, Herbert I., *Who Knows: Information in the Age of the Fortune 500*, Ablex, Norwood, NJ, 1981.

Toffler, Alvin, *The Third Wave*, Collins, London, 1980.

Wicklein, John, *Electronic Nightmare*, Beacon Press, Boston, 1981.

Reports
A Study of Remote Area Telecommunications in the Northern Territory, Implement Management Group Pty Ltd, Sydney, May 1980.
Annual Report, Telecom Australia, 1976-77, 1977-78, 1978-79, 1979-80, 1980-81, 1981-82.
Australian Communications Satellite System, Briefing for Industry, Briefing Papers, April 1980.
Australian Telecommunications Employees' Association, Submission to the Public Inquiry into Telecommunications, January 1982.
Business Telecommunications Services Pty Ltd, Submission to the Public Inquiry into Telecommunications, January 1982.
Cable and Subscription Television Services for Australia, Australian Broadcasting Tribunal, August, 1982 (The Jones Cable Television Report).
National Communications Satellite System, Commonwealth Government Task Force, July 1979 (The White Report).
Outcomes from the Telecom 2000 Report, National Telecommunications Planning Branch, Telecom Australia, July 1978.
Report of the Inquiry into Cable Expansion and Broadcasting Policy, London, October, 1982 (The Hunt Report).
Report of the Commission of Inquiry into the Australian Post Office, April 1974 (The Vernon Report).
Telecom 2000, National Telecommunications Planning Branch, Telecom Australia December 1975.
Telecom Australia Submission to the Public Inquiry into Telecommunications Services in Australia, February 1982.
Telecommunications in Transition: The Status of Competition in the Telecommunications Industry. Report by the majority staff of the subcommittee on Telecommunications, Consumer Protection and Finance, US House of Representatives, November 1981 (The Wirth report).
Telecommunications Services in Australia, Report of the Committee of Inquiry, November 1982 (The Davidson Report).

Third World Telecommunications Forum, International
Telecommunications Union, Geneva, September 1979.
The Modernization of Telecommunications, Post Office
Engineering Union London, June 1979.

Magazines
Channels of Communication, bimonthly, New York.
Communications International, monthly, London.
Communications Australia, monthly, Sydney.
Telephony, weekly, Chicago.
Communications News, monthly, New York.

Index

More about Penguins and Pelicans

For further information about books available from Penguin please write to Dept EP, Penguin Books Ltd, Harmondsworth, Middlesex UB7 ODA.

In the U.S.A.: For a complete list of books available from Penguin in the United States write to Dept DG, Penguin Books, 299 Murray Hill Parkway, East Rutherford, New Jersey 07073.

In Canada: For a complete list of books available from Penguin in Canada write to Penguin Books Canada Ltd, 2801 John Street, Markham, Ontario L3R 1B4.

In Australia: For a complete list of books available from Penguin in Australia write to the Marketing Department, Penguin Books Australia Ltd, P.O. Box 257, Ringwood, Victoria 3134.

In New Zealand: For a complete list of books available from Penguin in New Zealand write to the Marketing Department, Penguin Books (N.Z.) Ltd, P.O. Box 4019, Auckland 10.

Stuck!
Unemployed people talk to Michele Turner

Unemployment leaves a person powerless. Too poor to enjoy the enforced leisure, you are stuck. Your confidence erodes with each knock-back; money worries dominate life; you even start to believe you are the useless 'dole bludger' many people call you.

When Michele Turner saw what unemployment could do to people, she decided to interview them about their life without work. She spoke to ordinary Australians of different ages and occupations – shop assistants, scientists, labourers, clerical workers and many others. Their own lively accounts of work, families and being unemployed give an unusually detailed picture of Australian society.

Keith Windschuttle, in his introduction, says: 'Michele Turner has recorded an array of human experience that allows an insight into our current social predicament which no statistics could hope to provide.'

Australia: A Client State

Greg Crough and Ted Wheelwright

The expansion of transnational capitalism is causing the economic, social, political and cultural disintegration of individual nations. People know more about America than about neighbouring states; political repression has increased; elites run countries in the interests of foreign capital; client states are proliferating. The new world order imposed by transnational corporations jeopardizes national independence and encourages outside domination.

Australia too has sold out to these corporations whose goal is maximum profit. Instead of cheap resources and lower wages to attract more foreign capital, we need a policy of greater self-reliance to end increasing unemployment and a falling standard of living.

Micro Invaders
How the new world of technology works

Ian Reinecke

Micro Invaders is a guide to the technology built
around the micro chip, the influence of which has
begun to pervade our lives in offices, factories,
supermarkets, and our homes.

Ian Reinecke identifies the consequences of the
introduction of the chip, examines the pitfalls in the
headlong rush towards the use of new technology, and
counteracts the view of technology promoted by the
makers and sellers of computers.

He warns that their optimism is misplaced, even
dangerous, and argues that only by arming ourselves
with knowledge about the electronic revolution under
way can we work to make the benefits of the new
technology available to us all.